CLAIMING FREEDOM

CLAIMING FREEDOM

Race, Kinship, and Land in Nineteenth-Century Georgia

Karen Cook Bell

The University of South Carolina Press

Published by the University of South Carolina Press
Columbia, South Carolina 29208

www.sc.edu/uscpress

Manufactured in the United States of America

27 26 25 24 23 22 21 20 19 18
10 9 8 7 6 5 4 3 2 1

Library of Congress Cataloging-in-Publication Data
can be found at http://catalog.loc.gov/.

ISBN 978-1-61117-830-2 (cloth)
ISBN 978-1-61117-831-9 (ebook)

This book was printed on recycled paper with
30 percent postconsumer waste content.

To Clarence, Clarence Jr., Chris, and Kiara

Contents

Illustrations

FIGURES

TABLES

Acknowledgments

I owe a debt of gratitude to several persons and organizations who assisted me both directly and indirectly in unveiling the experiences of the men and women in this study. W. W. Law, who passed away fifteen years ago, and the Beach African American Cultural Center strengthened my commitment to writing about the experiences of rural African Americans. I am especially indebted to Law for sharing his wisdom and knowledge about the African American experience in Savannah. Gertrude Green, who worked incessantly with rural African Americans in Chatham County during the Great Depression, also shared her knowledge and insights about the Burroughs community and provided a deeper understanding of the plight of rural African Americans. I must also acknowledge the support that I received from Michael Sherman and the administrative services staff at the Chatham County Courthouse.

During the course of my teaching career at Savannah State University, I have had the good fortune to interact with several professors and community organizations who encouraged my work and supported my development as a professor and scholar. I am eternally grateful to Merolyn Stewart for her wisdom, patience, and foresight as chair of the Department of Social and Behavioral Sciences. I am likewise grateful to Otis Johnson, who supported and encouraged this project as dean of the Liberal Arts College. Johnson provided institutional support for research and study in Senegal, West Africa, which allowed me to gain a deeper understanding of the African background of this study. I am indebted to Alusine Jalloh, director of the Africa program at the University of Texas, Arlington, for directing the study abroad and allowing me to participate. I have been enriched by the experience on several levels, the most important of which is my understanding of community.

The paradigm of community is central to this study. Community organizations assisted in sharing their history and traditions through an oral history project that I directed in 2001. The Sapelo Island Cultural and Revitalization Society and the Sapelo Island community opened their hearts and minds and shared their collective memories. I must thank Maurice Bailey, Cornelia Bailey, the Grovenors, Carolyn Douse, and all of the student participants in the Sapelo Island Oral History Project. An American Dissertation Fellowship from the American Association of University

Women (AAUW) provided needed funding to write this study. I am grateful to the AAUW for their support. I am grateful to several scholars who read portions of this manuscript and provided direction for revisions. Daryl Michael Scott, Edna Greene Medford, Julius Akinyele, and Janice Sumler Edmonson shared their time and insights, and this study is a reflection of their generosity.

I am indebted to the staff at the National Archives; the Special Collections staff at the University of North Carolina, Chapel Hill; Bowie State University's Thurgood Marshall Library; and Savannah-Chatham County Live Oak Library for providing assistance accessing records and books used in this study. I must also acknowledge colleagues in the Department of History and Geography at Morgan State University, Towson University, and Bowie State University who vicariously aided in the completion of this study. I am indebted to several churches, which provided spiritual support: St. Paul Christian Methodist Episcopal Church, led by Pastor Henry Delaney; Overcoming by Faith, led by Pastor Ricky Temple; Immanuel's Church, led by Pastor Charles Schmidt; and Reid Temple A.M.E. Church, led by Lee P. Washington.

Finally, this book would not have been possible without the support that I received from my family over several years of research and writing. My husband, Clarence, endured my absence and time away from family functions and family events during the writing of this study. My children, Chris, Kiara, and Clarence Jr., missed their mother on numerous occasions and had to contend with my preoccupation with book-related matters. Their patience and understanding allowed me to press on to write and complete this project.

INTRODUCTION

Claiming Freedom in the Lowcountry

Absented from her master, a negro wench, supposed to be about 14 years old, named Lucia. She has a black stroke over each of her cheeks as a mark of her country; she has a very particular flesh mark on her upper lip right under the middle of her nose, it consists of a small round hollow spot, in the middle whereof is a smaller protuberance quite round and fastened underneath by a small shank. Whoever takes up said wench, and brings her to the subscriber, shall have ten shillings reward paid by John Reinier.

Savannah Georgia Gazette, November 19, 1766

Lucia, a young girl transported to the Georgia lowcountry during the 1760s, brought with her a deft understanding of her provenance. Prior to her forced migration, her father established her identity by placing "a black stroke over each of her cheeks" as a mark of her ethnicity.[1] Her family's conception of their historical reality no doubt included reverence for naming ceremonies, secret societies and the rituals associated with such societies, gendered roles, warrior traditions, and untrammeled freedom. It is likely that Lucia was a Mande speaking Malinke (Mandingo), as similar descriptions of country markings appear in advertisements for runaways identified as Mandingo.[2] For Lucia, running away was the final act of resistance to enslavement. It was a Pyrrhic victory against a system that sought to subsume her traditions and knowledge of herself. Within this system of inhuman bondage, however, enslaved Africans such as Lucia remained free. They retained a sense of themselves and relied on an informal network of both enslaved and free Africans for support, including the quasi-maroon communities developed by Africans who escaped enslavement.

The eighteenth century was foundational for the establishment of slavery in Georgia and represented the formation of oppositional communities in the lowcountry. Oppositional communities were communities of resistance that were based on shared transatlantic pasts; these communities were linked by regional origins, American destinations, and New World cultural developments.[3] *Claiming Freedom* investigates the ways in which African Americans created oppositional communities by delving into the complex networks of relations and tensions that were the products of contradictory and competing visions of freedom. The geographic region examined in this study is lowcountry Georgia, a five-county region that extends from Savannah to St. Mary's and served as the territorial nexus for African American social, political, and economic activism and resistance after the Civil War.

In lowcountry Georgia, as well as in other parts of the New World, enslaved Africans perceived themselves as part of a community that had distinct ethnic and national roots. Randomization was not a function of the Middle Passage. Although slave ships traversed the coast of Africa to secure Africans, in some instances slave ships drew their cargo from only one principal port. These included Gorée, Bonny, Calabar, Elmina, and the Biafra ports.[4] Slave ships bound for Georgia carried captive Africans who shared a similar linguistic heritage, for example, Mande speakers such as the Malinke and Serer. At the time Lucia absconded from her master in 1768, Georgia had imported 24 percent of its 2,325 Africans from Senegal, Gambia, and Sierra Leone. The ethnic and cultural makeup of the African supply zones for the Georgia lowcountry in the late eighteenth century included the Fula, Igbo, and Gola people, and Mande speakers such as the Malinke, Bambara, and Serer.[5]

The demand for African slave labor increased with the establishment of coastal rice and Sea Island cotton plantations during the late eighteenth century. As rice became a profitable export crop in coastal Georgia, merchants in Savannah imported Africans like Lucia from the Rice and Grain Coast of West Africa, which extended from the Senegambian region to Sierra Leone.[6] From 1755 to 1767, 53 percent of slaves imported into Savannah originated from the Caribbean, while 35 percent came directly from the Rice and Grain Coast.[7] Comparatively, during the intermediate period from 1768 to 1780, 68 percent of slaves imported into Savannah originated from the Rice and Grain Coast.[8] From 1784 to 1798, West African captives from rice growing regions accounted for 45 percent of slaves imported to Savannah (see Appendix).[9]

Runaway slave advertisements and oral narratives like that of Lucia provide a window for examining the aspirations of enslaved Africans. In this context, the act of running away marked the establishment of a dialectical relationship with the environment in which captive Africans lived. An examination of 270 advertisements for runaway slaves reveals that 126 advertisers designated fugitive Africans by nationality and included detailed descriptions of country markings.[10] Sydney, a young woman whose country marks were evident on her breast and arms, and who spoke "no English," took flight from the home of Elizabeth Anderson, well dressed with a cloth gown and coat.[11] Like many other new Africans, Sydney was unfamiliar with the environment in which she lived. She perceived potential for a successful flight from the oppression of bondage in the city and deftly concealed her country marks and her identity as a fugitive as she moved through the city of Savannah. Captive Africans such as Lempster, James, Peter, Fanny, and Silvia, who may have arrived on the same slave vessel, survived the Middle Passage and labored on the Ogeechee rice plantation of James Read. Identified as Gola slaves, they maintained ethnic and kinship ties through their forced migration and settlement and their collective escape from slavery.

Within lowcountry communities, the oral narratives of escaped Africans, which reveal acts of strategic resistance, represented human agency.[12] Illustrative of this is Ben and Nancy, who escaped their enslavement on James Read's rice plantation in early December 1789 by crossing the Ogeechee River with several other captives. Prior to their escape, Ben and Nancy had married. Their marriage and their plans to escape slavery by making their way to Spanish settlements in Florida underscored the determination of enslaved Africans to subvert slavery and the structures and powers that perpetuated the system.[13] Like Ben and Nancy, Patty and Daniel (of William Stephens Bewlie's rice plantation) planned to escape slavery by running away to Spanish Florida. Nine months earlier Patty had given birth to a son, Abram. Wearing a green wrapper and coat, and carrying additional clothing with which to change, Patty carried her son through the swamps of the Ogeechee Neck in route to Florida and freedom.[14] From the 1730s to 1805, 18 percent of runaways were women.[15]

The nineteenth century represented a watershed period for oppositional communities. The arrival of over 13,000 Africans in lowcountry Georgia led to the development of the distinct Gullah/Geechee language, an English-based creole dialect with West African origins. This shared language made possible the establishment of a sense of community in the new territory. The cultural identity of these oppositional communities emanated from shared African traditions and experiences and intersecting social relations and linguistic connections. Building on both their African background and their American experience, Africans in lowcountry Georgia retained much of their African culture and used it to mount physical and cultural resistance to their enslavement.[16] Cultural resistance represented a salient form of opposition.

As a system of physical and ideological bondage, slavery represented a daily assault on the humanity and dignity of bondmen and bondwomen. The ability of local, state, and national governments to violently suppress slave revolts with impunity led to the development of a dissident subculture within the slave community in lowcountry Georgia and other parts of the South. Accordingly the context and function of resistance retained an ambiguous meaning, a "private transcript," defined as an autonomous social space for the assertion of dignity, which existed on the opposite end of a continuum of resistance.[17] Slavery in the United States, as well as in the Caribbean and Latin America, rested on a basic contradiction that recognized captive Africans as property while simultaneously encouraging and recognizing their humanity. Both masters and enslaved Africans were caught up in a "complex web of compromise, adjustment, inconsistency, ambiguity, and deception."[18] Within slavery's broad spectrum existed a middle ground as bondmen and bondwomen struck a balance between resignation, rebellion, and accommodation to the realities of their enslavement and resistance to the dominance of their masters. They achieved this balance by seeking to assert a measure of autonomy in a situation where their lives could never be their own.[19]

In 1861 the largest freedom war in American history transformed the lives of African Americans in the Georgia lowcountry. This freedom war brought men and women into spaces where they challenged the slave system through individual and collective acts of resistance. They helped refugees escape to federal lines, and they served as spies, guides, and informants to Union forces. Lowcountry blacks "staged work slow-downs, refused instruction, resisted punishment, demanded pay for their work, gathered freely, traveled at will, and took freedom for themselves long before the Union Army arrived."[20] The emancipation of over 400,000 African Americans in Georgia produced a countervailing movement that was characterized by an ideological program conceived on ethnocentrism and native southern solidarity. Facing a combination of exceptional forces from federal, state, and local systems, which rendered economic subordination inevitable, African Americans maintained an expansive vision of freedom, which they defined as the right to resist authority, the right to political participation, and the right to secure and maintain economic independence.[21]

In the aftermath of the Civil War, oppositional communities resisted neodependency and neopaternalism by securing land, space, and the exclusive freedom to assert and agitate for political and economic rights. The first half-decade following the end of the Civil War witnessed the fermentation of resistance strategies as African American struggles for land redistribution, self-protection, the vote, and a fair settlement for wages stimulated group consciousness and unity. The formulation of overt collective acts designed to secure land and fair wages, and to undermine adverse federal, state, and local policies provide the context for examining what John David Smith refers to as change and discontinuity in "inherited geographies of race, space, and place."[22] Change and discontinuity were most evident in the triad counties of Chatham, Liberty, and McIntosh, where failed federal land policy sharpened the perceptions of African Americans, who developed myriad oppositional strategies to counter adverse federal, state, and local policies.

Throughout lowcountry Georgia, African Americans took action against native southern power, as well as federal policies that did not serve their interests. African American opposition included individual and community resistance, formalized organizational protest, and armed resistance. Through organizations such as the Union League and the Farmers' Alliance, African Americans developed a deft understanding of their political and social identity. The pursuit of self-governance, kinship, labor, and networks of communication transformed the political and social consciousness of African Americans during this period.[23] Concomitantly the development of "private transcripts" of resistance shaped the myriad ways they reappropriated ideas to define their lived experiences. Manifestations of this form of strategic resistance occurred in Chatham County, where African Americans in the Ogeechee rice district formed the first incorporated African American town in 1898, and on Sapelo Island in McIntosh County, where African Americans established an island within an island by purchasing over a thousand acres of land from the heirs of slave owner Thomas Spalding and establishing five thriving communities.

In many parts of lowcountry Georgia, rice remained a salient symbol of the postwar lowcountry landscape. Rice production and rice culture structured both the natural environment and the socioeconomic environment of freed men and women and thus became an integral part of their emancipatory ideology and cultural ethos. Obtaining proprietary interest in land suitable for cultivating rice for the market, as well as for home consumption, was a significant expression of their freedom during the first decade following emancipation.

Historians have debated several issues that have remained central to delineating the failure of federal land policy in the South and the concomitant economic marginalization of former slaves. In addition to excluding land in the public domain and preventing clear title of abandoned and confiscated lands, federal land policy ultimately failed in the South because Radical Republicans were not fully committed to the ideals of freedom and equality. The dream of "forty acres and a mule" died slowly for former slaves and became embedded in the historical memory of their descendants. The initiatives undertaken by African Americans to secure land through disciplined economic choices is central to understanding how African Americans claimed freedom for themselves. The extent to which African Americans were successful depended on regional demographic factors, the degree of economic elasticity, and the constancy of Republican political advantage. The spaces and terrain of the lowcountry landscape constitute an integral part of delineating African American agency in the New South. The environment provided the subtext for the ideas African Americans developed to secure autonomy and control of land.

A unique body of records that is vital to this study is the Records of the Bureau of Refugees, Freedmen, and Abandoned Lands (Freedmen's Bureau). Through the use of local materials in the Bureau's records for Georgia, lowcountry African Americans' concerns for civil rights, economic independence, and autonomy are illuminated. Although many of the conceptions are filtered through white perspectives, the beliefs and behavior of former slaves is apparent at every stage of the Reconstruction era. In conjunction with other supporting evidence, the Bureau records underscore the fact that African Americans actively participated in Reconstruction and endeavored to define the boundaries of race, space, and place.

The most incisive insights about the African American experience are found in the records of local agents and the Records of the Assistant Commissioner for the State of Georgia. The latter provide salient insights into failed federal land policy and the initiatives undertaken by African Americans to negotiate favorable terms to lease rice plantations. Specifically the Register of Land Titles, the Register of Complaints, the collection of Letters Received, the Records relating to Labor Contracts, and the Registers of Labor Contracts provide a composite picture of how former slaves began their adjustment to freedom and what some of their conceptions were about the society in which they lived.[24]

This analysis of the postwar period is culled from a variety of local records, such as Superior Court land records, tax records, probate records, and newspapers. These records help detail the meaning and significance of the postwar political economy of the region, which allowed the acquisition of land and the continuation of African American participation in the political process during the era of southern disfranchisement. These materials also illustrate the capacity of former slaves to rely on community and kinship networks to carve out and define their own spaces, as reflected in the political incorporation of the all black town of Burroughs in 1898. While recent scholarship on the lowcountry has emphasized tensions and an economic accumulationist strategy, which made for kinship and social ties,[25] this study departs from that paradigm by demonstrating, through deed records and probate records, that communities were committed to advancement and racial uplift irrespective of ties to property.

This study makes an important intervention in the historiography by providing a regional analysis of the contested terrain of slavery and freedom in the rice-producing region of lowcountry Georgia during the antebellum and postbellum period, with a clear sense of the importance of local institutions and the local political economy to understanding broader political and economic developments. An analysis of slavery and the wartime and Reconstruction experiences of former slaves in lowcountry Georgia provide invaluable insights into how they claimed freedom. As Jacqueline Jones's *Saving Savannah: The City and the Civil War* (2008) and Clarence Mohr's *On the Threshold of Freedom: Masters and Slaves in Civil War Georgia* (1986) have demonstrated, the escape of many black Georgians underscores the importance of freedom and family ties and simultaneously casts doubt on the depth of black commitment to the paternalistic ethos as they claimed freedom for themselves. The pages that follow demonstrate that the quest for freedom in lowcountry Georgia has also been a quest for community. The complex, fluid, and dynamic factors that constituted the lived social reality of enslaved and freed African Americans formed the core of the ways in which they claimed freedom.

1

THE SLAVE'S DREAM

Besides the ungathered rice he lay,
His sickle in his hand;
His breast was bare, his matted hair
Was buried in the sand.
Again, in the mist and shadow of sleep,
He saw his native Land.

Henry Wadsworth Longfellow, "The Slave's Dream"

The landscape served as the canvas upon which enslaved men and women forged a life and identity during the antebellum and postbellum period. This chapter establishes in lowcountry Georgia a sense of place, defined as a "feeling and understanding of a particular locale inscribed over time" by those who lived and traveled there.[1] The ambivalence of the landscape as a place of terror and community is narrated through the individual and collective voices of African Americans who reenvisioned their objective reality by challenging the isolation of their physical geography; they engaged in what Toni Morrison fashioned as remembering and (dis)remembering elements of their African culture through revisions of the past and through political activity.[2] In this chapter, political activity is understood as an organized collective action that affects power relations. Sterling Stuckey, Lawrence Levine, and Eugene Genovese have each looked beyond subversive acts for evidence of the deeper cultural and social resistance found in folkways, religious practices, and family life.[3]

Lowcountry Georgia emerged as the principal area for antebellum rice production. As late as 1860, twelve of the seventeen largest slave owners in the United States were rice planters.[4] Moreover, rice plantations were larger than other staple crop plantations in the South and in several respects resembled Caribbean estates. By 1830 rice had surpassed cotton as king in Georgia's five coastal counties: Chatham, Liberty, McIntosh, Glynn, and Camden. This region is divided into six natural ecosystems: barrier islands, coastal marine, estuaries and sounds, mainland upland, rivers, and swamps. The growth of rice in Georgia depended on the tide-flow method, the unusual requirements of the soil, and the knowledge and skill of enslaved Africans and African Americans. The tide-flow method required the flooding and draining of rice fields on the basis of tidal fluctuations. Because rice growth requires fresh water, rice lands were located above the saltwater lines on freshwater rivers. Furthermore, rice lands were positioned where the freshwater level could be raised by each high tide.[5]

The soil required for growing good rice crops consisted of clay and swamp muck. As a part of the subsoil, clay retained water well when flooded and thus prevented the fields from losing large amounts of water through leakage. The region's five large rivers, Savannah, Ogeechee, Altamaha, Satilla, and St. Mary's, were vital to the growth of rice and served as the focal point for settlement.[6] In coastal Georgia, transformation of the landscape emanated from the knowledge systems of Africans who were transplanted from rice-growing regions in West Africa. By 1860 three principal watershed rice districts had emerged: the Savannah-Ogeechee district, located between the Savannah and Ogeechee rivers; the Midway district, located between the Savannah and Altamaha rivers; and the Altamaha district, which stretched from the Atlantic between the Altamaha and St. Mary's rivers. By definition, a watershed is the land area which contributes surface water to a river or other body of water. The boundaries of a watershed are formed by a high point and all water flows down to the lowest point or watershed outlet. Settlement in watershed areas is characterized by a complex system involving social, ecological, and physical factors. The water served as a powerful unifying force in watershed districts.[7]

Along the Savannah and Ogeechee rivers, over 12,000 enslaved Africans labored on lowcountry plantations.[8] These plantations included Vallambrosia, Grove Point, Grove Hill, and Wild Horn, which were established by descendants of wealthy South Carolina planters. Daniel Blake of South Carolina purchased 1,321 acres of land, which comprised Vallambrosia plantation, from Stephen Elliott in 1827.[9] A few years later, Arthur Heyward, who married Blake's daughter, purchased the land and expanded it to 2,692 acres.[10] During this same period, Stephen Elliott consolidated Grove Hill plantation from the initial 840 acres purchased in 1797 to 1,340 acres. Elliott's son, Reverend Stephen Elliott Jr., sold the plantation to William and Stephen Habersham in 1849.[11]

Stephen Habersham began acquiring land in the Ogeechee area in 1848, when he purchased 900 acres from Francis H. MacLeod's estate.[12] MacLeod inherited Wild Horn plantation in the early 1800s from his grandfather Francis Harris, a speaker of the Colonial Assembly and a partner in the mercantile firm Habersham and Harris. Harris enlarged his initial 500-acre land grant to 3,400 acres.[13] Similarly Grove Point plantation initially consisted of 500 acres granted to South Carolina planter-merchant James Powell, who received a total of fifteen land grants

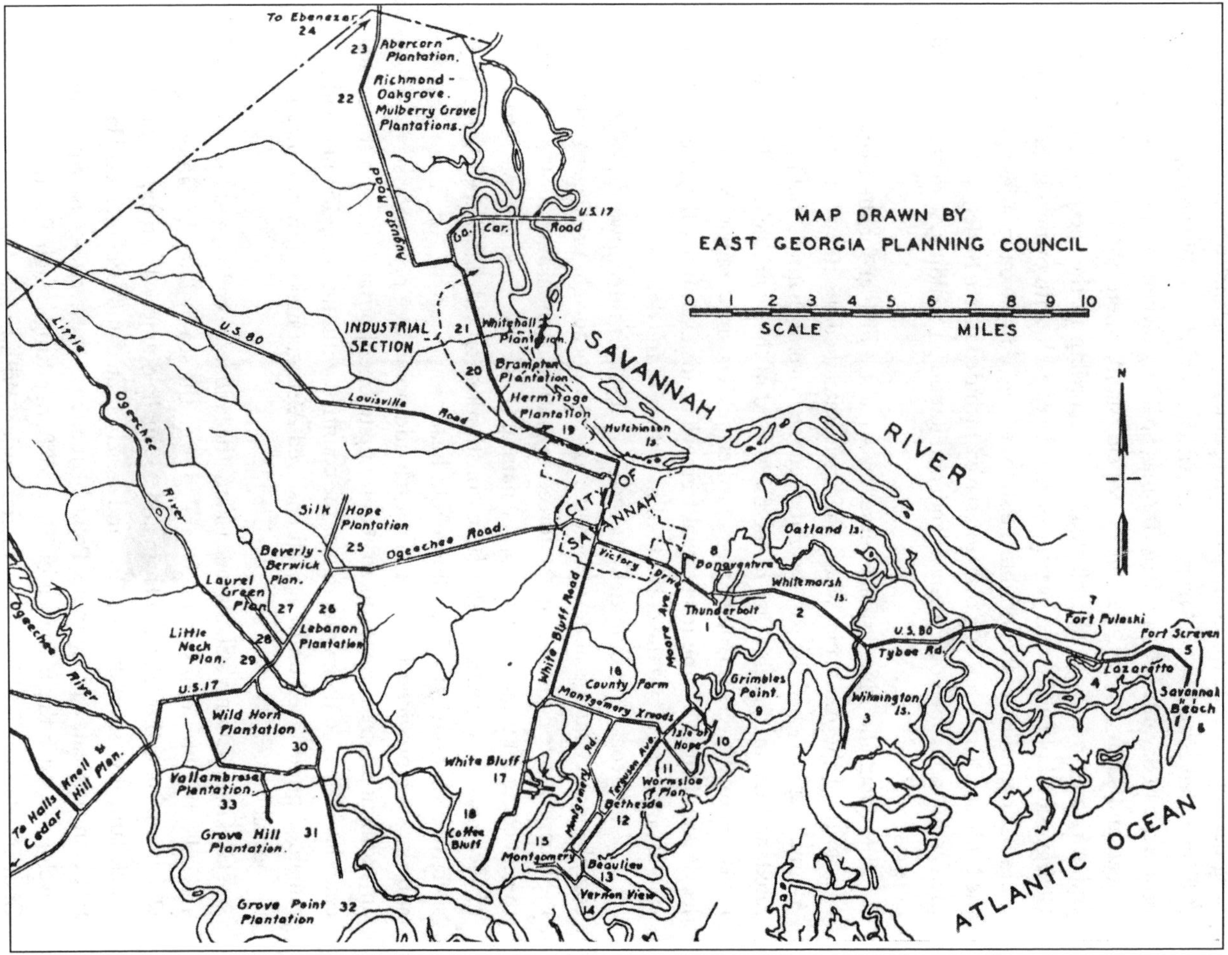

Plantation districts Savannah-Chatham County

in Georgia, totaling 6,645 acres.[14] In 1846 John R. Cheves purchased Grove Point plantation, which consisted of 1,500 acres.[15]

The Midway watershed community included Bryan, Liberty, and McIntosh counties; the latter was at the geographic center of Georgia's rice coast in 1860. Two of the earliest cotton and rice plantations were constructed on St. Catherine's Island in Liberty County and on Sapelo Island in McIntosh County. Jacob Waldburg developed extensive holdings on St. Catherine's Island, which at its peak, in 1853, included 255 enslaved Africans and African Americans. Waldburg also owned properties in Savannah.[16] Similarly Thomas Spalding owned extensive rice, cotton, wheat, and sugar cane plantations on Sapelo Island, where 300 enslaved Africans and African Americans labored in 1853.[17] According to the 1860 census, 41,084 Georgia slaveholders had an average of 11.2 slaves each, with owners in Liberty and McIntosh counties holding double the state average.[18] By 1850 the largest planters in the Midway district, holding over 200 slaves, included Pierce Butler, with 505 bondmen and bondwomen on Butler's Island; and Randolph Spalding, with 252 enslaved persons.[19]

The Altamaha River estuary served as a natural divider for the islands south and north of the Altamaha, where the third watershed district developed. As the Altamaha approached the sea, it partitioned into several channels that joined, separated, and rejoined each other in the marshland of the river's delta.[20] The marshlands and tidal rivers surrounding St. Catherine's, Ossabaw, Sapelo, St. Simons, and Jekyll islands provide the intellectual framework for examining the interrelationship of land, space, and the creation of narratives of freedom.

The rice coast communities emerged as a result of three inwardly related and complementary historical developments: extensive headright privileges granted in the Georgia state constitution, the forced migration of thousands of Africans, and the concomitant transformation of the natural landscape. To encourage settlement of Georgia's new counties, the state constitution provided headrights for prospective settlers in 1777. Each household head would receive two hundred acres, and the state provided fifty acres for each additional free person or slave. A 1783 amendment allowed applicants to acquire up to one thousand acres in the coastal counties.[21] By 1790 the population of the counties, with the exception of Chatham, remained under five hundred, with enslaved Africans making up the majority of the population.[22]

On Glynn County's St. Simons Island, the landscape epitomized the individual and collective ordeal of slavery. Separated from the sea by Little St. Simons Island, which confronts the Atlantic Ocean and Altamaha Sound with an expanse of hammock land, marshes, dunes, and sand beaches, St. Simons contained Hampton, Hopeton, Retreat, and Cannon's Point plantations. These rice coast communities developed under the influence of Thomas Butler King, Hugh F. Grant, John H. Couper, Thomas Spalding, and Pierce Butler. Within the Altamaha watershed district, 1,700 acres of land formed the nucleus of Butler's St. Simons properties, an expanse of land stretching across the northern end of Little and Greater St. Simons islands.[23] Butler's holdings consisted of four cotton plantations on St. Simons Island and a rice plantation on Butler's Island. Six hundred acres on the Altamaha delta that consisted of mostly marshland to the north and west of Hampton became known as Five Pound Tree, which symbolized the fractured lives and the submerged voices of enslaved African Americans in that it served as an isolated home for the unruly. Coterminous with Five Pound Tree was an expanse of two thousand acres of marshland that became what was called the Experiment plantation.[24]

Butler's Island serves as a spatial paradigm in which to view the conception of space within the coastal environment. Lying south and west of Darien and located ten miles upstream from Hampton, Butler's Island contained 1,500 acres of land, with more trees than marshland. Enslaved Africans banked and then cleared the land with hand tools for the cultivation of rice.[25] The high bank around the perimeter was nine miles in length. The removal of soil from the island side of the bank resulted in a large ditch that became a combination of aqueduct and canal. They placed floodgates and trunks (wood culverts) strategically in the high bank to facilitate the introduction of fresh water with the rise and fall of the river. Additionally they prepared a vast grid of banks, canals, and ditches, and drains and quarter drains from the heavy growth of the river swamp.[26]

The transition from long-staple cotton to rice production occurred following the perfection of the cotton gin in 1793. The exclusion of salt water from the incoming flood tides made the growth of rice possible along the Altamaha. From the beginning, enslaved African Americans directed the interior landscape by constructing a canal three hundred yards long, four feet wide, and eight inches deep that improved communications and access to Hampton.[27] Both the task labor system and the gang labor system were employed on Butler's Island and St. Simons Island. The growth of long-staple cotton required the use of the gang labor system. Moreover, seven horses and seven workers were required to operate the cotton gin, which freed the cotton of most of its seed. An ancillary step called moting required women to pick broken seeds and debris out of the cotton by hand and to winnow the cotton over a fan for further cleaning. On St. Simons Island, the cotton gin produced four hundred to five hundred pounds of clean fiber daily. The cotton was forced into three-hundred-pound bags by the compressing screw, and if it was sent on to Savannah or Charleston, it would be further compressed by more efficient equipment.[28]

On Butler's Island, four settlements determined the spatialized power relations within the natural landscape. The four settlements consisted of the overseer's house, located on the highest, most accessible land; the garden; the plantation complex, which consisted of the machine shops, the rice mill, and the sugar mill; and the slave quarters. Near the Champney River, located on the back side of the Altamaha, were the garden, the plantation complex, and the larger slave quarters.[29]

These settlements were protected from flooding within the island by their own lesser banks. As in other watershed communities, the river landing and its wharf were an integral part of this landscape. In the Altamaha watershed community of Camden County, Robert Stafford established extensive landholdings on Cumberland Island, consisting of over 4,200 acres for the cultivation of rice and sea island cotton worked by 348 enslaved Africans in 1850. By 1860 the Altamaha watershed community included 2,785 enslaved Africans and African Americans who worked 8,000 acres of land.[30]

Within the established watershed communities, resistance to enslavement became an integral part of the landscape. Materials as divergent as slave narratives, the post-Civil War petitions of former slaves, plantation records, and journals yield a composite picture of the complexities of the slave system that underscores the diversity of responses to the system. Collectively these materials demonstrate that narratives of resistance and freedom were a form of discourse within certain limits and with a conceptual language that established human agency. These narratives represented an attempt to construct an identity, a set of relationships, and boundaries for negation, resistance, and reinterpretation of their lived experience.[31] Resistance and freedom persisted in the consciousness of enslaved Africans and African Americans in lowcountry Georgia.

TABLE 1. Rice Production in Lowcountry Georgia, 1860

COUNTY	POUNDS PRODUCED
Chatham	25,934,160
Camden	10,330,068
McIntosh	6,421,100
Glynn	4,842,755
Liberty	2,548,382

SOURCE: *U.S. Census Manuscript Agricultural Returns,* 1860.

Within the first generation of Africans in the lowcountry, a substantial number were West Coast Africans from the Senegambian region and Sierra Leone. The nearly two dozen ethnic groups with representation along the west coast from Senegal to Sierra Leone, and from Angola at various times, provided the ideological superstructure upon which to express resistance and freedom.[32]

THE HURT OF THIS HURT WORLD

Narratives were central to the formation and expression of ideas of resistance and freedom within the community of the enslaved. As a central epistemological category, narratives represented a category of human experience and thinking, a body of ideas that explained relations, structures, and the conjuncture of discourse and power. Narratives that exemplified possible ideal ways of existence were the most ubiquitous in the identity of lowcountry African Americans. These utopian narratives were an integral part of the private transcripts of the enslaved.[33] Perhaps nowhere was this more evident than on Butler's Island. The degradation of the men, women, and children who labored on Butler's Island underscored the dichotomous nature of the task labor system, which until very recently has been equated with slave autonomy.[34] The records of Pierce Butler reveal a dismal experience. On Butler's Island, 50 percent of children age two to twelve months died as a result of being underweight and exposed to malaria, influenza, whooping cough, lockjaw, and winter fevers. On Stephen Habersham's, Grove Hill plantation, slave deaths occurred each month, with children under the age of five making up the majority of deaths recorded. Moreover, the health of women on the plantation was poor because women returned to field labor soon after giving birth. Women also suffered from a variety of ailments, including fallen wombs, spinal injuries from backbreaking work in rice fields, fevers, pulmonary illness, rheumatism, and foot rot caused by standing knee-deep in water.[35]

The belief that the enslaved could transcend their physical oppression by returning to Africa produced the symbol of a reversed transatlantic migration to escape an abhorrent reality. Narratives of flight back to Africa, preserved as intergenerational narratives within lowcountry communities, underscored the persistence of Africa in the consciousness of the enslaved. A persistent memory of Ryna Johnson, an enslaved woman on Hopeton plantation, and of several others in the St. Simons Island and Sapelo Island communities, was the legend of Butler's Island Africans who, resentful of the overseer's lash, flew back to Africa.[36] Similarly the narratives of Prince Sneed, Serina Hall, and Solomon Gibson, whose ancestors labored on St. Catherine's Island, reveal a parallel migration to Africa.[37]

Ideas are the environment in which people live, and thus the metaphor of returning to Africa expressed a determination to dream of and hope for a better life literally and symbolically beyond their present situation in slavery. The historical reenvisioning of returning to Africa remained a persistent theme in the ideology of African Americans who lived within the Georgia-South Carolina lowcountry continuum. Phyllis Green, a former slave in Charleston, South Carolina, described an event that took place on James Island, in which Africans who refused to submit to the seasoning process feigned accommodation and began their flight back to Africa. These oft-repeated narratives were represented as historical events, not myths, and underscore several themes of resistance, such as refusing to assimilate, plotting return back to Africa, pretending to accommodate, and flying home to freedom. In a similar vein, narratives of freedom through death provided the theoretical underpinnings for an alternate conception of historical reality. On St. Simons Island, newly purchased captive Africans sold to John Couper and Thomas Spalding by the Savannah firm of Mein and Mackay endured a second "voyage through death" down the coast from Savannah. Their confinement below deck created the conditions that led to a revolt against the crew and Couper's overseer. Landing near the marshlands, the Igbos began singing and wading through the waters of the Altamaha River, where twelve drowned in an attempt to reverse their forced migration.[38]

The struggle to resist enslavement created the conditions for severe punishments. Severe punishments for a variety of perceived offenses occurred frequently on the Butler's plantation. These punishments were gender neutral and deprived both men and women of their humanity and their dignity. Women such as Judy, Sinder, and Sophy, whose bodies were violated by the overseer and manager of the island, Roswell King Sr., and who bore children as a result of this violation, endured severe floggings at the behest of Mrs. King. Mrs. King meted out further punishment at Five Pound Tree, where the women were exiled for a week of additional floggings.[39] For women, slavery was even more terrible because overt resistance was not a viable option. The threat of retribution through physical violence such as whippings or the moral anguish that would result from separation from their family or surroundings if they were sold away was omnipresent. Sexuality, as Catherine Clinton has argued, was a central and significant element in the system of power devised by the slave society. The sexual abuse of slave women by white men marked the distinct convergence of racial, sexual, and economic systems. The life of Elizabeth Bernardey, a mulatto slave of Robert Stafford of Cumberland Island, is illustrative. By 1850 Stafford had owned 348 slaves and owned the largest tracts of land on the island, which totaled over 4,200 acres. Over the course of their thirty-year relationship, Bernardey gave birth to six children fathered by Stafford.[40]

Cruel and unusual punishments provided the impetus for flight from plantations. Implacable hostility was coeval with the task labor system, which was the cornerstone of lowcountry plantation management. Severe beatings, whippings, and floggings were convergent with chains, irons, and incarceration. Under these conditions, enslaved Africans seized opportunities for self-emancipation. The sea islands provided fluid egress for runaways to flee to the nearby pine lands and assimilate with the Seminoles in Spanish Florida. During the waning years of the war of 1812, 138 enslaved Africans from Butler's Island seized the opportunity to escape slavery when British forces occupied nearby Cumberland Island and several lesser islands.[41]

THE ILLUSION OF ISOLATION

The task labor system shaped the experiences of enslaved Africans on the plantation of Reverend Charles C. Jones.[42] The task system assigned each slave a certain amount of work each day, and depending on the season and the required tasks, it could be characterized by arduous labor and unhealthy weather conditions. A quarter acre to hoe in heavy rains, which occurred frequently in the lowcountry, meant slaves such as Sina and Eve on the Jones's Montevideo plantation and Patty and

Nancy on Stephen Habersham's Grove Hill plantation spent long hours completing their assigned task. Like men, women performed digging and cleaning tasks. Women used long-handled scoops "in which mud which had been accumulated in the ditch was dragged out."[43] On St. Simons Island, enslaved women on Kelvin Grove plantation performed much of the physical labor. The slave population on Kelvin Grove consisted of eighty-one slaves, of whom forty-five (56 percent) were women. Twenty-three were field hands who cultivated rice and Sea Island cotton. In 1853 Jane, Sarah, Hamit, Hester, and Nanny ginned and moted cotton, which yielded above sixty pounds per slave each day. While the task labor system provided slaves with "an economy of time" to plant and tend gardens and raise livestock, control and coercion remained the central elements of the system.[44]

The task labor system did create an internal slave economy that informed African American postwar strategies to secure economic independence and establish land-based communities. However, the ownership of property, like other aspects of slavery, remained outside of the law, which impeded formal recognition of this property when slavery ended. Public display and acknowledgement of property owned by slaves reinforced the informal economic system. The institutions that permitted the enslaved to accumulate property had been in place for generations and expanded during the nineteenth century. In the rural lower South, it was primarily an extension of slave gardens and livestock raising. In the urban areas of the lower and upper South, it evolved from African Americans hiring out their time. Gardens were used to supplement diets and in the process became the de facto land and property of the enslaved.[45]

The most extensive body of evidence relating to the property owned by enslaved Africans and African Americans are the records of the Southern Claims Commission, which was created by Congress to identify northern, and later Southern, loyalists who had lost personal property to Union soldiers during the Civil War and to provide restitution to them. The commissioners of the Claims Commission and their agents certified the loyalty of each claimant and the amount, nature, and value of the property taken, and reported their judgment on each claim in writing to Congress.[46] The issue of property ownership by enslaved African Americans has become central in the historiography of slavery. The work of Phillip D. Morgan, Thomas F. Armstrong, Loren Schweninger, and Dylan Penningroth has provided new insights that continually expand the framework for examining the complexity of slave life. Within this framework, questions concerning the relationship between kinship and property ownership have arisen. In his study of social relations and property ownership, Dylan Penningroth argues that property was one of the things that made social ties. Property's value, according to Penningroth "lay in the social relationships it embodied."[47]

The claims of African Americans reveal a great deal about kinship and the process by which a collective identity was forged. These narratives are a part of the politics of remembering life during slavery and other injustices. As a means of empowerment and identity formation, the testimony of formerly enslaved claimants and their witnesses underscores the fact that oppression created solidarity, irrespective of property-owning status. The oppression of slavery created and reinforced social ties and community. Thus kinship and race were inextricably interlinked. Moreover, the very nature of living life in a system of perpetual bondage meant that conflict within the slave community was diminished. Above all else, the majority of enslaved African Americans endeavored to survive slavery. This common experience and identity, as Wilson Moses has argued, was "the basis of a racial unity, unknown among the various African groups before the transatlantic slave trade."[48]

In this vein, the testimonies of claimants and their witnesses represent an indispensable link to an understanding of resistance to enslavement. These narratives of freedom hermeneutically convey what enslaved Africans and African Americans experienced during their enslavement. The images evoked and their vernacular style of speech originated from within their collective experience. African Americans such as Sandy Austin and Sambo Jefferson both revealed and concealed their protests against slavery. Austin, an enslaved laborer on the Joseph LeCounte plantation in Liberty County, saved his time under the task labor system to work for himself. He raised hogs and poultry for several years and expanded his property to include a mare by raising livestock and "selling the increase." Embedded within Austin's claim is the manner in which he secured de facto rights from LeCounte to own property.[49]

Contemporaneous with Austin, Sambo Jefferson had amassed a considerable amount of property, consisting of ducks, hogs, geese, rice, corn, and fence rail valued at $1,478. Jefferson, who was born a slave in South Carolina, had been freed by his master three years before the Civil War. During his enslavement, Jefferson cultivated five acres of cleared land for his own benefit. He continued to plant during the war, and through this process, he was able to secure property that consisted of 31 hogs, 49 ducks and geese, 178 bushels of rice, 75 bushels of corn, 43 ground nuts, and 2,000 fence rails.[50]

The communitarian character of social relations in the lowcountry is evident in the language and social practices bondmen and bondwomen revealed in their testimonies. These networks of communication and community informed power relations and the appropriation of economic spaces. Since the late eighteenth century, planters had acknowledged that the crops bondmen and bondwomen produced on their own time were their property. Interaction, exchange, and creativity allowed slaves such as James Anderson, who resided in Riceboro, to accumulate property, which consisted of hogs, cows, corn, potatoes, chickens, and clothing. Similarly Richard LeCounte "began raising chickens, and fowl and kept selling until he had saved up enough money to buy a cow." LeCounte raised chickens and fowl for over thirty years and negotiated with his owner, Joseph LeCounte, who purchased chickens and hogs from Richard for cash.[51] This supplement enhanced the social and economic position of Richard LeCounte and other bondmen and bondwomen who adroitly used the task system to mediate the oppression of slavery.

The accumulation of personal property was both symbolic and functional. Symbolic property, such as beads, pots, foodstuffs, and other homemade items, imparted feelings of self-worth and pride. Symbolic property represented a past material world that provided tools that not only were used for cooking and shelter, but also served as symbols that reinforced enslaved people's view of themselves as culturally distinct from others. In a similar manner, functional property, such as wagons, mules, chickens, and cows, engendered a sense of independence in its owners. Through the competence exhibited in their ability to acquire and make things, as well as through the trust manifested in their personal relationships, the LeCounte family derived a measure of power in their relations with planter Joseph LeCounte to raise hogs and poultry and to buy and sell rice, which they produced on their own. Like their brother Richard, Adam, Hercules, and Joshua LeCounte had owned property for many years and had secured additional food, shelter, and clothing by daily manipulation of the task system.[52]

The task labor system allowed women to manipulate their time to secure their own economic and social spaces. Slavery was a "system of many systems" that affected women on multiple levels. As Deborah Gray White has argued, "women deliberately dissembled their objective reality and masked their thoughts and personalities in order to protect valued parts of their lives from white and male invasion."[53] However, the hidden realm of women's lives was the primary realm in which they resisted the process of reduction. Their political, social, and economic struggle for full humanity is revealed in their narratives, which reveal that women's domestic responsibility informed their social reality. Within slave communities, women emerged as cultural interlocutors. They maintained a place of honor and a degree of political power derived from the contributions they made to the material and cultural life of the quarters. Women sustained family and kinship networks, anchored slave communities, and shouldered the dual burdens of field labor for their owners and domestic responsibilities for their households on a daily basis. The status of women in the slave community increased as a result of their work as nurses, midwives, and educators. On Retreat plantation Old Sarah, Ruthy, Polly, Lady, and Old Betty occupied nonagricultural positions as cooks, seamstresses, nurses, and housemaids.[54]

Women's marketing activities also provided a measure of economic influence within the community. The marketing activities of bondwomen had two significant consequences. First, they allowed the women to establish an economic link to the markets in Savannah, Sunbury, and Darien. River and coastal trading vessels provided important access to trade centers, enabling women to supplement their standard of living. Second, as consumers and producers, women traders resisted the legal constraints on their mobility. Linda Roberts, on January 30, 1875, testified that she had recently lost her husband and was relying on her children and grandchildren for support. But before the war, she had owned 20 head of cattle (valued at $400), 30 hogs, 40 beehives, 18 ducks, 50 chickens, 20 bushels of corn, 100 bushels of rice, a saddle and bridle, and a horse and buggy.[55] Family inheritance provided the means by which women such as Rachel Norman of Liberty County secured property. Rachel, who inherited livestock upon the death of her father and mother, resided in Riceboro on the estate of James Williams. Her property consisted of five heads of cattle, 15 bushels of corn, 12 bushels of rice, 12 chickens, and four hogs valued at $169.50. She had raised cattle for over twelve years prior to the arrival of Union forces.[56]

The shared narrative of Binah Butler and Moses Stikes reveals bondwomen's strength and endurance, and their commitment to earn as much as they could to support themselves. Butler and Stikes cultivated seven acres of land. They established a partnership and went to work raising garden vegetables to sell in the city, each owning half of all they earned. Both Binah and Moses hired out their time and paid wages to their master. Binah paid $10 per month, and Moses paid $21 per month. According to Binah, "it was hard work to keep ourselves and make money on anything more than what [we] would pay master. I was glad when the [Union Army] came; I hated to leave what we had but we were satisfied to get our freedom."[57] Binah and Moses claimed $864 of property, which included horses, fence rails, garden vegetables, hogs, chickens, cows, and rice. Gender influenced the credibility of claimants. According to the statistics of the Southern Claims Commission, only ten claims submitted by bondwomen in Liberty County were approved for recompense. Although in Chatham County fourteen claims by women were approved, former bondwomen had no successful claims in Bryan, McIntosh, Glynn, and Camden counties.[58]

MEMORY AND (DIS)REMEMBERING

The historical memory of the descendants of enslaved African Americans provides an important window through which to examine the language and religion of resistance in the discourse and cultural logics of the antebellum era. The emergence of a dissident subculture embodied by a complex system of religious and linguistic systems represented the third form of resistance along the South Carolina-Georgia continuum. In the case of language, African languages continued to inform the manner in which enslaved Africans expressed cultural autonomy. Enslaved Africans retained much of their African cultural identity as a result of three related factors. First, the ratio of the African and African American population to the white population remained disproportionately high; second, the importation of new Africans persisted in the years following the 1808 ban on the slave trade, reinforcing African cultural traditions and reducing assimilation; third, the lowcountry environment, with its string of barrier islands, separated the island communities from the mainland white population.[59] The language developed by lowcountry African Americans emerged as a central component in their ontological praxis. The communitarian character of the slaves' language and social practices provide salient insights into how bondmen and bondwomen understood and communicated their experiences and struggles through their use of language. The lucidity of their symbolic and metaphorical language provides crystalline insights into the ways in which they transformed their experiences into images that tell their stories of both oppression and liberation.[60]

The persistence of African languages is documented in the accounts of planters and of the progeny of bondmen and bondwomen in the lowcountry. Both John Couper and his son James Hamilton Couper, who owned several plantations on St. Simons Island and along the Altamaha River, including the well-known Hopeton plantation, wrote in 1827 that bondmen and bondwomen continued to speak and understand the Foulah language. The gradual creolization of African and English words to create a new linguistic category referred to as Gullah represented an important development in lowcountry communities. Through this language a rich expressive culture emerged in which bondmen and bondwomen articulated their feelings, hopes, and dreams and forged and maintained kinship networks. These networks were characterized by a common bond that included both blood relationships and social and economic relationships. As Margaret Washington Creel and Charles Joyner have demonstrated, the creation of Gullah allowed enslaved Africans to endure the collective tragedy of slavery.[61]

TABLE 2. *Population of Lowcountry Georgia, 1860*

COUNTY	AFRICAN AMERICAN	EUROPEAN AMERICAN	PERCENT AFRICAN AMERICAN
Bryan	2,379	1,636	59.2
Chatham	15,532	15,511	*50.0
Liberty	6,083	2,284	72.7
McIntosh	4, 417	1,429	74.2

*The white population of Chatham County was concentrated in the city of Savannah. The plantation districts held substantial black majorities.

SOURCE: *Compendium of the Ninth U.S. Census, 1870* (Washington, D.C.), 139.

In addition to language, religion played a key role in building and sustaining a dissident subculture in the lowcountry. Religion and religious activities helped Africans in diaspora societies cope with slavery. The fusion of Christianity with African religious beliefs has been viewed by scholars, most notably Albert Raboteau,

Robert Farris Thompson, Mechal Sobel, Melville Herskovits, and Sidney Mintz, as a form of cultural resistance. Captive Africans created a strong religious collective that shielded them from the physical and psychological effects of slavery. Their experiences were also based on an African worldview and cultural structure that was expressed in both Islamic and Christian terms.[62]

African traditional religion adhered to a form of monotheism. According to John Mbiti, within the African ontology there was always a supreme Creator. In Akan the creator was *Onyame;* in Bantu, *Nzambi;* in Mende, *Ngewo;* and in Gola, *Daya.* Second in the hierarchy were spirits capable of appearing within the world as living guardians. Humans, animals, and objects constituted the penultimate forces in the African cosmology. Creation stories, a supreme Being, spirits, and priest-healers were central to African religions, and enslaved Africans found similar features in Christianity that intensified conversion. In Liberty County, enslaved African Americans such as Lucy, who converted to Christianity while a slave of Reverend Charles C. Jones, embraced Christianity because it nurtured and kept alive the promise of equality and freedom and thus had both a liberatory and political meaning.[63]

Within lowcountry communities, slave preachers risked their lives to preach a message of liberation and resistance. The master of Preacher George in Chatham County threatened him with five hundred lashes if he continued to preach subversive messages to slaves. George disregarded his master's threat and continued to preach. After the discovery of George's activities, he was forced to flee across the Savannah River. He was captured after hiding in a nearby barn and burned alive before an assembly of slaves who were forced to travel twenty miles to the Greenville town square to watch what Moses Roper, a former slave and abolitionist, described as a "horrid spectacle."[64] Attending unsupervised religious slave meetings led to severe punishment. Enslaved men and women risked punishment and death if they undermined the power of the planter and the system of slavery. Tom Bucknie, a slave in Chatham County, received 150 lashes "washed with brine," for attending religious meetings. Bucknie continued to "attend the meetings and pray for his master," despite repeated threats and severe whippings.[65]

In addition to African traditional religion, the universe of African religious systems included Islam, which was introduced to West Africa in the eleventh century.[66] The ardor with which bondmen and bondwomen continued to adhere to Islamic traditions in the lowcountry represents a significant manifestation of self-determining identity and resistance. Evidence derived from narratives of the descendants of first- and second-generation Africans provides an incomplete but substantive picture of African-born Muslims, their progeny, and associated communities of believers who pursued their religion with diligence and purpose in an atmosphere charged with the teachings of Christianity and the attraction of African traditional religions. In addition, grandchildren and subsequent progeny spoke of

African-born Muslims with pride, suggesting a strong and clear identification with an Islamic heritage, if not an embrace of the religion.[67]

This community of extended multigenerational families, tied by bonds of kinship, was shaped by the cultural and ideological parameters of religious practices. First-generation Africans provided the cultural and linguistic homogeneity to sustain religious traditions. The capture and forced migration of Salih Bilali from Maasina in the Upper Niger valley floodplain is illustrative. Born in 1765, Salih was captured by slavers in 1790, during the period in which the Bambara were consolidating their control of the Upper Niger. After his confinement at Anamoboe, along the Gold Coast, slave traders purchased him. He arrived in North America in 1800 and became head driver on John Couper's Cannon's Point plantation on St. Simons Island. Although he had been given the name Tom, Salih remained a devout Muslim and continued to refer to himself as Salih.[68] The private language and intergenerational naming practices employed by Africans provide historical depth to their lived experiences. According to linguist Annette Kashif, the private, or "basket," names of Gullahs were invariably African homophones. Even though their memories regarding the meanings of their names faded with the passage of time, they continued to use these names, which were personal names in West African languages, because their older relatives did the same.[69]

In another context, eighty-eight-year-old Ben Sullivan of St. Simons, the grandson of Salih Bilali, remembered that in addition to his father, Bilali, and grandfather, two other Muslims in the community, "ole Israel" and Daphne continued to adhere to Islamic practices. Sullivan's narrative, which is written in dialect, places Islam at the center of religious life within the slave community. Islamic identity informed their use of language (in this case Arabic), their worldview, their ideas of time and space, their work, their social customs, and their historical traditions. According to Sullivan, "ole Israel he pray a lot wid a book [probably the Qur'an] he hab wut he hide, an he take a lill mat an he say he prayuhs on it. He pray wen duh sun go up an wen duh sun go down. . . . He alluz tie he head up in a wite clawt an seem he keep a lot uh clawt on hand."[70] Similarly Daphne prayed regularly, bowing "two an tree times in duh middle uh duh prayuh," and was usually veiled.[71] Sullivan, who was born during the 1840s, remembered many Africans whom he referred to as not "tame," an indication that a strong African ontology continued to shape their social reality. Within this African ontology, the desire to create and maintain structures that reflected an African identity persisted and conflicted with the worldview of planters, as Africans like "ole man Okra," of St. Simons Island built homes that were similar to their African homes and used their native languages to tell and retell narratives of Africa as a retention and coping strategy.[72]

Similar practices occurred in other areas of the lowcountry. On Sapelo Island, a Fulfulde-speaking slave from Timbo in the Guinea highlands, Futa Jallon, wrote in Arabic and instilled Islamic traditions into his twelve sons and seven daughters.

Bilali Mohomet, or Ben Ali, a Fula Muslim from present day Guinea-Conakry, wrote from memory his own version of a Muslim religious text, the *Risala* of Ibn Abu Zayd.[73] A contemporary of Salih Bilali, Ben Ali worked as a driver on the Spalding plantation. Although Ben Ali was African-born, his wife and children may not have been. According to Sapelo Island historian and Ben Ali's descendant Cornelia Bailey, Bilali's wife, Phoebe, came from the islands, meaning that she was either born or seasoned in the Caribbean. Ben Ali came with his entire family to Sapelo, where he underwent the seasoning process. He resisted those aspects of Western culture that conflicted with his African identity and accepted Western languages as alternate forms of communication. Ben Ali transferred this African and Islamic identity to his children, who were also multilingual Muslims. In addition to speaking Foulah and having knowledge of Arabic, they spoke French and English.[74]

Details of Bilali's religious practices are provided by Katie Brown, the great-granddaughter of Ben Ali, and one of the oldest inhabitants of Sapelo Island at the time of her interview in the 1930s. She enumerated Bilali's seven daughters as "Margaret, Bentoo, Chaalut, Medina, Yaruba, Fatima, and Hestuh."[75] Margaret was the grandmother of Brown, who went on to say: "Margaret an uh daughter Cotto use to say dat Bilali an he wife Phoebe pray on duh bead. Dey wuz bery puhticuluh bout duh time dey pray and dey bery regluh bout duh hour. Wen duh sun come up, wen it straight obuh head on wen it set, das duh time dey pray. Dey bow tuh duh sun an hab lill mat tuh kneel on. Duh beads is on a long string. Belali he pull bead an he say, Belamb, Hakabara, Mahamadu. Phoebe she say, Amen, Ameen."[76] In 1860 writer Georgia Bryan Conrad visited Sapelo Island in 1860 and described Ben Ali and his family as worshipers of Mahomet; she wrote: "they were all tall and well formed with good features."[77]

Ben Ali and his daughters maintained Islamic traditions within their families, as well as an interplantation communication network with other Muslims in the lowcountry. Shad Hall of Sapelo Island, a descendant of Bilali through his grandmother Hester, described Ben Ali's daughters who practiced Islamic rituals as follows: "Hestuh an all ub um sho pray on duh bead. Dey weah duh string uh beads on duh wais. Sometime duh string on duh neck. Dey pray at sun-up and face duh sun on duh knees an bow tuh it three times, kneelin on a lill mat."[78] In the context of communication, Brown referred to Salih Bilali of St. Simons as "cousin Belali Sullivan," an indication that Salih Bilali and Ben Ali had created a network based on a shared Islamic heritage and provenance. Both men originated from the kingdom of Bambara, spoke Foulah, and held positions as drivers. According to James Hamilton Couper, Salih Bilali (Tom) and Ben Ali were intimate friends.[79]

Although the data is fragmentary, the number of enslaved Muslims on Sapelo Island and St. Simons Island was significant. For example, in May 1802 two Muslim men named Alik and Abdalli escaped from Sapelo Island. Both men were probably African-born, as one spoke "bad English," while the other's command of the language was only slightly better.[80] Similarly, in March 1807, "Toney" Jacob, and eighteen-year-old Musa also escaped from Sapelo Island, having belonged to Alexander Johnston. It is conceivable that all three men were Muslims.[81] An 1827 document detailing the sale of Hopeton plantation on St. Simons Island by John Couper to James Hamilton Couper and his son James, 381 slave names are listed. On this list, the Muslim name Fatima is repeated six times, and Mahomet twice. Maryam is mentioned once.[82] In Liberty County, planter Joseph LeCounte recalled "an old native African named Philip," a Muslim who demonstrated the outward expressions of the religion "by going through all the prayers and prostrations of his native country."[83]

Islamic traditions retained and practiced by enslaved Africans and African Americans provided the religious underpinnings for the continuation of these practices by their progeny. The narratives of Sophie Davis of White Bluff, Chatham County; Ed Thorpe of Harris Neck, Liberty County; Rosa Grant of Possum Point, Chatham County; and Lawrence Baker of Darien, Liberty County reveal that their ancestors were also Muslim. Sophie Davis, whose ancestors were enslaved on St. Catherine's Island, remembered Africans who were brought to the island on slave ships. "They would pray at the rising and setting of the sun and would say Menna Mina, Mo."[84] Like the Bilali families, these early Muslims also prayed three times daily in the prescribed fashion, ending their prayers with "Ameen, Ameen, Ameen."[85] Rosa Grant said of her grandmother Ryna that "Friday wuz duh day she call huh prayuh day." This reference to the Muslim observance of Friday prayer, when Muslims congregate at noon, signified an attempt to keep alive the significance of the day.[86]

Both the First and Second Great Awakenings shaped the religious consciousness of enslaved Africans. Although the process of conversion varied according to the local environment and African ethnicity, Christianity appealed to lowcountry African Americans for two principal reasons. First, Christian customs, rituals, and beliefs paralleled the indigenous religious beliefs of West Africans, and West African religious thought and practice shaped their lives even through their conversion to Christianity. As did other diaspora communities, they syncretized elements of Christianity with their own sacred beliefs and traditions, and in doing so they influenced the contours of American religious culture. They retained a strong communion with the ancestors and developed a form of Gullah Christianity that excluded European Americans and provided recompense for past and present injustices. Because they lived continually in the presence of death, funerals were important ceremonies that symbolized the continuation of life after death. Thus decorating grave sites with important objects from this life, passing a child over the gravesite of the deceased, and orienting burial sites toward the east to symbolize the rising of the sun were important manifestations of the continuation of the spirit. Moreover, the sacrament of baptism conformed with their beliefs about bodies of water, which they regarded as sacred, and they performed the African circle dance known as the ring shout at funerals. Second, Christianity nurtured and kept alive the promise of equality and freedom and thus had both a liberatory and political meaning. The spirituals and shout songs of lowcountry African Americans demonstrate that they practiced a form of liberation theology that identified God with the condition of the oppressed and with the struggle for liberation.[87]

The gradual fusion of Christian and African beliefs in lowcountry watershed communities is evident in their dietary practices. In this context, sage observations of Islamic dietary practices in African American narratives reinforced the dissident subculture created by bondmen and bondwomen. Ophelia Baker of Chatham County provides a glimpse of this fusion by stating that members of the Holy Sanctified Church were forbidden to eat certain kinds of fish. Similarly Cornelia Bailey observed that Ben Ali's children would not eat wild animals or fresh meat and that some kinds of seafood, such as crab, were avoided.[88] Collectively, the testimonies of Ben Sullivan, Cornelia Bailey, Katie Brown, Rosa Grant, Ophelia Baker, and Sophie Davis provide the contours of Muslim life in early Georgia: prayer mats, prayer beads, veils, head coverings, Qur'ans, dietary laws, and ritualized daily prayer characterized their experiences. The composite picture represents a consistent and serious pursuit of Islam.[89]

As in the West African societies from which bondwomen and bondmen were transported, kinship relations informed the social, religious, and political foundation of the slave communities in lowcountry Georgia. As Steven Hahn argues, the obligations and responsibilities of kinship were crucial to the achievement of their short-term political objectives, which included protecting themselves and each other from slavery's violence and exploitation, carving out spheres of activity in which they could provide for themselves, and establishing relations and values suitable to a world of enslavement. The noncolonized imagination of bondmen and bondwomen was the space within which they turned a system based on the absolute power and personal domination of the master into one based on reciprocities. Their narratives of resistance and freedom reveal a uniquely political will to achieve autonomy, maintain dignity, secure use-rights to land, and engage in petty commodity markets.[90]

In the Chesapeake and lower Mississippi Valley, the vast majority of African Americans adhered to non-Islamic beliefs. In their struggle to retain a sense of identity, enslaved Africans had to determine which aspects or traits of their African heritage to retain and which to discard. The Christianization of Africans was an uneven process. It was welcomed by some and rejected by others. The demographic figures for Darien Baptist Church, near Sapelo Island, reveal that a significant number of enslaved Africans, 943, attended services in 1860.[91] In the process of acculturation, there were pressures to find points of agreement or similarity in religious expression, and the need to establish a community was intense. As the late nineteenth century progressed, planters became increasingly concerned with controlling the religious expression of their captive population. The number of Christian converts among bondmen and bondwomen increased rapidly as a result of their own desire to embrace an Africanized version of Christianity and of a post-1830 campaign within the "militant South" to use religion as a means of social control. As Africanized Christianity became more of a force, Islam in the lowcountry was contested and transformed. This transformation welded Christian and Islamic identities as evidenced by the practices of "Preacher Little, an itinerant preacher on Sapelo Island." A Mohammedan-looking man who wore a black skull cap, Preacher Little of the First African Baptist Church epitomized this fusion.[92]

Country markings, likewise, reveal the extent to which ideas concerning religion and African identity persisted. Rosanna Williams of Tatemville, Chatham County, received her father's country marks at a very young age. Her father, Lunnon Dennerson, and grandfather Golla Dennerson, whom Rosanna described as "King uh his tribe," labored on Charles Grant's plantation on the islands near Brunswick, Georgia. Rosanna, like other third-generation Africans, confidently expressed her family's origins in Liberia and revealed the circle marking on her chest as a symbol of her Gola identity.[93] As late as the 1930s, lowcountry African Americans continued to identify their African and Islamic roots with specificity. H. H. Miller, an educated, aged wealthy resident of Tatemville, recounted that he knew "many of the 'Golla' tribesman who were brought to this country" when he was a boy. The majority of these Africans may have been transported aboard the slave ship *Wanderer* and sold to local planter McMullen. According to Tonie Houston, Charles Lamar, the owner of the vessel, purchased these Gola Africans and sold them to McMullen.[94] The extensive Gola presence in lowcountry communities is apparent in naming practices, which affix the prefix Gola to the given name of African Americans, and in the continued use of words from the Gola language. Among the terms remembered by Houston were *musango* for tobacco, *mulafo* for whiskey, *sisure* for chicken, *gombay* for cow, and *gulluh* for hog.[95]

The process of religious acculturation proceeded unevenly during the antebellum period. However, with emancipation African Americans in the lowcountry demonstrated a passionate embrace of Christianity. On Sapelo Island, the progeny of African-born Muslims eventually began attending the Tuesday, Thursday, and Sunday night prayer houses established by each community on the island, while continuing their own Muslim gatherings With the establishment of the First African Baptist Church in May 1866, the open and collective pursuit of Islam became increasingly rare; however, remnants of the faith persisted. Despite pressure to convert to Christianity, the majority of African-born Muslims successfully resisted coercion to abandon their faith.[96]

The varied discourses of slave resistance illustrate that enslaved men and women created alternate geographies for themselves in lowcountry Georgia.

Enslaved Africans brought their bodies, their minds, and their cultures to the Americas, and they employed all three to address conflicting ideas of slavery and freedom. They carved out marginal spaces within slavery to engage in strategic resistance, and they established alliances based on ethnicity, occupation, kinship, and mutual oppression to contest their bondage. Slave insubordination crystallized into open defiance as they sought to gain individual and collective freedom by challenging the fissures within slavery. During this critical period, enslaved men and women reimagined, reformulated, and transformed the legal contexts in which they lived.[97] This form of political and strategic resistance, which allowed enslaved men and women to claim freedom for themselves, continued during the Civil War.

2

WAR AND FREEDOM

You may make my grave wherever you will
In a lowly vale or a lofty hill
You may make it among earth's humblest graves,
But not in a land where men are slaves

Frances Ellen Watkins Harper, "Bury Me in a Free Land"

Delia Garlic, a former slave in Virginia, Georgia, and Louisiana, knew the worst of slavery, including violent punishment and forced separation from family members. In an interview with the Works Progress Administration during the 1930s, she offered an unsparing assessment of her enslavement, saying the "days was hell . . . its bad to belong to folks [that] own you soul an' body."[1] Garlic provided a lucid narrative of her experiences as an enslaved woman. Her language suggests a bound and violently silenced black body where ruthless exploitation was a way of life, and where disorder and human degradation were commonplace.[2] Garlic's narrative captures the imagination precisely because it describes nearly unimaginable horror. The day-to-day experience of 250 years of bondage established interstices of slavery, marginal spaces where enslaved men and women struggled to create an identity that transcended their status as chattel property. Enslaved men and women employed these marginal spaces to their strategic advantage before and during the Civil War. This chapter interrogates how the chaos of the Civil War created a dynamic, layered backstory for self-emancipating men and women who sought to free themselves and their children from bondage in lowcountry Georgia and for the ways in which former slaves pursued economic justice through landownership.

This chapter argues that in lowcountry Georgia, self-emancipating men and women found in their experiences and emancipatory struggles the sources of inspiration for their own intellectual praxis. As political actors, they took actions during the war that were driven by the desire for freedom but were often constrained by wartime policies and physical terror. Freedom not only provided new and "socially liberated modes of being-with-others," but also created new opportunities to redefine community and construct a liberated identity.[3] But what exactly were the meaning and prospects for freedom in wartime lowcountry Georgia? And what were the meaning and prospects for a liberated identity?

MARGINAL SPACES OF FREEDOM

Opportunities for freedom in lowcountry Georgia were influenced by the natural landscape. The waterways, marshlands, and swamps provided transport and refuge from cruel masters, mistresses, and overseers, even if only temporarily. For a few, the waterways brought the city of Savannah within striking distance. Rice and sea island cotton plantations in lowcountry Georgia were positioned near the region's five large rivers: the Savannah, Ogeechee, Altamaha, Satilla, and St. Mary's, which were vital to the growth of rice and served as the focal point for settlement. The rice industry placed men and women in agricultural and nonagricultural occupations such as ricemilling and gristmilling. Additionally men worked as carpenters, brickmasons, and blacksmiths, and they staffed ferryboats, tugboats, drays, and steamboats, which sailed down the coastal rivers to transport rice and cotton to Savannah.[4]

The task labor system enabled many slaves to acquire property as they traded and sold the surplus of their gardens to each other, their masters, itinerant peddlers, and other consumers. Their experience with a market economy represented a hidden transcript of resistance as they negotiated the marginal spaces of freedom.[5] Women's marketing activities provided a measure of economic influence within the slave community. They allowed women to establish an economic link to the markets in Savannah. River and coastal trading vessels provided important access to trade centers, which women used to supplement their standard of living. Furthermore, as consumers and producers, women traders resisted the legal constraints of their mobility.

Women's access to markets also provided avenues for escape on the eve on the Civil War. At the age of eighteen in 1856, Jane, a slave of cotton and rice planter Charles C. Jones of Liberty County, Georgia, freed herself by stealing a boat and crossing the Ogeechee River, weaving around ponds, creeks, and drainage canals to the forests of oak and the cypress swamps, and on to the Savannah road. Wearing "fine-ear and finger-rings," the corpulent, self-confident African American woman traversed the thirty miles from Jones's plantation to the city of Savannah and renamed herself Sarah.[6] Jane had not been in the city more than a month before she was discovered. She had passed herself off as a slave from the Georgia upcountry who was permitted to hire her own time, and she found employment at $6.50 a week doing housework. A favorite house servant, Jane had run away several times before. The Jones's concern regarding her influence over other slaves on the plantation led to her confinement in the Wright slave broker's yard, from which she and members of her family from the Jones plantation were transported out of the city of Savannah and sold to an owner in Macon, Georgia, for $4,500.[7]

The experiences of Jane and other fugitive slaves underscored the tensions between what the enslaved thought and what they lived in the years preceding the Civil War. The act of running away marked the establishment of a dialectical relationship with the environment in which captive men and women lived. In this context, freedom in lowcountry Georgia emerged from the military realities of the Civil War. President Lincoln's Anaconda Plan, which imposed a naval blockade along the southeastern coastline, led to Union control of coastal territory from Virginia to Florida. The passage of the First Confiscation Act in August 1861 recognized fugitive men, women, and children who reached Union lines as "contraband of war" whose labor could be used to support the war effort.[8] As early as 1862, when Federal ships threatened the Georgia Sea Islands, which comprised the counties of Chatham, Liberty, McIntosh, Camden, and Glynn, enslaved men and women escaped in the midst of what historian Clarence Mohr refers to as refugeeing.[9] Through refugeeing, planters began relocating their slaves farther inland as the Union Navy blockaded the Sea Islands. In 1860 the enslaved population of the Sea Islands was 34,314.[10] By the end of August 1862, the number of persons classified as contraband of war had increased to over 500 on St. Simons Island.[11] Escapes were more numerous in 1862 than at any other period during the war.[12]

GENDER, WAR, AND FREEDOM

In lowcountry Georgia, the chaos of the war created a diegetic, layered backstory for a large segment of enslaved men and women in this region who experienced de facto freedom by escaping in the first two years of the war. These freedom narratives describe men and women with a keen sense of the binary structure of slavery and freedom. Despite what historian Stephanie M. H. Camp refers to as women's spatial illiteracy, women in lowcountry Georgia demonstrated a familiarity with the landscape and waterways and expressed a determined will to use flatboats and "dug-outs" to facilitate escape.[13] Union forces landed on Tybee and Warsaw islands in the final weeks of 1861, and by the end of March 1862 the entire Georgia coast came under Federal control. Gendered strategies of escape brought women into spaces where they reconceptualized the meaning of political leadership. In one poignant escape, a seventy-year-old Georgia woman used the marshlands to conceal her twenty-two children and grandchildren. Securing a flatboat, the emancipating fugitives drifted forty miles down the Savannah River and reached a Union gunboat to claim their freedom.[14] Under the terms of the Second Confiscation Act, of July 17, 1862, which freed slaves coming under Federal control, this grandmother and her children and grandchildren were free and could be used "in any military or naval service" to suppress the rebellion.[15] Such service included serving as cooks and laundresses and providing other forms of labor support.

The Emancipation Proclamation, issued on January 1, 1863, broadened the scope of the Second Confiscation Act by sanctioning the enlistment of free African American men in the Union Army. However, the Proclamation had very little immediate impact on freeing slaves in lowcountry Georgia because many had taken advantage of the chaos caused by the war to free themselves prior to 1863. General David Hunter's General Order No. 11, issued on May 9, 1862, had declared freedom to all slaves living in Florida, Georgia, and South Carolina.[16] Although President Lincoln rescinded Hunter's proclamation two weeks later, Hunter's order furthered the cause of freedom among enslaved men and women. On the Manigaults family's Hermitage and Gowrie plantations in Chatham County, Georgia, not only were the fields neglected during the war, but Louis Manigault reported frequent escapes of men and women who "piloted boats through the creeks, swamps, rivulets, and marshes" and who assisted the "Yankees in their raids."[17] Dolly, Manigault's washer for eight years, whom he listed as an "invalid," was among those who ran away in April 1863 while living with the Manigault family in Augusta.[18]

General David Hunter expanded on his freedom proclamation by recruiting fugitive slaves for the Union Army. Believing he was authorized to enlist "fugitive slaves" as soldiers in June 1862 by virtue of an order from Brigadier General T. W. Sherman to "employ all loyal persons offering their services in defence of the Union," Hunter aimed to recruit 50,000 black soldiers for the suppression of the Rebellion.[19] From Hunter's perspective, the experiment of arming fugitive slaves had been a "complete and marvellous success." The men were "sober, docile, attentive, and enthusiastic."[20] Hunter's description aimed to counter negative sentiments regarding the ability of black men to fight on par with white Union soldiers. Employing fugitive slaves as soldiers in 1862 was a radical departure from Union contraband policy, which placed black men in servile positions to white officers. Rufus Saxton, who served as the superintendent of contrabands in Beaufort, South Carolina, wrote disparagingly that "all the officers servants are negroes [and] large numbers are also employed in the Navy Department as sailors servants." Saxton supported the recruitment and enlistment of fugitive slaves into the Union Army and Navy as soldiers and sailors and commenced organizing the Second Regiment, composed of black soldiers.[21]

In March 1863, Federal policy mandated the conscription of Sea Island men by Union forces, which obligated these men to fight with the all-black regiments raised in South Carolina and Georgia.[22] During June 1863, military officials inaugurated a special draft for the Third South Carolina Volunteers on Ossabaw Island, Fort Pulaski, in Georgia, and in Fernandina, Florida, on Georgia's southern border.[23] In several instances, black men working on fortifications were impressed by Union Army commanders for enlistment against their will. At Fort Clinch in Florida, Major George Strong of the First South Carolina Volunteers impressed into service Jeff Houston, Peter Williams, Jake Forrester, Sam Major, and John Wanton. The men were working as military laborers on the fort, and under General Order No. 24 they were exempted from the draft because they were employed working on permanent fortifications. Captain Alfred Sears, army engineer at Fort Clinch, found the "kidnapping" of black men barbarous conduct.[24]

The Third South Carolina Volunteers combined with the newly formed Fourth and Fifth South Carolina Volunteers to form the Twenty-First U.S. Colored Troops (U.S.C.T). The need for soldiers augured changes in recruitment and enlistment. Major General J. G. Foster, commander of the Department of the South, expressed the need for all able-bodied men in the Sea Islands of South Carolina and Georgia to bear arms.[25] The Twenty-First U.S.C.T. numbered slightly over three hundred men until December 1864, when its ranks were filled by additional men who had followed General William Sherman to Savannah.[26]

Civic militarism in military camps was based on exclusive discourses that excluded women.[27] For instance, the language of military posters were grounded in the language of black masculinity. The presence of women and children behind Union lines was masked in one such poster, which contained the statement "all Negroes brought inside the lines at this place, will immediately on their arrival here, before any papers are drawn up, enlisting them as soldiers, be reported at the Provost Office in person."[28] Such military recruitment posters embodied the micro-techniques of power, such as laws, policies, and organizational norms and practices, to marginalize the presence of black women.[29] Women challenged the invisibility prescribed by military policies by taking individual and collective action as escape transformed them into emancipating "soldiers" of war and freedom.

An example from the Georgia Sea Islands is illustrative. In late December 1863, thirteen fugitives from McIntosh County, Georgia, boarded the U.S.S. *Fernandina* in St. Catherine's Sound. The leader of the group, a twenty-seven-year-old fugitive named Cain, had escaped from William King's plantation. Accompanying Cain was twenty-two-year-old Bella and her six-year-old son, Romeo; twenty-five-year-old Lizzie and her four children (Joseph, Sam, Eve, and Martha, age twelve years, four years, two years, and five months respectively); and thirty-two-year-old Sallie with her four children (Fannie, Joseph, Emma, and Ben, who ranged in age from eleven years to seven months). Early in 1864, Cain left the *Fernandina* to rescue his relatives from the vicinity of Sunbury, Georgia. He returned on January 7, along with ex-slave Sam, bringing forty-five-year-old Grace, her five children (Judy, Elizabeth, Phoebe, Victoria, and James), her son-in-law Charley, and her grandchildren (Arphee, Virginia, Clarissa, and Edward).[30] Free blacks from Darien, Georgia, reached the Union lines together with those who were escaping slavery.[31] Approximately two-thirds of the escapees were women and children, who were mustered into service.[32] Behind Union lines, women served as cooks, nurses, and seamstresses. As the case of Susie King Taylor illustrates, women also served as educators to soldiers of the U.S.C.T. Literate former slaves like Susie King Taylor and her husband,

Sergeant Edward King of Darien, Georgia, performed much of the educational work in military camps and established a model of educational leadership, which allowed men to begin or expand their formal education.[33]

Attempts toward liberation in many areas of the lowcountry were characterized by violence. Confederate soldiers met the advance of Union pickets by retaliating against African Americans in the vicinity. In one instance, Confederate soldiers from Fort Chapman in South Carolina burned a plantation home on Hutchinson Island near Savannah and murdered and terrorized over one hundred men, women, and children in the area.[34] These frequent skirmishes between Union and Confederate forces in the lowcountry placed men, women, and children in precarious positions and underscored the virulent nature of warfare. Confederate soldiers, responding to drum beating at night on the north end of Hutchinson Island, opened fired with the expectation that Union soldiers were on the island. Union soldiers had left the island a week earlier, and malevolent Confederate forces killed fifteen men, women, and children.[35]

During the war, diseases also afflicted enslaved men, women, and children. The cycle of life and death continued unabated as enslaved women gave birth and unyielding diseases consumed young and old. At Hermitage and East Hermitage plantations, seven women gave birth during the early years of the war.[36] Manigault, who served as medical assistant to Confederate surgeon Joseph Jones, reported deaths from the following conditions at Gowrie and East Hermitage plantations from 1861 to 1864: dropsy, sunstroke, cancer in the stomach, and dysentery. The most severe afflictions occurred in the years preceding the Civil War when a virulent cholera epidemic swept through Gowrie plantation.[37] On the field and behind Union and Confederate lines, camp fevers, typhus fever, and common fevers were the most prevalent wartime medical conditions. This issue led S. P. Moore, surgeon general of the Confederate States of America, to task Jones with instituting extended treatment of fevers and studying the relationship of climate and soil to disease.[38]

As the early years of the war brought coastal regions under Union control, the coasts of Virginia and Louisiana also served as havens for emancipating men and women. On March 13, 1862, Congress passed legislation prohibiting the employment of Union soldiers to return fugitive slaves to former masters. The Second Confiscation Act contained a provision referred to as the Militia Act, which freed the mothers, wives, and children of freed men whose labor and service were used to suppress the rebellion.[39] The act declared "forever free" the mothers, wives, and children of black men who had belonged to disloyal masters and then rendered service to the United States, but only if the family members were also owned by disloyal masters—a qualification that excluded the families of most border-state black soldiers.[40] The federal government did not resolve this exclusion until March 3, 1865, when Congress, by joint resolution, provided for the freedom of the wives and children of all men serving in, or subsequently mustered into, army or navy service.[41]

The Militia Act provided the official imprimatur for soldiers to claim freedom for their wives and children during the war. African American soldiers of the reorganized, Union-supported First Louisiana Native Guards seized horses, carts, and mules in St. Bernard Parish for the purpose of transporting men, women, and children from the surrounding plantations to the city of New Orleans. In one instance, five soldiers demanded the freedom of their wives from loyal planter Mr. E. Villerie in August 1863.[42] Similar demands for freedom occurred in other areas of the South, particularly in the border states of the Union. In Kentucky, Mary Wilson, the wife of Lewis Wilson, of the United States Colored Infantry, claimed her freedom under the Militia Act from master William Adams by leaving his plantation and setting up residence in the city of Lexington. Adams reclaimed Mary with the assistance of the city constable, "tied her in a Slaughter house, . . . and inflicted upon her naked body a severe beating and bruising.[43] Through these instances of on-the-ground relations, the political struggles of husbands and wives demonstrate the myriad challenges they faced in claiming freedom during the war.

From 1862 to 1865, the issue of wage labor emerged as the focus of military officials in the transition from slavery in wartime Louisiana. During the era of slavery, enslaved women in southern Louisiana labored on plantations, worked as domestics and market women, nurtured their children, loved their husbands, and endured episodes of physical and mental terror. The enslaved female population of southern Louisiana, which comprised twenty-three parishes in 1860, consisted of 43,898 women between the ages of fifteen and sixty.[44] During the Civil War, as Union forces occupied much of the region, women expected and demanded fair payment for their labor. Their expectations were often at odds with those of military officials and their former masters and mistresses.

The case of Dinah is illustrative of the conditions women faced in Union-controlled New Orleans. Dinah and her three children were denied fair compensation for a day's work performed for Mr. Elin in New Orleans. According to Dinah's complaint, "Mr. Elin told her he would pay her what was right. He gave her three [children] ten cents each and refused to pay more."[45] Dinah received one dollar for her labor.[46] A sample of twenty-two registers and payrolls of freed people employed on plantations in Terre Bonne Parish from November 1863 to February 1864 indicate that the agency hired 139 women, 111 men, and 72 children to work on plantations.[47] As during their enslavement, government officials valued women's field labor above the domestic work women performed for their families.[48] In her seminal study of black women's labor, Jacqueline Jones has demonstrated that newly emancipated women did not have the luxury of choosing between different kinds of work. Women with children found that "economic necessity bred its own kind of slavery."[49]

In her study of Virginia, Mary J. Farmer argues that the Freedmen's Bureau believed that supporting "black women was more acceptable than supporting black men. Black men had to find employment or face persecution as vagrants."[50] But the court records from Louisiana's Bureau of Free Labor indicate that vagrancy charges were levied against a significant number of women, as well as men. Women filed complaints for nonpayment of wages and resisted vagrancy charges, which military officials implemented to control newly freed people without regard to gender. Women such as Elizabeth White, Henrietta Henderson, Caroline Starks, Charlotte Ann Hall, and Amelie Candole, who filed complaints in New Orleans for nonpayment of wages, are representative of the ways in which women actively pursued their own objectives for fair compensation and economic justice.[51] In comparison, emancipated women in the Sea Islands of lowcountry Georgia often labored behind the lines of the Union Army and Navy without recompense as contraband of war. Freedom brought its own kind of reward in January 1863 as women who were skilled market women received remuneration for goods supplied to the Union Navy.[52]

The arrival of General Sherman's army in Georgia provided an additional opportunity for men and women to claim their freedom. The capture of Atlanta in September 1864, following Confederate general John Bell Hood's evacuation, led Sherman to propose to General Grant a destructive march across Georgia to force Confederate capitulation.[53] As Sherman marched through central Georgia in November 1864, 19,000 men, women, and children left the plantations to follow his army.[54] Before the capture of Atlanta, Sherman had received some indication of what he might expect in the execution of his plan to cut and burn a path up to sixty miles wide through central and southern Georgia to Savannah. Wherever he encountered African Americans, a considerable following of men, women, and children joined in what they considered a march for freedom.[55] Sherman's Special Field Order No. 120, issued on November 9, 1864, endorsed the use, in the march through central Georgia, of "able bodied Negroes" who would constitute a "pioneer battalion" to repair and reinforce roads as they followed the advance guard.[56]

General Sherman divided his army into two wings: the right wing, commanded by Major General Oliver Otis Howard, and the left wing, commanded by Major General H. W. Slocum. According to Slocum, "At least 14,000 of these people joined the two columns at different points on the march, but many of them were too old and infirm, and others too young, to endure the fatigues of the march, and therefore were left in the rear. More than one-half of the above number, however, reached the coast with us. Many of the able-bodied men were transferred to the officers of the Quartermaster and subsistence departments, and others were employed in the two corps as teamsters, cooks and servants."[57] While Slocum's description masks the presence of women and children, the metalanguage of his description suggests that not only men, but also women and children, were among the young and the "too old and infirm."

The large number of men, women, and children following the Union Army led to drastic measures at river and creek crossings to reduce the number of refugees. One Union officer illustrated these measures by writing:

> "When the lower and less fruitful lands were reached, the embarrassment and military annoyance increased. This was more particularly felt in the left wing, which was then the only one exposed to the attacks of the enemy. Losing patience at the failure of all orders and exhortations to these poor people to stay home, Gen. Davis (now commanding the Fourteenth Corps), ordered the pontoon bridge at Ebenezer Creek to be taken up before the refugees who were following that corps had crossed, so as to leave them on the further bank of the unavoidable stream and thus dis-embarrass the marching troops. . . . Those who could not swim as well as those who could swim, were drowned. The loss of life was still great enough to prove that . . . it was literally preferable to die freeman rather than to live slaves."[58]

Sherman defended the actions of General Davis as "militarily necessary," thus reconciling emancipating men and women's moral quest for freedom with his desire to reach the sea. Northern newspapers reported that hundreds of refugees drowned or were reenslaved.[59]

General Slocum's left wing was under constant harassment from Confederate forces led by General Joseph Wheeler's cavalry corps. The Confederate general believed this harassment led Union forces to abandon African Americans at Ebenezer Creek.[60] It was impossible to determine the number of African Americans who followed the army. Some joined for brief intervals, became discouraged, and returned to their homes. Many found it difficult to associate freedom with the harsh measures applied by General Sherman's troops on their way to the sea. Frequently the inherent racism of many Union soldiers gave a grim view of what the future promised. When they encountered such treatment, African Americans soldiers of war and freedom turned away from the jubilant march and awaited an uncertain future.[61]

The Civil War devastated much of the state of Georgia. Sherman's campaign aimed at destroying the physical, economic, and cultural landscapes of the region. Widespread destruction of physical structures, including hundreds of miles of railroads, and an economic depression, inherent in the ravages of war, left men, women, and children destitute and in need of food, clothing, and medical care.[62] Sherman's army arrived outside the city limits of Savannah on December 12, 1864, after traversing through forty-two counties in the state. On January 16, 1865, Sherman issued General Field Order No. 15, which reserved the Sea Islands and abandoned inland rice fields for former slaves. Sherman and other Union officers were under investigation by Secretary of War Edwin M. Stanton for acts of cruelty against African American refugees. The general issued Field Order No. 15 after meeting with African American religious leaders in Savannah. It represented Sherman's effort to recast himself while simultaneously jettisoning the newly emancipated from the lines of the Union Army. Men and women who were heads of households received from five to forty acres of "abandoned land" under Sherman's order.[63] President Andrew Johnson later reversed Field Order No. 15, but former slaves in Georgia and other parts of the South continued to believe that the federal government would provide forty acres of land as compensation for enslavement.[64]

Sherman's march represented the end of emancipation and the beginning of African American freedom. Although the city of Savannah was physically intact, it was desolate in spirit and desperately poor. Thousands of African American refugees, including a significant number of women, wandered aimlessly, in need of food, shelter, and clothing. Sherman sought help from General Rufus Saxton in Beaufort, who was already overwhelmed by 15,000 refugees.[65] Saxton reported, "Every cabin and house on the islands is filled to overflowing."[66] He suggested that soldiers from a black regiment protect the islands of St. Simons in Georgia and Edisto in South Carolina, which would also serve as refuge for the homeless. Sherman accepted the suggestion as meritorious, especially for women and children; he believed that most, if not all, able-bodied men could be put to work by the quartermaster corps.

LESS THAN FORTY ACRES

The subjugation of the lowcountry by Union forces during the winter of 1864 provided the impetus for the region's metamorphosis into "abandoned" land settlements for emancipated individuals. Federal officials classified plantations as abandoned if the owner was voluntarily absent and engaged in aiding or encouraging the rebellion. Rufus Saxton, who later became supervisor of Freedman's Bureau affairs in Georgia, advised freed men and women, in a meeting held at Second Baptist Church in Savannah, to locate abandoned lands where they could work and support themselves.[67] Freed men and women who had followed Sherman's trek into Savannah undoubtedly joined with those who returned to plantation lands and carved out family plots. These plots of land represented shared places of intersecting relations, culture, and language that reinforced preexisting kinship and community networks.[68]

Landownership was problematic from the beginning and necessitated a demarcation in land titles. Sherman's land policy did not confer permanent title. Instead, Captain A. P. Ketchum, adjutant general of the Freedmen's Bureau in Georgia, issued possessory titles that placed the recipients in a state of economic purgatory by granting them ownership of the crops they produced but not ownership of the soil. Permanent title to the abandoned lands hinged on presidential confirmation, a condition that Sherman outlined in Special Order No.16.[69] The assassination of President Lincoln in April 1865 made permanent land titles untenable. Lincoln's successor, Andrew Johnson, pursued a lenient Reconstruction policy that would

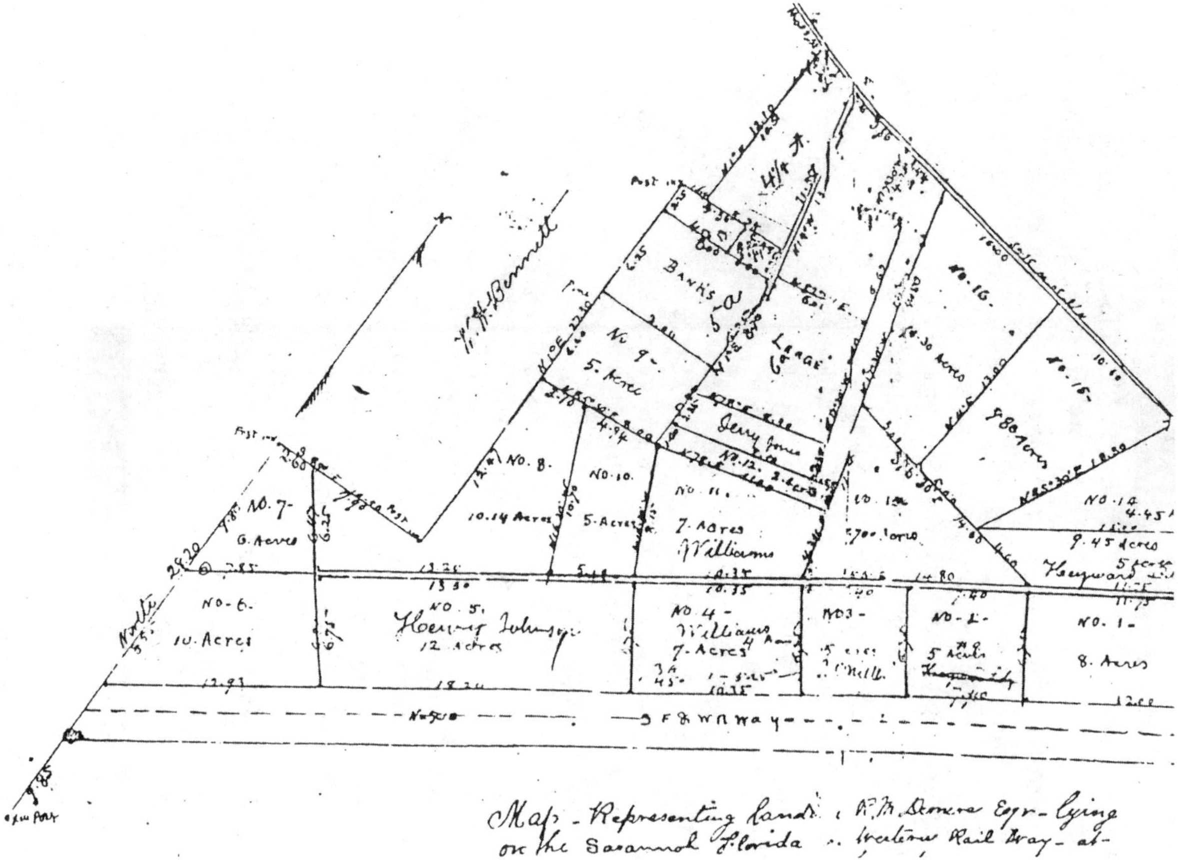

This 1883 map shows the subdivision of land on the Ogeechee Neck. During the 1870s and 1880s African Americans on the Ogeechee Neck purchased between four to ten acres of land near Miller's station and at Wild Horn plantation, providing the foundation for the town of Burroughs. Subdivision of Land, William Miller's Plantation, 1883. Records of the Chatham County Superior Court, Savannah, Georgia.

allow the original owners to return and claim rights of ownership. Johnson's Amnesty Act of May 29, 1865, offered a pardon and the restoration of all rights, including right to abandoned property, to Southerners who swore an oath of allegiance to the Union. Additionally each former Confederate state had to ratify the 13th Amendment. Under Johnson's plan, all of the former Confederate states were readmitted, including Mississippi, which refused to ratify the 13th Amendment, and South Carolina, which refused to repudiate its Confederate war debt.[70]

Despite the defeat of the Confederacy, planters hoped to reestablish what historian Allan Kulikoff termed "domestic patriarchy" by exerting control over their land and former slaves. John Cheves, the owner of the 2,014-acre Grove Point plantation, applied for restoration to his land in July 1865. Cheves had not only abandoned his plantation but had also engaged in building torpedoes for Fort McAllister and had employed his slaves in maintaining the fort. By the time of his return, twenty-five families had received possessory titles to 245 acres of land (see Table 3).[71] Planters began returning to plantation districts during the flooding and draining of rice fields in the summer of 1865. The Ogeechee plantations, like those on Skidaway Island, had been spared the wartime destruction that had occurred on several Savannah River plantations. Union officials had controlled and operated several of the plantations in the district. They established their headquarters in the plantation house at Wild Horn during the attack on nearby Fort McAllister, and also maintained a signaling station at the rice mill on Grove Point plantation.[72]

On Grove Hill plantation, owned by William and Robert Habersham, fifty families received title to 641 acres (see Tables 4–5). Grove Hill consisted of 1,100 acres, of which 200 acres were highland. Jacob Shellman, Charles Brown, and Billy Williams, land recipients at Grove Hill and Grove Point, became petitioners in the articles of incorporation for the town of Burroughs in 1898.[73] On nearby New Hope and Shaftesbury plantations, owned by William H. Gibbons, the land was also subdivided. Nineteen families received possessory title to 213 acres at Shaftesbury.[74] Both Grove Point and Grove Hill plantations were located on the Ogeechee Neck, an area that also contained the Wild Horn and Vallambrosia plantations. Former slaves on Wild Horn and Vallambrosia did not receive possessory titles but rented the land from the Freedmen's Bureau, paying one-quarter of their crop as rent.[75]

TABLE 3. Families Who Received Land Titles in 1865, Grove Point Plantation, John R. Cheves

SETTLER	NUMBER OF ACRES	NUMBER IN FAMILY
Pat Taylor	20	3
Thomas Glover	15	6
Dinah Glover	15	3
Francis Singleton	15	4

SETTLER	NUMBER OF ACRES	NUMBER IN FAMILY
Peter Singleton	30	7
Rosana Edwards	10	3
Ned Richardson	30	9
Toby Taylor	5	2
Richard Lachison	15	5
Amy Wilkins	5	1
Billy Williams	5	1
Susie Wright	5	3
Catsey Cheves	5	5
Sambo Greene	10	3
Nebison Barnard	10	2
Lucian Footman	15	3
Titus Neal	10	2
Collins Larrie	15	6
Lucy Barnard	15	5
George Sella	20	4
Richard Bennett	10	6
London Lowman	10	3
David Rollabid	10	4
Major Young	15	2
Anderson Grant	20	3

SOURCE: Register of Land Titles Issued, Savannah, RG 105, Bureau of Refugees, Freedmen, and Abandoned Lands, National Archives, Washington, D.C.

TABLE 4. Families Who Received Land Titles in 1865, Grove Hill Plantation, William Habersham

SETTLER	NUMBER OF ACRES	NUMBER IN FAMILY
John Cuthbert	30	4
Lucy Wilson	10	4
Peter McKnight	25	4
Samuel Howard	20	4
Davis Williams	20	3
Wally Large	10	3
Jermiah Jones	40	6
Aliok Campbell	25	4
Daniel Morton	25	9
Scott Butler	30	4
Hannah Butler	5	3

Table 4 continued

SETTLER	NUMBER OF ACRES	NUMBER IN FAMILY
Pompey Jackson	4	1
Dandy McNeal	10	5
Tina Jones	5	5
Titus Quarterman	5	5
Sambo Mack	5	5
March Marshall	10	5
Mary Bush	30	3
S. Davenport	10	3
Charles Brown	5	7
Collin Williams	5	2
Jacob Shellman	10	3
Ben Telfair	10	6
Joseph Waltower	6	3

SOURCE: Register of Land Titles Issued, Savannah, RG 105, Bureau of Refugees, Freedmen, and Abandoned Lands, National Archives, Washington, D.C.

TABLE 5. Families Who Also Received Land Titles in 1865, Grove Hill Plantation, William Habersham

SETTLER	NUMBER OF ACRES	NUMBER IN FAMILY
Polly Burroughs	11	2
Jane Jones	6	3
Dick Jones	10	4
William Joiner	25	6
Caesar Malone	15	3
Billy Williams	10	3
Henry Emory	5	6
January Hamilton	10	2
Abraham Jacob	10	5
Jane Hargrage	10	3
John Broker	10	5
Caesar Mallard	10	3
Sandy Flowers	30	4
Augustus Johnson	10	5
Peter Sweet	10	2
Sleigh Dunham	10	3
George Agner	10	5
Toby Roberts	10	5

SETTLER	NUMBER OF ACRES	NUMBER IN FAMILY
William Coleman	15	2
Susannah Grovllon	10	2
Hannah Davis	12	4
Gabriel Roberts	5	4
John Campbell	5	3
May Anderson	10	7
Joe Monroe	12	6
Adam Habersham	5	3

SOURCE: Register of Land Titles Issued, Savannah, RG 105, Bureau of Refugees, Freedmen, and Abandoned Lands, National Archives, Washington, D.C.

Note: Tables 4 and 5 are similar in nature but based on two separate documents in the records.

Bureau enumerations for the islands south of Sapelo Island reveal the fluid conditions within which both agents and settlers negotiated. Both time and distance remained intrinsic weaknesses in the land grant process. In August 1865, the Reverend William F. Eaton, whose jurisdiction included the islands from Sapelo south, found it difficult to survey the land claims of the freed men and women within his jurisdiction due to the distance between the Sea Islands and Savannah. Eaton's figures, according to historian Paul Cimbala, may not accurately reflect the actual settlement of the islands.[76] Nonetheless, Eaton reported 352 African Americans residing on Sapelo, 606 on St. Simons, and 60 on Cumberland. Farther north, on St. Catherine's and Ossabaw islands, the reports of the Reverend Tunis G. Campbell revealed a similar discrepancy. In December, Campbell reported 369 freedmen claiming four thousand acres of improved and unimproved land on St. Catherine's; on Ossabaw there were 78 freedmen claiming two thousand acres of land.[77]

African Americans on Skidaway Island and Butler's Island adopted similar strategies. Under the leadership of Ulysses Houston, who served as pastor of the Third African Baptist Church in Savannah, African Americans on Skidaway Island carved out plots of land on eight plantations and received possessory title to a total of 2,875 acres under Sherman's order.[78] They elected Garrison Frazier as governor, and also elected a sheriff and three inspectors. Frazier and Houston were among twenty African American religious leaders who met with Sherman to advocate for the establishment of oppositional communities. The formation of oppositional communities occurred through nationalist ideology and processes, when a shared ideology and a sense of common destiny converged to challenge both the promise and the failure of federal land policy. Concomitantly, on Butler's Island, fifty-six African American families occupied land that they claimed under Sherman's field order. In many instances, the abandoned lands they claimed had not been registered with Bureau agents. On both Skidaway and Butler's, African Americans turned inward to reestablish community and kinship ties on land where their enslavement harbored transcendent memories of oppression. These communities did not represent an escape from reality, but they were rational attempts by African Americans to manipulate the hostile environment in which they lived. Maintaining their occupancy of land where their forced labor had produced millions of pounds of rice underscored the belief in both a natural and specific right to the land.[79]

Sherman's order affected barrier islands that were on the periphery of time and space. For almost a century, African Americans labored on Georgia's six largest offshore islands, producing rice and Sea Island cotton within the confines of an existentialist environment. The marshlands and tidal rivers surrounding Cumberland, Jekyll, St. Simons, Sapelo, St. Catherine's, and Ossabaw islands separated the islands from the mainland, reinforcing their collective identity and consciousness.[80] This ideological landscape also included a host of smaller barrier islands and inland rice districts, such as Skidaway, Butler's, Argyle, and Whitemarsh islands, where Sherman's order altered the spatial parameters of former plantations. In this context, the Sea Islands and the inland rice districts became a nexus for newly freed slaves, many of whom not only maintained ancestral ties to plantation lands, but also believed that they had a natural right to the land. The majority of men and women who returned to coastal Georgia had worked the same land during slavery. They had loved, borne children, and buried their dead on this land, and had developed a spiritual, if not religious attachment to it.[81]

The enduring vitality of African American culture in the lowcountry stemmed from the employment of absentee plantation management, which provided enslaved African Americans with a greater degree of autonomy than existed on cotton and sugar plantations. Consequently African Americans developed an attachment to the land that found reinforcement in consanguineal relationships. The demographic majority held by the slave population in the region was an additional factor that shaped the ideology of African Americans. In 1860 the region had a population of 34,314 slaves and 23,184 whites, most of whom resided in the city of Savannah.[82] This demographic majority shaped the worldview of former slaves in the immediate postwar period as they sought to gain control of land and their labor.

As African Americans gained social and economic spaces in the lowcountry, they also created myriad political networks to promote political advocacy and self-governance. The political channels established to protect and influence communities in the lowcountry included mustered militias and organized governments. African Americans on the Ogeechee Neck established the largest settlement of freed people in the Ogeechee district, receiving title to 886 acres of land.[83] Slavery and emancipation served as the prism for nationalist unity, as evidenced by the election of a committee of three on each plantation to represent the communities. The functional authority of these committees included serving as "cabinets of advisors" to the Freedmen's Bureau in Savannah. In addition to selecting representatives, freed people also organized the Ogeechee Home Guards, which provided freed men with an important collective political identity. Moses H. Bentley, under the auspices of the Union League, had formed the Ogeechee Home Guards, which at its peak in 1867 mustered in two hundred men. The Union League encouraged progressive political action by counseling African Americans to insist on "setting up for themselves to secure homesteads."[84]

For many African Americans, the barrier islands were important symbols of cultural memory and identity. African and African American knowledge systems had created and maintained the technologies of rice production for decades. In addition to its value as the principal plantation cash crop for lowcountry Georgia, rice was valued as a market item and a dietary staple in the years following emancipation. In areas such as the Ogeechee district and Sapelo Island, obtaining proprietary interest in land suitable for cultivating rice for the market, as well as for home consumption, was a significant expression of their freedom during the first decade following emancipation.[85]

Rice cultivation figured prominently in the lives of slaves and planters during the antebellum period. Constrained by geography, rice plantations clustered at a distance of between five and twenty-five miles from the sea and required the maintenance of an elaborate irrigation system and a threshing mill. They required investments from $50,000 to $500,000 at the outset and required year-round attention. By 1862 the Sea Islands had been abandoned by planters, who considered it vital to protect their valued property by forsaking rice production as Union forces gained control of nearby Tybee Island, and patrolling the defenseless, exposed Sea Islands in Georgia. Prior to the Civil War, enslaved African Americans living within the six counties in the region had annually produced 51,686,141 pounds of rice.[86]

During the process of restoration, planters were forced to adjust to the reality that former slaves possessed keen knowledge about the cycles of rice production and were now in a position, as freed men and women, to manipulate the lowcountry landscape and subvert land restoration to fulfill their economic objectives. Rice plantations functioned as "huge hydraulic machines," which necessitated the construction and maintenance of floodgates, trunks, canals, banks, and ditches. They were massive engineering achievements that slaves had erected and had maintained for nearly a century.[87] In addition to coordinated labor, rice cultivation also required skill. Workers began preparing the soil for cultivation in January and continued until early March. They planted the seeds in straight-line trenches four inches wide and eleven inches apart. After flooding the fields for eight to nine days, workers drained the water, and the fields were allowed to dry for ten days. Referred to as the "sprout flow," this initial flooding resulted in the sprouting of seeds.[88] A second flow, referred to as the "point flow," occurred for eight to ten days. This flooding and draining of fields occurred repeatedly until the final flooding, referred to as the "harvest flow," in September. Gathering rice required the use of sickles; rice workers grasped a handful of rice stalks with the left hand and swung the sickle with the right hand in a rhythmic pattern. After harvesting, they threshed the rice at the threshing mill to remove the seeds. Workers pounded rice used for home consumption with mortars and pestles and winnowed it in reed baskets made in West African fashion.[89]

During the early months of the Freedmen's Bureau's existence, its policies supported the distribution of land to former slaves. Rufus Saxton, as inspector of plantations and settlements and the Freedmen's Bureau assistant commissioner, moved expeditiously to place agents in the Ogeechee district and on St. Catherine's and St. Simons islands to execute the land provisions of General Sherman's field order. Saxton, who directed one of the first emancipation laboratories in the South Carolina Sea Islands, sympathized with the plight of former slaves and articulated policies that reinforced the nationalist ideology of lowcountry African Americans.[90] During his tenure as assistant commissioner, 40,000 freed men and women on abandoned plantations in the lowcountry received possessory titles to plots of land ranging from five to forty acres. However, along the Georgia coast, the number of African American families receiving land in the official register did not conform to the reality of ad hoc settlement and emancipation in the rice and cotton fields. According to the official records, 242 African Americans claimed 1,645 acres, receiving possessory titles from 62 land grants on Ossabaw, St. Catherine's, Sapelo, and St. Simons islands.[91]

By the end of 1865, most of the planters in the district had received a presidential pardon and "informal possession" of their lands. Robert Habersham received a special pardon from President Johnson in September 1865. Although planters had been given possession of their land, the bureau maintained that freed people had control over the crops. By year's end, former slaves had produced a rice crop, which they marketed despite the constraints of the postwar environment. They insisted on selling their rice in Savannah as opposed to selling it directly to agents of the Bureau, who imposed a mill toll and a rice tax.[92] The tide of federal land policy turned quickly at the end of 1865. Major General Oliver Otis Howard, commissioner of the Freedmen's Bureau, countermanded Sherman's order following Johnson's nullification of the Bureau's enabling land provisions on September 12, 1865. Although planters' lands were returned to them, the Bureau maintained that former slaves had control over the crops they produced and could not be removed until after they marketed their harvest. Although Bureau agent Captain A. P. Ketchum recognized the economic rights of freed men and women, reorganizing the labor supply to provide discipline and control became the Bureau's first priority. In very important ways, the Freedmen's Bureau served as the agent of dispossession because of its role as mediator in the restoration process.[93]

THE OGEECHEE TROUBLES

Adverse changes in the contract labor system, which resulted in less autonomy and more direct supervision from new managers, overseers, and their guards, propelled freed men and women to force a distribution of land. In 1867 the owners of Prairie and Southfield plantations decided to rent their lands to Major J. Motte Middleton and Captain J. F. Tucker. Tucker also became part owner of John Cheves's Grove Point plantation. Middleton's expulsion of men who refused to sign labor contracts under his terms immediately engendered hostility and bitterness on the part of black laborers. According to William Burroughs, they also "felt dissatisfied with anyone having possession of the lands because they had the plantation pretty much to themselves."[94]

On Saturday, December 31, 1868, two years after Johnson rescinded General Field Order No. 15, the Ogeechee troubles erupted. The *Savannah Morning News* provided sensationalized accounts of the five-day revolt, which at its core was more than a struggle over land. It was an ideological struggle to test the breadth and the limits of economic democracy.[95] Dissatisfied with the imposition of labor contracts and the transgression of what had become a sacrosanct doctrine on the Ogeechee Neck, the leaders of the revolt, Solomon Farley, Paul Campbell, Jack Cuthbert, and Captain Green, began mobilizing the Ogeechee Home Guards, a military and protective unit. Moses H. Bentley, under the auspices of the Union League, had formed the Ogeechee Home Guards in 1866. The Union League encouraged African Americans to secure homesteads, counseling them to insist on "setting up for themselves."[96] Union League meetings provided black men with an important collective political identity that served to reinforce their ideology. The officers of the Union League's Ogeechee district included Farley as president, Campbell as vice president, Cuthbert as assistant vice president, and Sam Howard as secretary. Union League meetings had been held regularly on Grove Point plantation since 1866. However, in February 1868 Major Middleton disallowed the meetings, effectively eviscerating a viable political organization on the Ogeechee Neck that promoted political and social activism. Middleton's actions forced the men to meet in secret, which ultimately contributed to the escalating hostilities.[97]

The cycle of the "insurrectionary'" events continued on New Year's Day. Deep in the Ogeechee woods, just before sunrise, two hundred members of the Ogeechee Home Guards divided into military companies and armed themselves with muskets and bayonets. The men had putatively secured weapons in Savannah months before the revolt. Plantation managers had also provided muskets to "trustworthy" African Americans on the Ogeechee Neck to drive off the ricebirds.[98] As the men marched toward the plantations, they met George Baxley, one of Middleton's overseers, who had gone to investigate the commotion in the woods. The men lurched toward

Baxley, surrounded him, confiscated his weapons, and struck him with the butt of a musket. Baxley recovered after the men had left, found a canoe at the Ogeechee River, and made his way to Savannah. By dint of threats, the insurgents also forced Middleton to leave the Ogeechee Neck and used their weapons to intimidate and force others who did not support their objectives to flee. The strategic objectives of the men and women did not include murder. Their primary objective was to force the former landowners and their agents to abandon the Ogeechee Neck. The rebels also excoriated obsequious black guards like Fortune Brown and George Bunyan, who were reluctant to join the rebellion. As the insurgents traveled from the Ogeechee plantations to the Atlantic Gulf train station, a strategic rallying point, they proclaimed that "no white man should live between the two Ogeechees."[99]

Despite the pandemonium that engulfed the Ogeechee Neck, the actions of the men and women were purposeful. They established their headquarters at Middleton's house on Southfield plantation, constructed a fortification at Peach Hill, and established a watch on the main roads. In the late evening on New Year's Day, Farley issued the "Ogeechee Manifesto." This manifesto was more than an attempt by a semi-literate freedman to justify his resistance to local authorities; it was an apocalyptic plea for recognition of the economic rights of former slaves, as indicated by the document's last statement "Ogeechee Until Death."[100] Freed people from nearby Bryan and Liberty counties, as well as from Augusta Road on the outskirts of Savannah, had joined what the *Savannah Morning News* proclaimed the Ogeechee insurrection. The paper's supercilious verbiage and stinging condemnations of the participants fed rumors of a mass movement of former slaves to the Ogeechee Neck and contributed to the belief that the men and women had perpetrated mayhem and murder.[101]

The objective of complete autonomy over the region seemed feasible to most freed people and a few of Savannah's black religious leaders, whom the insurgents invited to begin the process of negotiation and settlement. The African Americans in the district constituted an overwhelming majority: in 1870 they numbered 4,201 as opposed to a white population of 411, a decline of two from the 413 in 1860.[102] In other areas of lowcountry Georgia, freed men and woman had already achieved the autonomy that African Americans on the Ogeechee Neck desired. At Belle Ville on St. Catherine's Island, for instance, the Reverend Tunis G. Campbell had established an autonomous community of African Americans and appointed himself governor on the basis of the promise of Sherman's order. After troops removed Campbell, he purchased a 1,250-acre plantation in McIntosh County and established another black settlement.[103]

The possibility that the Ogeechee revolt could succeed and spread entered the minds of white Savannah residents as white families who were reportedly "driven out" boarded the Atlantic Gulf railway or sailed down the Ogeechee Canal for Savannah. The railway's Miller's Station, located near the land of planter William H.

Miller, became an important rallying point. A distance of only two to three miles separated the plantations on the Ogeechee Neck; hence, freed people maintained an interplantation network. Through this network they maintained close associations that strengthened the bonds of family and community. This bond was particularly evident on January 2, when Savannah sheriff James Dooner arrested Solomon Farley at New Hope plantation. As president of the district's Union League, Farley was viewed as the leader of the insurrection. When authorities attempted to transport him to Savannah, hundreds of blacks, in military formation and armed, rallied at Miller's Station. This show of force led to Farley's release, but it also prompted civil authorities to seek federal military assistance.[104]

The tranquil marshlands and tidal rivers that extended across the Ogeechee landscape were manifest symbols of rice production and important symbols of the revolt. During the five days of unrest, the insurgents secured possession of thousands of bushels of rice from Grove Hill, Grove Point, Prairie, and Southfield plantations. The acquisition and disposition of the rice crop became a cogent display of their freedom to exist as independent "rice planters," an appellation rice workers believed reflected the apotheosis of their life and labor.[105]

During the revolt, the insurgents received consul from Aaron A. Bradley, a labor activist. Bradley, who escaped slavery in Georgia during the 1830s, had studied law in Boston and positioned himself to serve as an advocate for African Americans. When slavery ended, he settled in Savannah and became an ardent political agitator for dispossessed freed men and women. Bradley, in fact, had been charged with using seditious and insurrectionary language in 1865, when he led the first campaign in Chatham County to retain the land promised under Sherman's order. The plangent and iconoclastic oratory of Bradley reinforced the Ogeechee resistance campaign and set the stage for the penultimate stage of defiance.[106]

During the final two days of the revolt, prayer meetings, which had accompanied the violence from the outset, intensified as word of military reinforcement spread. These meetings helped the people to sustain faith in their objectives. They were augmented by drumming, which in the culture of West African society summoned the spirits of their ancestors to appear. Drumming was also an integral part of the "ring shout" that followed prayer meetings and represented a continuing African cultural manifestation among lowcountry African Americans. Shout songs like "Time Drawin' Nigh (I See the Sign)" provided group affirmation that their campaign for land, autonomy, and control could be sustained.[107]

The inexorable sequence of events culminated on January 5 when the Ogeechee men and women received word that U.S. military forces had arrived in Savannah. The arrival of troops exacerbated anxiety and division among the insurgents that intensified as discussion of surrender emerged. Nonetheless, possible surrender did not result in the capitulation of the majority of African Americans on the Ogeechee Neck. In a final attempt to resist authorities, freed men and women led by Solomon

Farley, Captain Green, and other Union League officers destroyed the bridge over the Ogeechee River and sabotaged the plantation mansions at Grove Hill, Grove Point, and Southfield. But the flurry of activity did not quell the division within the Ogeechee Home Guards. In anticipation of the army's arrival, fourteen men and one woman surrendered to authorities at the Oglethorpe Barracks in Savannah.[108]

With tensions building, Sheriff Dooner, after meeting with Savannah mayor Edward C. Anderson, requested military assistance from General George G. Meade, military commander of the Georgia district. Meade emphatically refused the request, stating that "only after men and means had been exhausted" could the military act.[109] After forming an ineffective *posse comitatus,* Sheriff Dooner on January 5 surrendered his duties to military officials. As a result of this action, the Sixteenth Infantry Regiment prepared to disembark for the Ogeechee country. Commanded by Major Thomas W. Sweeney, the unit consisted of Companies A and I from Augusta and Companies B and C from Atlanta. The soldiers' duties were to restore the peace and assist civil authorities in arresting the insurgents. During the five days of unrest, Savannah judge Philip M. Russell Jr. issued 150 warrants against the participants, charging them with "insurrection against the State of Georgia, robbery by force, robbery by intimidation, assault with intent to murder and larceny."[110] On January 6 at one o'clock in the afternoon, companies A and I, led by Major Sweeney, arrived on the Ogeechee Neck and gained possession of the plantations. For nine days, the soldiers aided civil authorities in arresting 141 individuals. By January 15, the entire Ogeechee Neck had been abandoned. Those who were not arrested crossed the river to Bryan County in fear of later retribution from civil authorities.[111]

The Ogeechee troubles occurred just at the moment when Radical Republicans in Congress were deciding the state's fate. The Georgia House of Representatives, early in September 1868, had expelled twenty-eight of the thirty-two recently elected black representatives on the grounds that the right to vote did not imply the right to hold office. This affront against the Reconstruction Act of 1867 prompted Republican leaders in Washington to reevaluate the status of Georgia. Thus Georgia remained imperiled during the Ogeechee revolt.[112]

In the pretrial proceedings, which began on Friday, January 15, and lasted for fourteen days, the case of the *State of Georgia v. Captain Green* became a litmus test for determining whether insurrection charges could be sustained. As spectators filled the gallery and lower hall in the Chatham County courthouse, the twenty-five prisoners sat on the south side of the courtroom, "hard looking" and filled with trepidation.[113] While Captain Green awaited his fate, Solomon Farley, who could not be located by authorities, had fled the county. Defense attorneys Henry S. Fitch, a state-appointed counsel; James Johnson, a Savannah attorney who voluntarily provided his services; and A. W. Stone, whose presence was requested by interested parties in Savannah, represented Captain Green and the other accused men and women, who consistently denied participating in the revolt. Their refusal to confess heightened the atmosphere of the court's proceedings.[114]

In presenting their case, the prosecuting attorneys for the state, Henry R. Jackson and Alfred B. Smith, relied on the testimony of Sheriff Dooner, his deputy Julius Kaufman, Captain Tucker, and Major Middleton. Other persons who were driven out of the Ogeechee country provided collateral testimony. The four witnesses for the defense—Jack Cuthbert, a drillmaster for the Ogeechee Home Guards; Thomas Benedict, an officer in the Union League; and two plantation owners, William Burroughs and William Miller—provided counterfactual testimony that relegated the Ogeechee insurrection to a dispute over labor contracts.[115] Miller, who maintained amiable relations with the African Americans on the Ogeechee Neck, had not lived on his plantation for three months prior to the violence. The sympathetic testimony of both Burroughs and Miller cast a moderate light on the revolt, but did not influence the decision of Judge Russell. On the last day of the proceedings, "black spectators filled the court gallery as white spectators congregated around the main door" to hear Judge Russell commit Captain Green and 116 of the insurgents to trial. Twenty-six African Americans who were not identified by the state's witnesses were released.[116]

The public had already decided the fate of the Ogeechee prisoners, but most believed that Governor Rufus Bullock would issue a pardon. Throughout his term as governor, Bullock had made extensive use of his pardoning powers and had also encouraged Radical Republicans to reimpose military rule in Georgia after the expulsion of the black representatives. Whites in Savannah believed that Bullock and Aaron A. Bradley had prearranged the trouble in the Ogeechee district. Supporters of a pardon also viewed a trial as an unnecessary expense.[117]

Although public outcry over the Ogeechee troubles had dissipated by the start of the trial on May 12, 1869, interest in the fate of the prisoners remained salient in Savannah. The lead prosecuting attorney for the state, C. W. West, secured guilty verdicts against Captain Green, Dandy McNeil, Ned Edwards, Jack Cuthbert, Thomas Benedict, and Nick Bailing for insurrection, robbery by intimidation and assault with intent to murder in connection with the Ogeechee riot. Larceny and assault charges were levied against the other participants, who invariably were found not guilty in the absence of corroborating testimony. Judge William Schley, in a climate of profound disdain, sentenced the six men charged with insurrection to five years of hard labor in Milledgeville. Hard labor in the state prison ended two months later. In July, Governor Bullock issued amnesty proclamations, which absolved the men of all charges.[118]

During the 1870s, the new Republican agenda increasingly catered to northern businesspeople and southern political interests, and this combination resulted in the abandonment of an economic platform for freed men and women. The issuance of enormous grants of land and government bonds for railroad development in the West and the development of a program capable of capturing white support in the South meant that tangible economic restitution in the form of land was not forthcoming. The failure of the Ogeechee men and women to force a distribution of land led them to devise an alternative strategy to secure a measure of economic independence.[119]

The wartime and postwar experiences of men and women in lowcountry Georgia provide valuable insights into both slavery and the Civil War. Viewed from an antebellum perspective, the escape of many black Georgians underscores the importance of freedom and family ties and simultaneously casts doubt on the depth of black commitment to the paternalistic ethos as they claimed freedom for themselves.[120] During the Civil War, Delia Garlic and many enslaved men and women pursued their freedom in marginal spaces where public and private history unfolded.[121] The myriad challenges they faced during and after the war represented distilled expressions of freedom and a desire for economic justice.

3

"FULL AND FAIR COMPENSATION"

The plant of freedom upward sprung
And spread its leaves so fresh and young
Its blossoms now are blowing

Paul Laurence Dunbar, "Ode to Ethiopia"

On the eve of emancipation, abandoned rice lands on Butler's Island stood as symbols of African American suffering and dislocation. Half a decade earlier, 450 enslaved African Americans from the island had undergone the humiliation of public auction and sale at Ten Broeck Race Track in Savannah, Georgia. Their dislocation from family and community punctuated seventy years of arduous labor under horrifying conditions that denied their humanity. Yet following the end of the Civil War, Dandy Stewart and other former slaves auctioned at Ten Broeck Race Track returned to the island, "a little community [where] for generations all sorts of relations of blood and kinship [were] established."[1] Their return to Butler's Island mirrored the decision of other former slaves in the Georgia lowcountry to return to ambiguous sites where kinship and community coexisted with their pain and suffering.

Upon his return to Butler's Island in the spring of 1865, Dandy Stewart reasserted the prewar title listed in the 1859 auction as "engineer and blacksmith."[2] The rice lands that Stewart had helped to maintain were now subject to the provisions of General William Sherman's General Field Order No. 15, promulgated in Savannah on January 16, 1865. Sherman's field order, which reserved the Sea Islands and abandoned inland rice fields south of Charleston, South Carolina, to St. John's River in Florida for former enslaved persons, structured the experiences of African Americans in lowcountry Georgia.[3] As the territorial testing ground for federal land policy in the former Confederate South, lowcountry Georgia provides a window into former slaves' definition of the boundaries and spaces of freedom.[4] Former slaveholder's control of space and enslaved people's resistance to that control resulted from conflicting dialectical ideas regarding the meaning of free labor. As carpenters, brick masons, engineers, "rice planters," seamstresses, weavers, cooks, and foremen; and as lumbermen, fishermen, and hacks, former slaves created on an everyday level a space for pragmatic economic practices as they employed their skills.[5]

The reestablishment of a post-Civil War rice economy required negotiation with people, the landscape, and nature. As an engineer and blacksmith, Dandy Stewart had constructed and maintained the banks to protect against flooding from the Altamaha River; carved out and maintained ditches and dikes to support the tide-flow method of producing rice; and fashioned work implements and tools for the production of rice and the maintenance of the plantation.[6]

The flood of January 1865 posed a significant threat to rice production in the lowcountry as the Civil War entered its final stages and General Sherman's Field Order No. 15 altered the politics of land and space. The rising waters of the Savannah River and other major arteries, such as the Ogeechee, Altamaha, and St. Mary's rivers, suspended business activity and created swamp conditions in the region as water moved through the city of Savannah at the speed of twenty miles per hour and rose thirty-seven feet above the low water mark.[7] Unlike the case in previous flooding, the now-former slaves were not inclined to perform the work of draining, repairing, and rebuilding the rice fields and plantation mills. The chaos of the aftermath of war left plantations throughout Georgia idle as former slaves tested the new spaces of freedom by taking day trips to nearby towns and refusing to work as slaves on plantations.

For many, the return to abandoned plantations left them "bad off and short on provisions."[8] The privations of war and the spread of diseases also created a demographic crisis as 17,000 freed men and women died during the years of 1865 and 1866.[9] As it did other areas of the former Confederacy, the Civil War devastated much of the state of Georgia. Widespread destruction of physical structures, including hundreds of miles of railroads, and an economic depression, inherent in the ravages of war, left men, women, and children destitute and in need of food, clothing, and medical care.[10] Adding to the distress of many in the city of Savannah, a disastrous fire occurred on the evening of January 28, 1865, that destroyed more than a hundred homes and covered twenty acres of land.[11]

The men and women who returned to the Georgia Sea Islands formed "liberating communities" through a digetic process in which land served as the experiential tie that bound people together.[12] For former slaves in Georgia and throughout the South, the Civil War inaugurated a social, political, and economic revolution, and the tension between slavery, free labor, and modernity eroded. Ideas regarding the meaning of free labor emerged from the expressive culture of emancipated men and women, whereby freedom and social justice were inextricably linked. Former slaves received inspiration for liberation and social justice ideology from biblical texts that promised freedom for the enslaved, justice for the oppressed, and an inheritance here on Earth.[13] Following the Civil War, this system of beliefs directed their transition to freedom. A corollary idea wedded to liberation and social justice emerged through former slaves' understanding of free labor ideology. Beyond the ideology that promoted equality of opportunity, free labor represented the hopes, visions, and dreams of former slaves for control of their own labor.[14]

Free labor implied self-ownership and the possession of productive property. In this context, African American churches became sites of democratic political discourse on self-determination and Black nationalism.[15] Former slaves believed that securing their freedom was incompatible with continuing to work for their former masters. Freedom from white supervision implied land ownership and freedom to control their lives and the disposition of their labor. The devolution of the Freedmen's Bureau labor policy, which failed because contract labor was antithetical to former slaves' understanding of free labor, meant that liminal spaces of freedom would be the inheritance of former slaves.

FREE LABOR IDEOLOGY AND LIMINAL SPACES OF FREEDOM

Emancipated men and women challenged liminal spaces by expropriating ideas concerning free labor and establishing a coda of "full and fair compensation."[16] As free labor ideology transformed the southern economy following the end of the Civil War, the Republican view that all Americans shared common economic interests undergirded their belief that slavery was inimical to the principles of free enterprise and economic liberalism. Freedom of choice, the ideological underpinning of economic liberalism, implied equality. However, southern leaders and many northern leaders could not accept this proposition following emancipation. Emancipation revolutionized southern society by destroying bondage and, in theory at least, leaving former slaves and planters free to create new ways of existing.[17]

The Thirteenth Amendment completed the process that northern Republicans felt was necessary to make African Americans a part of the free labor system. It also expanded federal power, as it promised freedom that the national government would theoretically guarantee; thus this amendment served as a pivotal legal and moral connective that linked former slaves to the national government.[18] Throughout 1865, in the face of presidential restraint and southern defiance, Republicans increasingly became united in the belief that the government had to enforce a true free labor system in the South. Thus the new status of African American labor was the linchpin of Reconstruction.[19]

The Thirteenth Amendment, however, had very little effect on deep-seated white attitudes about former slaves. Southern whites continued to see freed men and women as constituting an inferior order with no rights a white person was bound to respect. The Freedmen's Bureau presided over the transition from a slave economy, in which decisions about work resided with planters, to a free labor economy in which former slaves could make their own choices, but in which poverty and a lack of opportunity raised major barriers to economic mobility. Resistance to economic equality remained pervasive as free labor institutions were reshaped by a culture of racism.[20] Significantly, as the North lost its will to maintain the occupation of the South, social, political, and economic Reconstruction dissipated. By 1877 the question of labor, capital, work, and wages occupied the political landscape as the urban labor movement eclipsed southern Reconstruction.

As southern legislatures enacted a series of vagrancy laws, apprenticeship systems, and criminal penalties for breach of contract to control the labor of former slaves, they relied on an economy of antebellum stereotypes to justify their actions.[21] The Black Codes reflected postwar "status anxiety" over the place of former slaves in southern society.[22] As a regressive mechanism, the Codes vitiated the Thirteenth Amendment by regulating the labor of former slaves through the legal process. Georgia's Black Code permitted whippings as punishment for misdemeanors; and by means of laws on labor contracts, it set up enforcement machinery to drive former slaves back to agricultural work at starvation wages.[23] In other parts of the South, particularly in Mississippi and South Carolina, which enacted the most severe Codes, the laws governing the labor of former slaves reinforced a slave-servant status. Mississippi required freed men and freed women to possess written evidence of employment for the coming year. Similarly South Carolina's Code barred African Americans from following any occupation other than farmer or servant unless they paid an annual tax, which ranged from ten to one hundred dollars.[24]

In lowcountry Georgia, as in other regions of the former Confederate South, planters resisted the creation of a free labor market after emancipation. In Chatham County, Harris Phillips continued to hold Morris, his wife Jane, and several other former bondmen and bondwomen six months after General Sherman's arrival in the city of Savannah. Morris sought redress for his condition and payment for his labor by filing a complaint with the Freedmen's Bureau in Savannah.[25] The Bureau arranged for the resolution of contract disputes, and agents often made unilateral judgments when one party sued with a complaint. In other cases arbitration boards or military courts handed down decisions.[26] Bureau policy during the summer of 1865 remained sympathetic to the economic rights of former slaves. Captain A. P. Ketchum, who served as chief officer of the Sherman reservation, advised Phillips to make amicable arrangements with freed men and women and to pay them for their labor. According to Ketchum, they were also entitled to payment for work already performed on producing the crops.[27] General James H. Wilson, who occupied Macon, Georgia, in April 1865, articulated a similar position when he outlawed the dismissal of freed men and women without compensation for work they had already performed.[28]

Planters' proprietary interest in the crops produced by the labor of former slaves following President Johnson's May 1865 reversal of General William Sherman's General Field Order No. 15 stimulated contentious discourse on the preternatural duties of military commanders tasked with implementing Bureau labor policy. Military commanders' and local agents' wide-ranging mandates to implement and effectively administer the agency's multitudinous tasks escalated tensions between planters and former slaves. Throughout the state, the end of the idea of land redistribution hastened the development of a system of compensated labor to produce rice and cotton.[29] On John G. Lawton's plantation, confrontation over the crops and labor of former slaves magnified opposing views on property rights and the meaning of a free labor system. Former slaves on Lawton's plantation planted their own crops during the war and continued to plant the lands in Lawton's absence until June 1865. According to Bureau policy, which provided the legal imprimatur to labor relations in postwar Georgia, Lawton's land had been abandoned, and former slaves were entitled to remain on the place until they gathered their crops. The Bureau required Lawton to make "full and fair compensation" for crops, labor, and expenditures for the entire year to freed men and freed women should he not abide by this established arrangement.[30] Throughout lowcountry Georgia, however, planters sent former slaves away unpaid for their labor.[31]

Former slaves' complaints about planter intransigence regarding a free labor system clearly articulated ideas concerning the meaning of work in the context of free labor ideology. Prince Morrel, who labored on Julia Spiers's plantation, complained to the Bureau that Mrs. Spiers did not intend to pay the former slaves for the work they had performed during 1865. Morrel's complaint led to the placement of a lien on all crops and Bureau-mandated "full and fair compensation" to recure amicable relations with former slaves.[32] In St. Mary's, Georgia, former slaves Samuel and Dawson likewise filed a grievance with the Bureau regarding a buggy they had furnished to planter Jesse Butler. Butler agreed to pay the men eighteen dollars by securing an installment note in December 1867. However, the men had not received payment by June 1868 and commenced to demand payment for this commercial transaction with Butler.[33]

Complaints over property reinforced freed people's ideas concerning their proprietary rights to symbolic and economic property. Moreover, the complaints of former slaves demonstrate a shift from a two-dimensional space with sharp boundaries defined by their enslavement to a multidimensional space with unbounded subspaces. Illustrative of this is Mungo Davis's trespassing complaint against planter William Miller and his mule. According to Davis's complaint, Miller's mule was "in the habit of trespassing upon his rice fields, to the great detriment of his crop." The complaint continued: "He has represented the cases to you but was met with the answer that you would not keep your mule in for no niggers' crop and further that you threatened to shoot him if he injured your mule."[34] Bureau agents upheld Davis's economic rights by admonishing Miller to control his animals and to fence them in, because the "very life and prosperity of the freedmen for the next year depend upon a proper care of this year's crop."[35]

Cases adjudicated by the Provost Court in Savannah, however, invariably treated former slaves with enmity. The fulminations of Reverend James Simms, who served as the legal advocate for the vast majority of former slaves in Chatham County, had very little impact on military officers who were sympathetic toward planters.[36] Indeed, throughout the South, planters jettisoned from their plantations former slaves who were too old or infirm to labor. In many instances, former slaves were evicted without any means to provide for themselves. In the lowcountry, former slave Sally Paeche complained to Bureau agents that planter Andrew T. Eyck had ordered her to vacate her house without the opportunity to gather her crops.[37] Planters, moreover, transformed "rights" that had been enjoyed by slaves—clothing, housing, access to garden plots—into commodities for which payment was due.[38]

Judgments promulgated by the Freedmen's Bureau subverted planter notions of property rights. In the case of *Raymond R. Kay v. Charles Walthour, Peter Way, and Billy Gillman,* the court ruled that Walthour, Way, and Gillman, all former slaves of Raymond Kay, retained title to the horses they claimed as their property during their enslavement.[39] For the majority of former slaves, however, their relationship with planters remained unresolved as ideas hermetically sealed during slavery continued unabated in freedom. Negotiating with former slaves for fair wages was anathema to planter beliefs. Fanny Andrews, the daughter of a Georgia planter, expressed humiliation at being compelled to negotiate with former slaves for wages.[40]

The postwar labor system evolved out of the establishment of operations of power by the army. As a military organization established in the War Department, the army staffed the Bureau, and army personnel served as the connective tissue linking the southern economy to the political will of former masters and freed men and women. Contracts represented not merely the location of domination and resistance, but all manner of complex interrelationships and hybridization.[41] Contracts, enticement, and vagrancy laws contradicted the tenets of free labor ideology; however, these mechanisms were implemented by the Freedmen's Bureau to regulate the labor of former slaves. Historian James Schmidt has argued that "Union Army officers did not act solely or even centrally out of racial reasons to create a free-labor system based upon Northern ideology."[42] However, ideas regarding race, work, and the enslavement of Africans permeated the consciousness of northerners and southerners. The policies promulgated by the Freedmen's Bureau, which advocated contracts with former masters, can be viewed as an extension of this racial ideology.[43]

The judicial work of the Bureau expanded to include legal relationships with non-Bureau tribunals. As civil governments were restored, Bureau courts were discontinued, and jurisdiction was transferred to civil authorities.[44] In civil courts,

Bureau agents acted as counselors and advisors of former slaves and also appeared in court as attorneys for those unable to procure counsel. In the cases involving land and labor, where civil courts were reestablished, the Bureau retained jurisdiction over cases involving disputes between planters and former slaves. This policy, which sought to promote equitable justice for former slaves, varied in regional distribution. In North Carolina, Governor Holden commissioned bureau agents as regular magistrates; in Alabama, Mississippi, and Georgia, the assistant commissioners authorized provisional governors to constitute civil courts and freedmen's courts.[45] By the end of 1865, the Bureau consisted of 799 men, including officers, agents, and clerks; this group included 424 soldiers and 375 civilians.[46] By 1869 its workforce had dwindled to 158.[47]

The contract system developed out of the assumption that freed people would work for former planters out of economic necessity. This system had its origins in the antebellum northern economy, where ideas concerning discipline and hard work helped to regulate the labor of vagrants. The northern judicial system affirmed the right of employers to impose labor discipline with long-term contracts. One of the first Union-controlled areas to implement a contract labor policy was southern Louisiana. The capture of New Orleans and Baton Rouge in April and May 1862, respectively, by naval commander David G. Farragut and General Benjamin Butler brought both cities under Union military control.[48] Farragut, a former resident of Louisiana, led an expedition of forty-four ships up the Mississippi River with the intention of taking New Orleans, closing the Confederacy's main source of supplies and severing the South. After a five-day bombardment of Fort Jackson and St. Philip near the mouth of the river, Farragut successfully took seventeen ships past the forts on April 24, 1862, and two days later occupied the city of New Orleans without opposition.[49] On May 1, General Butler brought 15,000 Federal troops to New Orleans and imposed military rule. Farragut continued up the Mississippi River and captured Baton Rouge and Bayou Sara.[50]

After the occupation of New Orleans and surrounding areas, army officers searched for ways to organize labor and poor relief. The Confiscation Acts of July 17, 1862, freed slaves coming under national control and authorized the president to use former slaves to suppress the rebellion. They also freed the mothers, wives, and children of freedmen whose labor and service were used to suppress the rebellion.[51] The Confiscation Acts led to the formation of the Bureau of Negro Labor in wartime Louisiana to address the reality of emancipation in 1862. Enslaved men and women fleeing plantations formed "contraband colonies" north of the city of New Orleans, where General Butler inaugurated a mass program of public works and promised Unionists the support of the army in enforcing plantation labor in surrounding parishes provided that wages were paid.[52]

Under Louisiana's first Superintendent of Negro Labor, George H. Hanks, emancipated men and women were required to work in return for support. In Terre

Bonne, Louisiana, freedmen received ten dollars per month; freed women received six dollars per month; and children between twelve and sixteen received two dollars per month to continue laboring on sugar, cotton, and rice plantations.[53] Each labor agreement incorporated the language of "fair prices" for labor; however, the wages were far from fair given the inability of former slaves to sell their labor in the market place. In an ideal market, free labor removed both the legal restraints of contracts and the paternalism of the master-servant relationship.[54] The devaluation of women's labor was consistent with the formulation of nineteenth-century policies that marked masculine identities in hegemonic and patriarchal terms. However, as Julie Saville demonstrates, women in the South Carolina lowcountry endeavored to control agricultural production by "disputing what they would plant, where they would plant it and in what amounts."[55] Women also demanded higher wages for task work. According to Amy Dru Stanley, emancipation meant "female self-ownership," which included the right to demand fair prices for labor.[56] During the Civil War, the Bureau of Negro Labor, under the auspices of the federal government, created a market in labor that seemed to contradict free labor ideology. This contradiction undergirded federal policy during the Reconstruction period as contracts controlled the ability of former slaves to sell their labor power freely in the market.[57]

On rice plantations, the lack of capital to repair the destruction wrought by the war, combined with the effects of neglect, made it virtually impossible to revive the rice industry on a large scale. Concomitantly an increase in rice production in Louisiana following the Civil War shifted the locus of money and profit from the crop. In 1864 Louisiana produced 1.5 million pounds of rice.[58] By 1866 rice production had increased to 4.7 million pounds of rice, and by 1876 the total was 22 million pounds.[59] New Orleans became the center of the rice trade, and a decade after the war it furnished both South Carolina and Georgia with rice seed.[60] Planters in the lowcountry initially employed the contract system to revive the rice industry. Through lease arrangements with former slaves, planters endeavored to perpetuate an unequal economic system in which they controlled and benefited from the labor of former slaves. On William Gibbons's Shaftesbury plantation on Argyle Island, 119 freedmen and freedwomen entered into an agreement on March 1, 1866 in which they would cultivate 400 acres of rice land and furnish the rice seed, agricultural implements, and supplies "of all kind" to cultivate the land. Gibbons did not incur any expense for supplies, subsistence, clothing, maintenance, or medical aid.[61]

Although freedmen and freedwomen retained equity and commercial rights to the crops produced, the puissance of the contract favored Gibbons. At the termination of the agreement on January 1, 1867, Gibbons would receive possession of the premises with all improvements. Concurrently the foreman, Abelard Shigg, meted out tasks each day and penalized persons who did not abide by the contract terms, which included provisions against violating the "peace and good order" of the plantation with discharge and removal.[62] Controlling property such as livestock reflected Gibbons's interest in extending his authority over the economic property of former slaves as he sought to control the new boundaries and spaces of freedom. Stipulated within the contract was the provision that no hogs would run at large and that if they were found they would be killed. Gibbons also mandated that no other stock could be kept without his consent.[63]

The economic effects of uncompensated emancipation forced former slaves into unfavorable contracts. However, in some instances, former slaves secured advantageous contracts in which they in effect "mortgaged themselves."[64] On John and Thomas Screven's plantation in Chatham County, freedmen and freedwomen signed a twelve-month contract on January 18, 1866. The contract terms displayed the profundity of former slaves' negotiating skill and enterprise. In addition to supplying wages and rations, which included medical attention and medicine, John and Thomas Screven agreed to pay "for all right to work double the amount "pro rate" of their stipulated wage.[65] Former slaves received half of their wages in money at the beginning of each month and the remainder at the expiration of the contract in rice or other produce "in an amount of sufficient market value to compensate for the full amount of wages remaining unpaid."[66]

The development of joint ventures involving planters and former slaves in the rice country represented a cogent manifestation of the destruction of wealth and capital caused by the Civil War. With emancipation, the slave South was much poorer because the most valuable asset, slave property, ceased to exist. Similarly death and injury eliminated hundreds of thousands of productive people from the economy, and the war destroyed buildings, farms, bridges, railroads, horses, mules, cows, and other livestock. Securing land through lease contracts embodied a nascent form of temporary proprietorship, which allowed former slaves to rent land for later purchase.[67] In Chatham County, Romeo Howes, a former slave of Reverend Benjamin Burr, established a rental arrangement with William Burroughs, administrator for the Burr estate. Howes rented ten acres of land on Magnolia plantation in the White Bluff district on February 26, 1866, paying fifty dollars in four installments, with the first quarter paid at the time of signing his agreement, the next quarter on April 1, the third quarter on July 1, and the remaining quarter on October 1.[68]

As in other parts of the South, social dialectics were a function of power relations and were negotiated relationally. Freedmen endeavored to exercise the authority and power denied them during slavery both economically and socially. Husbands sought to protect the honor of their wives from abusive planters and overseers by lodging complaints with the Freedmen's Bureau. Former slave Phillip Gaston lodged a complaint against his foreman, Bailey Forster, for using abusive and insulting language toward his wife, Amelia Gaston. Bureau agent William Royal mediated the dispute by mandating that Mr. Rowe, the employer of Forster, control his foreman and advise him "not to use threatening or abusive language toward the hands."[69]

WOMEN OF FREEDOM

The labor of African American women remained central to the southern economy in the years following the end of the Civil War. For women, the complex interrelationships of gender, class, and race produced varied responses. Emancipation required finding ways to give meaning to freedom within a society devoted to circumscribing the attempts of black women to assert their freedom. In later decades, industrialization and urbanization influenced and altered the location of the transformation of the lives and work experiences of the majority of African American women. The proliferation of racial and sexual stereotypes during the late nineteenth and early twentieth centuries affected how African American women defined themselves in relationship to each other and to the larger society.

As mothers, daughters, wives, and sisters, women had to contend with the problem of finding and keeping employment and depending on white employers for payment.[70] In May 1866, "a worn, weary, woman with 11 children, and another with three," spent ten days in the forest near Columbus, Georgia, before entering the city to seek assistance.[71] According to their testimony, the women had been driven off the plantation because "wese no account with our childer," they told sympathetic northern teachers.[72] Nancy Johnson returned to work for her mistress following the war as a seamstress; according to her testimony to the Southern Claims Commission, she "wove 40 yds. of dress goods for [her mistress] that she promised to pay me for; but she never paid me a cent for it."[73] In like manner, a mother of five, evicted from a North Carolina farm by a white man who declared their "keep" would cost him more than they could earn, responded that "it seemed like it was might hard; she'd been made free, and it did appear as if thar must be something more comin."[74] Their only choice was to take whatever work was available, and that was not much. Freed with nothing but the clothes on their backs and unable to provide for themselves, women relied on the assistance of the Bureau to meet their basic needs.[75]

The tenuous economic position of field hands and domestic servants necessitated relying on their children to support the household economy. In cases where children were held as "bound laborers" in violation of the Thirteenth Amendment, both women and men appealed to the Bureau for the release of their children and grandchildren.[76] In one such case, the grandparents of Peter, a former slave who had lost his mother and had been held by William Dickinson in Pierce County, Georgia, maintained to the Bureau that Dickinson had violated Peter's labor rights as a freeperson and that, as grandparents, they retained custodial rights.[77] In the case of Ann Phillips of St. Mary's, Georgia, whose son Charley "went away with W. B. Folks to work for him," in February 1868, the lines of demarcation between bound laborers and free laborers were contested.[78] Charley had been away for two months, and the longevity of his absence worried his mother, who had written a formal letter to Folks requesting his return. Phillips pressed the issue of her son's labor further with the Freedmen's Bureau by lodging a complaint to have her son returned.[79]

In other cases, women whose children were held as bound laborers for extended periods sought to secure their children by force. Dorca Samuels, the mother of Nannie, whose labor had been indentured for five years by Miller Hallows in 1866, attempted to end the indenture by threatening to bring "a band of freed people to take Nannie by force."[80] In some cases, the Bureau approved apprenticeship arrangements between employers and minor children above the age of fifteen years.[81] Such approvals may have also stemmed from the Bureau's desire to employ minor children since the Bureau could not properly staff Freedmen's Bureau schools on the islands and relied on the American Missionary Association to supply teachers.[82]

Employers habitually defrauded women of the small amounts they had earned as they worked to sustain themselves and their families; in several cases employers forced women to leave without recompense. Under the Freedmen's Bureau complaint procedure, women asserted their right to full and fair compensation. Compensation complaints represented the largest single category of grievances initiated by black women.[83] In the inland cotton districts, few planters had cash on hand after the war since Confederate bonds were worthless and they could not mortgage their former "human property" to secure loans. Planters charged their employees such exorbitant prices for supplies that workers were lucky if they ended the year even, rather than indebted to their employer. Women who achieved less than the required production quota received a lecture on the virtues of hard work and deductions from their wages. Planter Ivey White, for example, lodged a complaint against his field hand Angeline Sealy. According to the complaint, "Sealy is lazy and does not pick more than 35 to 40 pounds of cotton per day."[84] The agent, Charles Rautchenburg, sustained the charge and gave Sealy a lecture on her duties, emphasizing that if she did not average from seventy-five to one hundred pounds of cotton per day, a deduction would be made from her wages.[85] According to Bureau agent Douglass Risley, "in nine cases out of ten," complaints arise because "white men are still reluctant to permit [a former slave] to enjoy his rights freely."[86]

The acrimony displayed against former slaves created new opportunities for women to demand fair compensation. Women like Rachel Hunter, a launderer in St. Mary's, Georgia, imbued with values and beliefs regarding the meaning of free labor, prepared a "due bill" of fifteen dollars for services rendered to Miller B. Grant.[87] Grant failed to pay, so Hunter filed a complaint with the Freedmen's Bureau to secure the wages owed to her. As in other cases, Bureau agent William Royal protected the economic rights of a former slave by demanding payment for services rendered.[88]

The year 1866 was a year of far-reaching political and economic significance in the city of Savannah and the state of Georgia. On April 3, 1866, President Andrew Johnson issued his Peace Proclamation, which lifted trade restrictions on the former Confederate states. Trade in Georgia benefited from this Act as commercial activities increased exponentially.[89] Restoration of the Atlantic and Gulf Railroad and the Central Railroad led provost marshals to combat vagrancy with compulsory labor. As historian Joseph P. Reidy argues, "in Macon and other parts of central Georgia, many vagrants were women and children whose husbands worked on the railroads or on outlying plantations where accommodations were denied to nonworkers."[90]

Collective acts of resistance by women occurred when women organized themselves through economic networks. In the immediate postwar years, domestic workers organized mass labor protests for higher wages. Launderers in Atlanta, Georgia, and Jackson, Mississippi, in particular, succeeded in organizing to raise wages to support themselves and their families.[91] In the lowcountry rice districts, women faced a peculiar dialectic as they sought to withdraw from work in the fields. The specialized knowledge and labor of women remained a key requirement for the successful cultivation of rice for the local market. Women valued rice as a dietary staple and market crop, and the technologies employed in producing rice were created and maintained through the intellect and cultural knowledge of women.[92] During their enslavement, rice was grown, processed, and cooked in styles that marked the African diaspora in the Americas. According to Judith Carney, "women fashioned mortars by using fire to burn into a cypress or pine tree trunk a cavity or receptacle in which to place unmilled grain. With the mortar hollowed out to waist height, they milled unprocessed rice with a wooden pestle that weighed between seven and ten pounds."[93]

In the lowcountry, women's attitudes toward work depended on the extent of their freedom from white supervision. On Butler's Island, Charity, a former slave who represented herself to Frances Butler Leigh as "unable to move," walked six miles almost every day to sell eggs from her own chickens on a neighboring plantation.[94] Finding physical strength from self-reliance, Charity used her feigned infirmity to receive patronage from Leigh while simultaneously empowering herself by refusing to sell eggs to Leigh and engaging in political masking to conceal her economic activities.[95] Asserting their independence through "ingenious" coded behavior provided women with the means by which they could forge strong personal identities and voices. A significant number of freed women released their anger by publicly denouncing planters, taking their grievances to local bureau agents, or goading other former slaves who were more reticent or fatalistic. Women were particularly outspoken and aggressive in their willingness to confront white authority figures.[96]

Through the narrative of Frances Butler Leigh, the voices of liberated women reveal that they did not submit to the pressures of planters and that they were among the most militant fighters for their rights among former slaves. As they reinterpreted the free labor ideology of the Republican Party to claim freedom for themselves, women assumed a vital role in establishing political platforms, often through mutual associations in religious institutions, which reflected their concerns as women, mothers, and workers.[97] Controlling their own labor and contributing to the family economy were central economic concerns. Through their engagement in political struggles women sought to alter power relations. Moreover, women asserted a new cultural aesthetic and exercised power in cultural practices as they abandoned wearing head kerchiefs. On Butler's Island, women acted with temerity in abandoning their headscarves, not only to display and assert their natural coiffures, but also to assume a status of equality with white women.[98]

For women, control of their labor and access to land had multiple concurrent political meanings that can be bracketed off into symbolic and intellectual categories of analysis. The symbolism of land ownership redefined the individual's existence because freedom in nineteenth-century America rested on the ownership of productive property. Intellectually the land represented the body, mind, visions, and dreams of women like Phoebe Robinson, an independent farmer on Sapelo Island. Robinson inherited forty-four and one-half acres of land from her husband and made careful provisions in her will to bequeath the land to her four sons, Samuel, June, Marmaduke, and Esau, and to her niece Annie.[99]

Sewing or working as a launderer or cook proved profitable in some cases and provided women with the resources to purchase land. Elizabeth Edy, whose husband, James, had predeceased her, sewed to provide for son, Abram, and daughter, Mary Elizabeth. She had managed to purchase real estate valued at three hundred dollars in 1870. As a member of First Bryan Baptist Church, Edy had benefited from the religious network, which emphasized saving and black landownership. Edy made her own contribution to the building fund of First African Baptist Church, paying three dollars per month to rebuild the parent church on a new site.[100] Like Edy, other African American women sought the security and independence land ownership engendered. Maria Johnson, who also sewed to earn money, purchased land valued at eight hundred dollars in 1870. Johnson, who served as president of the St. John the Baptist Society, functioned as the head of household and provided support to sixteen-year-old August Watch, who resided with her and whom she taught to sew.[101] Women landowners also engaged in entrepreneurial activities such as selling fish, fabricating various items such as woven mats and brooms, and selling excess produce from gardens. Savannah depended on market women for fruit, fish, oysters, crabs, clams, and shrimp. This form of economic activity proved profitable for women such as Dolly Williams, whose husband, John, had left her. Dolly, a member of First African Baptist Church, maintained a savings account with the Freedmen's Bank and purchased land valued at six hundred dollars.[102]

CLAIMING FREEDOM FOR THEMSELVES

Plantation management proved difficult for Northern investors who purchased Sea Island estates in the immediate postwar period. On St. Simons Island following the death of James Hamilton Couper, owner of Cannon's Point plantation, a northern investor who believed he could "simply put former slaves to work and pay them regular wages," failed in his attempt to manage the labor of freedmen and freedwomen.[103] Continuing strategies of resistance that emerged during their enslavement, they forced "Mr. G" to abandon the place by working slowly or leaving the estate. For two years following his departure, fifty families controlled and possessed the land.[104] African Americans sought to create their own vision of a postwar southern economy that was diametrically opposed to the interests of northern investors and southern planters. Former slaves wanted self-sufficiency that would allow freedom from the exploitation of their labor. In this sense, personal autonomy superseded pecuniary interests.

Unified by the common experience of their enslavement, former slaves on Sapelo Island refused to return to the antebellum status quo. Recognizing that commercial cotton and rice production could not be sustained at its pre-Civil War level, the heirs of Thomas Spalding sold 1,000 acres of land on Sapelo Island to the Hillery Land Company, organized in 1871 by three former slaves: William Hillery, his brother-in-law John Grovner, and Bilally Bell (an appellation that suggests an Islamic retention). The Hillery Land Company enriched the island community of Sapelo by providing an institutional network to secure land. Hillery, Grovner, and Bell pooled their money to make a five hundred-dollar down payment on land in Raccoon Bluff near Belle Marsh that was being sold for $2,000.[105] The men paid another five hundred dollars upon signing the purchase agreement and provided three-year notes for the five hundred dollars due on January 1.[106] The Hillery Land Company created an island within an island by parceling out twenty plots of thirty-three acres each, which Sapelo Island families purchased to establish homesteads.[107] Intracommunity networks such as that established by the Hillery Land Company reinforced fictive and nonfictive kin relationships. These relationships were important in the sale and transfer of land in lowcountry African American communities.[108] The community of interests served as the cohesive force for political activism over landownership and fair compensation.

Historian Eric Foner identified landownership as the central component of the black economic agenda. Black landownership would have a transformative impact on the southern economy and foster self-sufficiency. However, only in the lowcountry rice region did the ideal come to fruition. Although rice production in the lowcountry never regained its prewar profitability, the power of local black politicians was paramount for establishing the region as a symbol and stronghold of black economic and political clout through landownership. The failure of land reform in the remainder of the South, Foner argued, led to alternative strategies to transform the economy. Most Reconstruction governments resorted to railroad construction as a vehicle to effect economic change. According to Foner, this vision appealed to a broad array of southerners and cut across party lines.[109]

During the waning years of congressional Reconstruction, intimidation and violence by vigilante organizations such as the Ku Klux Klan, the Jayhawks, and the Regulators proscribed the enaction of free labor ideology throughout the South.[110] The activities of the Klan had its origins in the labor troubles that emerged with the destruction of slavery. The enfranchisement of African American men politicized the Klan's reign of terror and led to the success of what John Hope Franklin termed "counter Reconstruction." In the 1874 elections, only three counties in the state of Georgia maintained a black voting majority and elected African American men to the state legislature: Liberty, McIntosh, and Glynn counties.[111] The redemption of the state government, which involved the election of 41 Democratic senators and 156 Democrats to the House, succeeded in diminishing the Republican presence in state politics. By 1884 only Liberty and McIntosh counties elected an African American representative to the state legislature.[112]

Throughout the 1870s and 1880s, local African American leaders labored to ensure the longevity of the Republican Party by organizing rallies and attending state Republican conventions, not only to encourage high voter turnout in local elections, but to foment support in national elections.[113] In McIntosh County, Republican voters assembled in front of the old courthouse in Darien in July 1876 to choose two delegates to attend the district convention scheduled to convene on August 10 in Savannah. The meeting was called to order by Allen C. Gould, whom the convention elected on motion as convention chair. Daniel Spaulding served as secretary. The committee elected Gould and Samuel Russell as delegates. The biracial convention adopted strong resolutions endorsing Rutherford B. Hayes and William A. Wheeler for president and vice president of the United States. The convention's executive committee consisted of Gould, Hamilton Curry, Lectured Crawford, P. C. Dollie, and Peter Maxwell. Each of these local leaders and least two local white leaders attending the convention, W. H. Way and J. W. Corker, made a series of copacetic speeches in support of the Republican Party.[114]

The Republican Convention of the First Congressional District of Georgia met at St. James Tabernacle in Savannah on Thursday, August 10, 1876. Attorney and vice chair Louis B. Toomer called the meeting to order and read the call for the convention in the absence of James Atkins, who served as chair of the district committee. John H. Deveaux, owner of the region's only black newspaper, *The Savannah Tribune,* was unanimously elected temporary chair, and J. H. Perry was elected secretary. At the Republican District Convention, members nominated J. E. Bryant unanimously for Congress and John T. Collins as a district elector; and they elected John H. Deveaux chair of the district committee.[115]

Local leaders in Chatham, McIntosh, Liberty, Glynn, and Camden counties were connected to leaders in Savannah through political and fraternal networks. The *Savannah Tribune* provided access to public community space for political activism. Political networks derived from inter-island ties established with the assistance of local leaders such as former slaves William A. Golding of Liberty County and J. C. Legree of Chatham County, who became mayor of Burroughs, Georgia. Golding, who served as a "delegate" of local freedmen and freedwomen through his employment by the Freedmen's Bureau, held court sessions in Liberty County in which he, along with other former slaves, wrote letters complaining of the conditions in the lowcountry.[116] In one such letter Golding stated: "We cannot labor for the landowners and know that our infirm and children are not provided for and not allowed to educate or learn more than they were permitted in slavery. We are a working class of people and we are willing and are desirous to work for a fair compensation. But to return to work upon the terms that are at present offered to us would be we think going back into the state of slavery."[117]

Like other lowcountry leaders, such as Aaron A. Bradley and Tunis Campbell, Golding wedded politics with a desire for social and economic justice.[118] His service in Georgia's constitutional convention of 1867, the Georgia House of Representatives in 1868, and the Georgia labor convention reflected a trope of leadership committed to the advancement of fair compensation. Although the Georgia House of Representatives expelled Golding, along with other African American legislators, on the grounds that the right of black men to vote did not necessarily translate into a right to hold office, Golding continued to give voice to the labor concerns of African Americans in the lowcountry.[119]

Leaders such as Bradley and Golding used their social capital to promote identity politics in the lowcountry. *Identity politics* refers to "collective sensibilities and actions that come from a particular location within society, in direct defiance of universal categories that tend to subsume, erase, or suppress this particularity." In this sense, *location* implies a distinctive "social memory, consciousness, and practice, as well as place within the social structure."[120]

Former slaves continued to demand full and fair compensation throughout the late nineteenth century. Through organizations such as the Union League and the Georgia Colored Farmers' Alliance, they endeavored to push against neodependency and neopaternalism. After the end of the war, the Union League provided former slaves with a platform to express their views on political, social, and economic matters.[121] Men such as engineer and blacksmith Dandy Stewart relied on these organizations to maintain political spaces for their own intellectual praxis. Stewart was elected to the Darien County Board of Commissioners in 1878. He

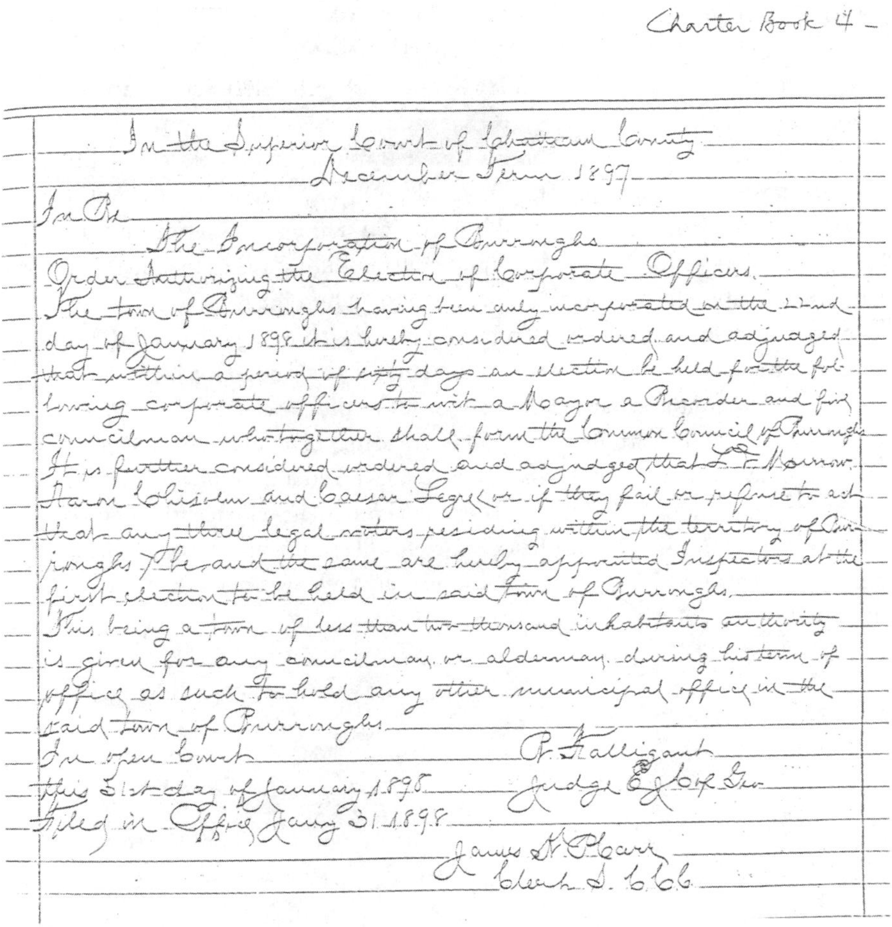
Charter Book 4 -

In the Superior Court of Chatham County
December Term 1897

In Re
The Incorporation of Burroughs
Order Authorizing the Election of Corporate Officers.

The town of Burroughs having been duly incorporated on the 22nd day of January 1898 it is hereby considered ordered and adjudged that within a period of sixty days an election be held for the following corporate officers to wit a Mayor a Recorder and five councilmen who together shall form the Common Council of Burroughs.
It is further considered ordered and adjudged that L. F. Monroe, Aaron Chisolm and Caesar Legree or if they fail or refuse to act that any three legal voters residing within the territory of Burroughs the be and the same are hereby appointed Inspectors at the first election to be held in said town of Burroughs.
This being a town of less than two thousand inhabitants authority is given for any councilman or alderman during his term of office as such to hold any other municipal office in the said town of Burroughs.

In open Court
this 31st day of January 1898
P. Falligant
Judge E. C. S. C. Ga.

Filed in Office Jany 31 1898.
James K. P. Carr
Clerk S. C. C.

Article Authorizing the Election of Corporate Officers, Burroughs, Georgia, 1898. Records of the Chatham County Superior Court, Charter Book 4, 123–24, Savannah, Georgia.

and his son Dandy Stewart Jr., who labored as a farmer, remained commissioners throughout the 1880s.[122]

During the late 1880s and early 1890s, the Georgia Colored Farmers' Alliance became the principal vehicle for welding free labor ideology to fair compensation. Organized in Troup County in 1884, the Colored Farmers' Alliance at its peak boasted a membership of 90,000, which included a large number of women.[123] The significance of this movement became evident with the construction in the 1880s of a Farmers' Alliance Hall on Sapelo Island, where residents held political meetings to discuss the community's economic concerns.[124] Alliance members elected African Americans to local county positions and were instrumental in electing two

African Americans, Lectured Crawford of McIntosh County and J. M. Holzendorf of Camden County, to the Georgia state legislature in 1890.[125] The gradual decline of the Colored Farmers' Alliance in 1893 was coeval with deteriorating race relations throughout the state.

Dandy Stewart lived on Butler's Island throughout the Reconstruction and post-Reconstruction periods. He remained politically active in lowcountry politics throughout 1890s until his death on May 23, 1891.[126] His service on the Board of Commissioners for Darien, Georgia, and his duties as coroner for McIntosh County, a position he assumed in 1879, had earned him the respect and admiration of black and white citizens. Like other former slaves, Stewart carved out liminal spaces of freedom from former plantation lands, and through his labor as an engineer and blacksmith he earned enough wages to purchase thirty acres of land on Butler's Island.[127] Stewart, like many other African American men in the lowcountry, continued to pay a poll tax until his death to remain politically active in the county and give voice to the region. Not unlike other late-nineteenth-century African American families, Stewart left a legacy for his son, who continued his father's political activism as the economic and political challenges of the 1890s continued unabated in spite of African American resistance.

4

THE STATE OF FREEDOM IS THE STATE OF SELF-RELIANCE

A people, to be free, must necessarily be their own rulers.

Martin R. Delany, *Political Destiny of the Colored Race on the American Continent*

On June 4, 1870 Joshua C. Legree opened an account with the Savannah branch of the Freedmen's Bank. Three years earlier, Legree had been among the first to register to vote under the terms of the 1867 Reconstruction Act. Both his political activity and his desire to save the fruits of his labor underscored his determination to establish an independent life for himself, his wife, Mary, and daughter, Rina. For four decades, Legree remained politically active in the lowcountry, consistently paid a poll tax to retain voting rights, and built an economic foundation that included land and other forms of property. Elected as the first mayor of Burroughs, Georgia, in 1898, Legree relied on a network of men and women in the Ogeechee district, who shared the same collective experience of dispossession, to build a political base.[1] The postemancipation conduct of former slaves serves as an important frame of reference for delineating how they created meaningful structures of resistance out of what Clifford Geertz termed "webs of significance."[2] In lowcountry Georgia, these webs of significance consisted of elements of culture, which African Americans created and re-created both during their enslavement and after slavery ended.

African Americans defined their existence through kinship and community solidarity. They established autonomous communities, separated from white religious institutions, and created their own religious bodies. Lowcountry Georgians also maintained a rural-urban link through cooperative associations and cultural commonalities.[3] A rural-urban link developed as a result of railway transportation networks that connected the city of Savannah, the county seat, to plantation districts. These coastal areas maintained substantial black majorities and had been the centers of rice production. This rural-urban link was particularly salient after the Civil War, when African Americans established communities on the outskirts of Savannah. African Americans who settled on the rural fringes of Savannah became a group of "country dwelling city people" who held various occupations in Savannah, but who resided in rural and semirural areas. Rural and semirural African Americans shared a common cultural and religious bond.[4] A shared political and cultural consciousness provided the ideological foundation for the emergence of Black nationalism and its multiple manifestations. Black nationalism developed in response to the slave trade and slavery and is predicated on the idea of racial unity and political unification. Political unification refers to the belief that the entire race has a collective destiny, comparable to that of a nation. Black nationalism and the formation of oppositional communities were a part of the same historical continuum.[5]

The ideology of white supremacy defined American social reality during the second half of the nineteenth century. The half decade which witnessed the redemption of the South reinforced white supremacy and the idea of a democracy for whites only. The Compromise of 1877, which certified Rutherford B. Hayes as president, marked the end of a tumultuous era. As the federal government abjured interfering in the affairs of the South and consented to the removal of federal troops, the Republican Party frayed into two factions, which ultimately weakened the viability of the party in the South and underscored the Republican Party's weakened position toward protecting the political and economic rights of formerly enslaved people.[6]

In the lowcountry, African Americans remained the demographic majority and continued to hold office at the local and state level during the post-Reconstruction period, despite a decline in the size of the African American vote. Indeed, the year 1877 was a watershed year for African American voting as the new state constitution disfranchised all persons who owed city taxes levied since 1876, the year in which the new state constitution was adopted. By 1888 the number of African American legislators was cut to two: Anthony Wilson of Camden County and S. A. McIvor of Liberty County.[7] Wilson and McIvor were among the first to register to vote in 1867 under the Reconstruction Act. The men had carved a political niches for themselves in their respective counties by serving as school teachers and political leaders.[8]

Coterminous with disfranchisement, Ku Klux Klan activity intensified throughout the state. Klan violence escalated in counties where African Americans were numerically in the minority. As the collective position of African Americans declined, there was a corresponding increase in the number of lynchings. Although most lynchings were not systematically recorded, the year 1899 represented the peak year for documented lynchings in Georgia, with twenty-seven recorded.[9] This period was characterized by a "global awakening of whiteness," as lynching, colonization, imperialism, and the consolidation of whiteness, led to what W. E. B. Du Bois described in *The Souls of White Folk* as a "descent into hell."[10] Legal scholar Mark Weiner observed that "the vast majority of southerners, depended on lynching to maintain their distinctive social and cultural order"; lynching thus served as a defining act of justice and community for southerners.[11] In the lowcountry, African Americans maintained a demographic majority that mediated the development of insurgent Klan violence as African Americans could retaliate against such violence.[12]

The post-Reconstruction period was significant for the extension of self-determination strategies in lowcountry communities. Both Henry McNeal Turner and Martin R. Delany were central to this discourse on self-determination strategies, espousing both emigrationism and separatism.[13] The establishment of the Liberian Exodus Joint Stock Steamship Company, formed in 1877 by Delany, B. F. Porter, and other prominent clergy in Charleston, South Carolina, advocated emigration to Liberia as a panacea for race hatred in America.[14] Emigration represented the first salient effort by enslaved and free African Americans to establish an autonomous national state in order to gain freedom, independence, and self-reliance. Unable to function as citizen members within American society, African Americans who emigrated to Liberia would be able to acquire property, build institutions, and enjoy the rights and privileges of freedom.

The creation of an African American entrepreneurial class during the second half of the nineteenth century did not preclude social immunity to race prejudice and aspersions on their character. Former slaves who responded to the persuasive rhetoric of Henry McNeal Turner, pastor of Savannah's St. James Tabernacle A.M.E. church, included entrepreneurs who accepted Turner's proposition that "being sick or dying with fever in Africa was better than dying at the hands of a lynch mob in the U.S."[15] In 1877, 197 men and women influenced by Delany and Turner left Savannah for Liberia. The emigrationist thrust continued during the last two decades of the nineteenth century as 400 African Americans emigrated to Sierra Leone in 1887; in 1895 the steamship *Horsa* left the port of Savannah with 202 emigrants.[16]

The historical burden of enslavement, which carried with it the characterization of African Americans as lazy, irrational, and licentious, cast them as a discernible and separate group, a problem within the social framework of America. As former slaves remained engaged in politics, they husbanded their resources in support of emigrationist and separatist platforms that reinforced private and public transcripts of resistance. For the vast majority of African Americans, separatism, not emigrationism, emerged as the most viable alternative. Their cultural identity as descendants of Africans remained deeply rooted in the American past; thus many

Rice cultivation on the Ogeechee near Savannah. *Harper's Weekly,* January 5, 1867

perceived America as their home and endeavored to build communities and institutions there.

KINSHIP AND LAND IN THE LOWCOUNTRY

A prominent feature of lowcountry communities was the presence of three pivotal institutions: the family, the church, and mutual associations. These institutions served as reinforcements for the individual and the community as a whole. To a large extent, the self-defined thought and behavior displayed by former slaves emanated from the roles they assumed within these institutions, through which a network of kinship relationships developed. Kinship communities were not simply bound together by blood relations. Instead, community institutions structured relationship patterns that encompassed the entire community. For instance, churches functioned as extended kinship groups by providing emotional closeness and support in times of crisis.[17]

African Americans developed several strategies to sustain access to and control of land. In several communities, their land supported the growth of rice, which they valued as both a market crop and a dietary staple. The initiatives undertaken by African Americans to secure land through disciplined economic choices is central to understanding how they seized freedom. The extent to which they were successful depended on regional demographic factors, the degree of economic elasticity, and the relative fluidity of race relations. The formulation of overt collective acts designed to secure land and establish autonomous communities in opposition to federal land restoration represented a salient effort to translate emancipation into substantive freedom.

Landownership was the symbol of group interactions and represented status to all those related to it. Landowners held a higher status than tenants or sharecroppers because they had gained a small foothold in the earth that provided a measure of independence. In the Burroughs community, located in the Ogeechee district of Chatham County, twenty-four men and women had obtained this measure of independence between 1870 and 1888. Their ages ranged from twenty-six to seventy-two at the time of their land purchase.[18] Chatham County's agrarian-industrial economy enhanced the opportunities for African Americans to acquire land. In addition to wage labor, African Americans engaged in commercial farming and in entrepreneurial activities such as marketing produce and selling fish, shrimp, oysters, and crabs. These various forms of economic activity persisted into the twentieth century and expanded or contracted with structural changes in the county's economy. Although the vast majority of African Americans found it difficult to save and invest in land, the number of African American landowners in the county increased steadily between 1870 and 1900. Their landholdings averaged between nine and twenty-six acres. In the state of Georgia, African Americans owned 1,252,714 million of the 31,203,973 acres of improved land, or 4 percent of the total farming area.[19]

In spite of economic restrictions, African Americans in the state of Georgia continued to increase their landholdings. In the Ogeechee district, rural and semirural African Americans secured a measure of independence through the purchase of land and the establishment of communities such as Brownsville, Burroughs, Dittmersville, Fort Argyle, and Millersville.[20] Brownsville and Dittmersville maintained the highest property values, with average valuation at five hundred dollars.[21] Freed people cooperated to purchase land and homes in other areas of Chatham County throughout the 1870s. Between 1873 and 1874 African Americans established the Southville community, where they built thirty homes with an aggregate value of ten thousand dollars. They also established mutual associations such as the Sons and Daughters of Southville, which paid $150.00 for three parcels of land.[22] This pattern of cooperation also developed in Brownsville and Dittmersville, where African Americans accumulated tracts of real estate valued individually between two hundred and two thousand dollars.[23] William Morgin, a farm laborer and member of First African Baptist Church, opened an account with the Freedmen's Bank in Savannah in 1867. Two years later, he purchased land for one hundred dollars in Dittmersville, located on the outskirts of Savannah in White Bluff.[24] Dittmersville and First African Baptist Church served as kinship communities for Morgin and other African Americans, such as Diamond Williams, a steamboat pilot, who paid two hundred dollars for land in Dittmersville in 1868, and Robert Watt, a farm laborer, who paid one hundred dollars for land in Dittmersville in 1869.[25]

African American families in the lowcountry adhered to a nuclear model. The desire for a stable family and their aspirations for land and other economic opportunities were interrelated. In Burroughs, 87 percent of the landowners maintained nuclear households in 1880.[26] For farmers, the family functioned as an economic unit. However, this varied with respect to the age of the children and the particular needs of the family. The wives of three out of the seven farmers remained at home as opposed to working in the fields. For instance, Fortune Watson, who produced 10,208 pounds of rice in 1879, recognized the importance of having his wife, Tilla, devote her time and energy to raising their four children who had not reached working age. In most farming families, however, every family member who was physically able engaged in some type of work. Invariably families utilized the savings of all family members to invest in land.[27] In a few cases, however, rice farmers also hired laborers to assist in performing arduous field work, paying between two and nine dollars per week for the time hired. Their economic activities revolved around the Atlantic and Gulf Railroad, which provided the means by which they transported locally grown vegetables and rice to Savannah.[28]

Successful farming, whether commercial or for subsistence, required access to property other than land. Livestock, such as chickens, cows, draught animals, and pigs, provided farmers with the instruments to provide for their families and to earn additional income from marketing produce, including eggs, corn, sweet potatoes, and, in a few instances, cotton. In cases where women worked on family farms, they performed tasks such as planting, harvesting, and marketing produce. Family farming encouraged solidarity, individual initiative, and responsibility.[29] Both Sam Black and Toby Roberts were among the original land recipients after General William Sherman's Field Order No. 15. Although they found it difficult to save and invest in land, both men relied on the labor of their family and the draft animals they owned to meet their economic needs.[30]

Landowners placed a high value on providing land for their children. For instance, William Ferguson paid $130 for six acres of land (lot number nine) from January Stoney in 1876 "to hold in trust for Andrew Bryan," Ferguson's eight-year-old step-son, and "Matilda Ferguson," his eleven-year-old daughter.[31] Stoney, who paid $266 for seven acres, or lot number nine of Wild Horn, in 1874, may have migrated out of the area and purchased land in another area of Chatham County, as James Grant did in 1882.[32] Grant, who paid $373 for eighteen acres (lot number one) at Wild Horn in 1874, sold his holdings to Adam Young for $300. Grant remained in the Ogeechee district but migrated closer to Savannah.[33] Affinal relations played a part in land transfers between David Roulabit and Elze Green. Roulabit, one of the original 1865 land recipients, purchased three lots (numbers six, seven, and eight) of the Miller-Demere tract on November 1, 1888. On December 1, 1888, he sold five acres to Elze Green for $60.11.[34]

An important factor in examining property ownership among rural African Americans is their "level of living."[35] The first generation of freedmen and freedwomen in rural districts lived for the most part as did other groups in agricultural areas during the late nineteenth century. In lowcountry Georgia, they raised their own poultry and vegetables, fished, hunted, produced a cash crop of rice or cotton, and engaged in some form of commerce. However, they still faced obstacles to economic advancement. Their small holdings precluded expanding their level of output. They were also vulnerable to fluctuations in national and international markets and faced natural disasters such as floods and hurricanes. Like their poor white counterparts, they were economically marginalized.[36]

LANDOWNERSHIP AND WOMEN'S COMMUNITY NETWORKS

The establishment of an identity as self-sufficient agriculturalists and the concomitant reaffirmation as property owners provided women with a new ideological orientation. Caroline Ealy purchased twenty and three-quarters acres on January 10, 1873, paying $415. Ealy's estate consisted of "lot number three," which bordered Chevis Road on the east.[37] Apart from Plenty Ancrum, Caroline Ealy held the largest tract in the Burroughs settlement. Other women who purchased land secured modest acreage. Hannah Green and Sarah Davis owned seven and five acres, respectively. Both Green and Davis held fiduciary deeds. Mingo Broughton served as trustee for Green, who paid $140 for her property, which ran parallel with Chevis Road and which bordered the lands of Norris Weston on the north. Likewise, Robin Davis and Prince Wright acted on behalf of Davis, who paid $200 for five acres "lying near Chevis road."[38]

The process by which women created networks and developed survival strategies to manage living during their enslavement provides important insights into gender, race, and class, and into the role of women, particularly women classified as head of household, in oppositional communities. These women struggled to give form and meaning to their lives through their participation in female benevolent societies, which encouraged women to save and invest in land. The issuance of possessory titles to women under Sherman's Field Order reinforced the conditions under which women sought to establish new economic and political realities.

For single and widowed women, the ownership of land emerged as the focal point of their struggle. Most embraced the end of institutionalized slavery by locating loved ones and rebuilding their families. For many women, however, the prospects of seeing children and husbands who had been sold away during slavery were dim. The plight of Mary McGill, who migrated to Savannah from South Carolina, underscores the painful circumstances that invaded the lives of many freedwomen.

McGill's husband, Joe, died shortly before the war ended. Together they had lost four children who had died at birth, and they had witnessed the sale of two daughters, Diana and Margaret, twenty years before the war began.[39]

Freedwomen sought comfort from the personal pain slavery inflicted and the economic hardships they faced as a result of their gender and race through community networks that stemmed from the African American church. The experiences of African American women created a shared belief system or worldview that informed their roles in extended kinship institutions such as the church and mutual aid and benevolent societies. These institutions inculcated the doctrines of self-help and solidarity.

In the process of institution building, nearly every African American community in lowcountry Georgia sought to secure title to land for church purposes. In the A.M.E. church, as well as in other churches, committees on deeds and homesteads were established in each district of South Georgia for this purpose. In this arena, women enhanced the material foundation of the church not only through fundraising, but in some instances by providing land. Selina Stewart, who inherited the thousand-dollar estate of her father, James Stewart, sold a small parcel of the land to Mt. Zion C.M.E. church in order to "promote the welfare of the church."[40]

To a large extent, African American churches were the institutional backbone of the Savannah branch of the Freedmen's Savings and Trust, which operated in the city from 1866 to 1874. In other areas of Chatham County, the trustees of the C.M.E. church in the Ogeechee district, Hillard Jackson, Limus Greene, Caesar King, Jacob Grant, and Francis Shaw, purchased one acre of land in 1879 from the Burroughs family. Additionally the Burroughs family, which owned Wild Horn plantation in the Ogeechee district, sold land to Mount Olive Baptist Church and the New Ogeechee Baptist Church, which maintained majority African American congregations. In 1864 Francis MacLeod bequeathed one thousand acres of Wild Horn to William Burroughs to hold in trust for his wife, Ann A. Burroughs (MacLeod's daughter), and their children, William Burroughs Jr., Joseph Burroughs, and Alethea Burroughs. Specified in each deed is the consent of Burroughs's wife and children. Church accounts were used to make improvements on buildings and to support educational activities. Moreover, church-related benevolent societies, such as the Mary Magdalene Society, the Ladies Galatian Society, and the Daughters of Nehemiah, complemented the mission of the church while promoting habits of mutuality.[41]

Female benevolent societies enabled African American women to form an independent power base within their communities. In Savannah-Chatham County, women assumed leadership positions in most female benevolent societies. On the basis of Elsa Barkley Brown's paradigm of female leadership, African American women led and served as community influentials, community activists, and elite leaders. Women categorized as community influentials held secondary positions within the associations, such as secretary and treasurer. Community activists, on the other hand, were women who served as president and vice-president and who were chosen to lead at least twice.[42] Similarly the elite leaders were women elected to primary positions more than three times. Between 1865 and 1885, 922 persons served as officers in Savannah's African American organizations. Women comprised 28 percent of the officers. Ninety-six percent of the 922 officers were former slaves.[43]

The balance of power in a number of associations was not always equal; however, all members played some role in constructing a vision of community. Members in associations such as the Sons and Daughters of Jerusalem, the Sons and Daughters of Mount Sinai, and the Sons and Daughters of Zion coordinated their activities to achieve their objective of buying land. The Sons and Daughters of Mount Sinai, for instance, raised two hundred dollars to purchase a lot for the society. Likewise, the Jerusalem and Zion associations paid seventy-five dollars in 1883 and forty dollars in 1888, respectively, for small parcels of land.[44] Through their involvement in more than two hundred mutual aid and benevolent associations, African American women in Savannah played an instrumental role in building the material and spiritual foundation of Black institutions. Through these institutions, they formed intracommunity networks that provided support for self-reliant women seeking to build a land base.[45]

Church-affiliated societies such as mutual aid benevolent associations played a pivotal role in the economic arena of women's lives. In the process of working together to enhance the institutional structure of the community, women, particularly those who were widowed, benefited from the various means by which these institutions taught saving to buy land. Women, like men, maintained deep-seated aspirations to invest in land, which was a tangible manifestation of their independence as well as an asset that might strengthen kinship and family ties. However, single and widowed women, particularly in rural areas, found it difficult to purchase land because of low wages and familial responsibilities. In spite of economic hardships, African American women in Savannah-Chatham County became landowners. By 1876, 117 African American women in Chatham County, most of whom were former slaves, owned land.[46]

Compared with the total number of landowners in Savannah in 1870, the number of landowning African American women is significant. Savannah's rural-urban economy and the conterminous development of a plantation and industrial economy placed African American men and women in a comparatively good position to accumulate real and personal property. In 1870 their total value of land and personal property amounted to $425,013. By 1900 this amount totaled $914,320, an increase of 54 percent.[47] African American women emerged as landowners during this period through inheritance and through individual and collective efforts. Many of the women functioned as the head of the household due to the death of a spouse or because of voluntary separation. Some landowners, moreover, were single women who sought to establish security for themselves. In 1870 and 1880, women headed one-fourth of the African-American families in Savannah.[48]

Kinship played an instrumental role in the community network of African American women. In some instances, landed kin helped landless family members acquire land. Illustrative of this is the Sheftall family, who helped family members acquire land by selling them portions of their property. Susan Sheftall and Eve Johnson each secured land from the estate of Margaret Sheftall, their grandmother, for ten dollars. Susan Sheftall, who worked as a launderer, had accumulated real property valued at two thousand dollars by 1870.[49] In most cases, women who purchased land secured modest acreage averaging between five and ten acres. Holdings that were large enough to build a home and maintain a garden represented an economic investment in a family estate. Women often took great care to include their children as co-owners of land. For instance, the premises of Kate Brown's deed stated "this indenture made November 4, 1882 between William Burroughs, Ann Burroughs, and Joseph and Alethea Burroughs, parties of the first part, and *Kate Brown and her children* [emphasis added] parties of the second part."[50]

In other instances, women purchased land for their children. Illustrative of this is Nancy Singleton, who on behalf of her children paid one hundred dollars for five acres of land in the Burroughs community.[51] Affinal relations also governed rights to land. Plenty Ancrum, for instance, "in consideration for the natural love and affection" and the sum of five dollars, conveyed one and one-half acre of his twenty-three acres to Tenah Murray.[52] Thus, through an "internal land trade," women gained access to small parcels of land, which they equated with economic and personal independence. Through landownership self-reliant African American women redefined and reordered their lives and preserved their personal autonomy. For the most part, they relied on community networks that stemmed from the Black church to construct their vision of community. These networks were forged in the process of institution building and were strengthened by their collective efforts to build a land base for their communities.

Although not all whites in Savannah opposed selling land to African Americans, many conspired to keep African American landless by not selling to them. Out of a population of 27,515 in 1880, only 648 African American families owned land. An inverse relationship between the percentage of African American families in Savannah and the percentage who owned land persisted primarily because Chatham County maintained the highest land value per acre in the state of Georgia. This condition prevailed even during the 1870s, when land values dropped by 50 percent because of an economic depression. Moreover, although the amount of land African Americans owned more than doubled, from 1,055 acres in 1874 to 2,687 acres in 1880, the aggregate value of land decreased due to the economic depression, from $192,000 in 1870 to $79,000 in 1880. Similarly the per capita wealth of African

Americans declined from $17.79 in 1870 to $7.31 in 1880.[53] In Bryan and Liberty counties, which offered land at two to thirty dollars per acre, African Americans had greater success in purchasing land.[54]

THE TOWN OF BURROUGHS

As economic and social oppression intensified at the turn of the twentieth century, the Burroughs community sought to obtain economic and social independence through self-segregation within the protective confines of an all-Black community. Burroughs became the only incorporated town in Chatham County in 1898, with residents serving as mayor, town council members, and constable. The town's boundaries extended six miles southwest of Chevis Road, encompassing the Miller and Fort Argyle communities. The incorporation of Burroughs reinforced the bonds of family and community, which informed the transfer and sale of land.[55] The "internal land trade" became the primary mechanism that gave other community members access to land. For instance, Apollo Blount and Frank Gladden, both of whom were over seventy in 1890, sold small plots from their holdings. Blount, whose wife, Binah, may have predeceased him, sold two and one-half acres of his ten acres to Elizabeth Agnew on April 21, 1890. Similarly Gladden sold one acre of his four and three-quarters acres to Bishop C. K. Nelson, who paid thirty-four dollars.[56]

The subdivision of small tracts into even smaller parcels signaled a shift from cash crop farming to primarily subsistence agriculture. The small lots that men and women purchased were only large enough to build a home and maintain a small garden. This pattern continued in the 1890s and into the twentieth century. Between 1890 and 1907, fourteen African Americans purchased land from the Burroughs family.[57] During this seventeen-year period, they purchased seventy-seven acres, paying $1,447 for plots which ranged in size from three-quarters of an acre to eleven and one-half acres, paying as much as $18.85 per acre.[58] Six had made arrangements with Joseph and Alethea Burroughs, the son and daughter of William Burroughs, to purchase their land in installments. In most cases, they made final payment for their land but did not receive the actual deed until three to four years later, primarily because of the deaths of both Joseph and Alethea Burroughs.

Eight of the landowners were women whose husbands may have predeceased them and who continued to make payments on the land. Comfort Blake's title, for instance, specified that the land consisted of "seven acres set forth in the name of Amos Blake."[59] At age forty-nine, she made final payment to Joseph and Alethea Burroughs on November 27, 1899, and received the deed from Nina Burroughs, the granddaughter of William Burroughs, in 1904.[60] In other cases children took over payments and purchased the land. For instance, the heirs of Sallie Legree, J. C. Legree, Fred Legree, and C. Bradley paid $230 for eleven and one-half acres at Wild Horn. Other women purchased land ranging from three-quarters of an acre to nine and three-quarters acres. Five of the women worked as farm laborers and also relied on the contributions of their children to the family economy.[61]

Although rural African Americans were economically marginalized, they continued to profit from a community network that provided social and religious reinforcement. In Burroughs the "church became the center for everything" and played a major role in holding the community together.[62] Three churches provided spiritual and social uplift: Mount Olive Baptist, New Ogeechee Baptist, and St. Bartholomew's Episcopal. At these institutions parishioners learned the price of rice and heard about upcoming elections. Moreover, weddings, funerals, summer revivals, church suppers and bazaars provided much of the community social life, and youth groups, women's missionary societies, and meetings of deacons and elders gave African Americans the opportunity of self-government denied them in the larger society. Residences and farmlands were clustered around these institutions, which not only underscored their centrality, but were also an indication of the settlement's growth into a town with social institutions. These institutions were less than one mile apart and were connected by Chevis Road, the main artery of the community. Hence, for the Burroughs community, land and religion had complementary roles in that these two elements structured the community.[63]

Churches, moreover, served as institutional linkages between rural and urban African Americans. For instance, Mount Olive Baptist Church at Burroughs included in its membership Brother Richard H. Howard, who was also a member of St. James Tabernacle A.M.E. Church in Savannah. Additionally the New Ogeechee Baptist church at Burroughs was the site of the Tenth Session of the Zion Baptist Association's teachers convention, which included representatives from Darien (McIntosh County) and Brunswick.[64] Mutual associations also provided support and promoted solidarity. Illustrative of this is the Labor Union Protective Association (LUPA) and the Georgia Benevolent Fishermen's Association (GBFA), which promoted economic independence by directing various business enterprises. In 1892 the LUPA, which opened a grocery store on the Ogeechee Neck, consisted of carpenters and other skilled African American tradesman who united as a result of exclusion from all white unions. The LUPA also provided burial services to members who invested a percentage of their savings for such purposes. The LUPA was a vital link between rural and urban African Americans. Its board of directors included J. C. Legree, the mayor of Burroughs, and S. Snelson, an African American surgeon and physician in Savannah. Similarly the GBFA, chartered in 1894, encouraged business enterprises in the oyster industry by securing a lease of two thousand acres of oyster ground in the county; at one time it reported over one thousand dollars in income.[65]

Burroughs, like other African American communities, regarded institutional property as an essential element in establishing oppositional communities. Mars Ward, who owned four hundred dollars in real estate, bequeathed one acre of his fifteen acres on Burkhalter Road in the district to the Second Baptist Church in Savannah.[66] African Americans also purchased land to house mutual associations and secret societies, which were the centers of rural and urban social life. Both mutual associations and secret societies encouraged savings from their members in the form of monthly dues. At Burroughs, the Burroughs Union Club purchased eight and one-half acres of land for $250.[67] By 1880 a total of 193 mutual aid societies and clubs were formed by African Americans in Savannah and the outlying districts of Chatham County. Their primary purpose involved providing burial services and aid to the sick. They also sent money to cities hit by disaster and worked with associations when epidemics plagued Savannah.[68]

In addition to mutual societies, African Americans in the town of Burroughs held membership in secret societies, such as the Masons for men and the Order of the Eastern Star for women. These societies promoted solidarity and reinforced individual self-esteem. The Burroughs Union Club, adjacent to St. Bartholomew's church, served as the meeting place for the societies.[69] An integral feature of these associations was the opportunity they provided for members to unite for community-related activities that were often held in Savannah, including celebrations commemorating Emancipation Day, Liberian Independence Day, the adoption of the Fourteenth and Fifteenth Amendments, and President Lincoln's birthday. Summer excursions, which included picnics and steamboat rides, also reinforced community networks. These activities strengthened the bond between rural and semirural African Americans.[70]

Freedom's first generation had fostered the development of kinship and solidarity through the reinforcement of individual self-esteem, a sympathetic understanding of their mutual plight, and various expressions of love, manifested in the sale and transfer of property. As freedom's second generation matured, they inherited not only the institutions that served as the cornerstone of Burroughs and similar communities throughout the South, but also their parents' land, and they maintained an ethos of cooperation that helped others become landowners. Land was the primary economic asset that they could pass on to their children. Although they owned a comparatively small amount of land, it represented their portion of the "tree of life" that they could pass on to their children.

Children secured land not only by inheritance, but also through their own efforts. However, their holdings were much smaller than those of their parents, primarily as a result of the division of land among heirs and also because of the scarcity of available land. Industrial magnate Henry Ford purchased nearly all of the former rice plantations on the Ogeechee Neck and in Bryan County. As land became scarcer, African Americans relied on kinship networks to secure small parcels.[71] Kinship and co-residential relationships informed the transfer and sale of family land. Men and women relied on these bonds for intergenerational land transfers, as well as for fictive kin land sales. Moreover, members of the community had a mutual responsibility for one another, which they maintained through shared experiences. Inheritance patterns generally took the form of exclusive rights of ownership, such as heir and successor property, or usufruct rights, in which an "activator" of the estate maintained a right to the house or land.[72]

Landowners typically transferred land by means of deeds and, in a few instances, wills. Through the warranty clause of each deed, landowners held fee simple title, which protected the rights of their heirs to the land. Referred to as heirs' property, this type of arrangement was most prevalent among rural African Americans, who often maintained family land in the names of their parents. Although wills were not very common among rural African Americans, particularly among those with small holdings, a few African Americans in the district made legal provisions for the disposition of their property. Deeds often reflected the pronouncement of wills.[73] Emanuel Heidt's will, for instance, provided for the distribution of one-half acre of his estate to his daughter Crispy Arkwright, and three-quarters of an acre to his granddaughter, Pinkey Sheppard. Each paid one dollar to Sambo Crawford, who served as administrator for Heidt's estate. Both Sheppard and Arkwright had maintained independent households in close proximity to Heidt's.[74]

Providing land for one's children and controlling land deeds and land use were important ways by which the members of the first generation ensured rights to their children's labor and secured for themselves care and support in old age. Accordingly they generally retained control of their land until well into their old age and made legal provisions for the disposition of their property prior to their deaths. For instance, at age seventy Jacob Shellman, who had received ten acres under Sherman's Field Order in 1865, "in consideration of love and affection, and the sum of $5.00" conveyed his five acres, which contained the family home, to his children Lizzie, Ralph, Lucretia, and Mary Shellman, on January 20, 1907.[75]

While agriculture continued to provide a livelihood for the majority of African Americans in lowcountry Georgia, most barely scratched out a living from the land. Moreover, obtaining capital to reinvest in their small holdings was difficult for rural African Americans. However, some landowners secured capital by issuing debt deeds against their property. Richard Crawford, for instance, issued a debt deed in 1907, using his ten acres as collateral. Crawford, who had paid $200 for ten acres at Wild Horn in 1872, received $140 from H. A. Fountain, one of the few white residents in Burroughs. In two years, Crawford repaid the total amount.[76]

By 1910 farming for most African Americans in Chatham County entailed cultivating small plots that averaged between three and nine acres. This represented a 300 percent drop in total farm acreage from 1890 to 1910.[77] Both the older and younger generations of landowners at Burroughs continued to farm, planting small plots of rice and sugarcane. They also earned income from fishing, dipping rosin from pine trees, and distilling turpentine. The lumber industry proved attractive, especially in nearby Bryan County, where it had superseded the rice industry. From the Ogeechee Neck, men sometimes traveled daily back and forth to Bryan County, where they worked at the Ford lumber mills.[78]

Sons generally followed the occupation of their fathers, while daughters assumed the familial role of their mothers, which included engaging in farm labor. However, in Burroughs a few men held high-status positions, such as mayor, sheriff, and town council member, in addition to working as farmers. In 1910, 44 percent of the landowners in Burroughs made their living as farmers; in 1920, 81 percent of the landowners were farmers. In contrast with the 1910 landowners, the vast majority of African American landowners in 1920 (73 percent) were over the age of forty (see Tables 6–8).[79]

Acquiring small parcels of land, however, did not solve the economic plight of rural African Americans in Chatham County in the first two decades of the twentieth century. As the larger society denied them access to credit and the market, their economic prospects were limited due to the land-based economic and political power of the new ruling class, which included Henry Ford. As historian Eric Foner aptly writes, "the autonomy offered by landownership was defensive rather than the springboard for sustained economic advancement."[80] All-black towns such as Burroughs did not prosper economically, primarily because the communities were a closed economic group with a relatively small population. In 1912 the town's population was two hundred.[81] From 1913 to 1917, the population remained listed at two hundred. Moreover, reinvestment in the community remained proscribed due to the persistence of race-based economic exploitation and the lack of adequate monetary resources.

In the political arena, Burroughs created its own system of governance. However, in the areas of trade and education it remained dependent on the urban center. Nonetheless, the autonomy and group cooperation offered through self-segregation within the protective confines of an all-Black community may have compensated for the low material condition of Burroughs.[82] The urban center maintained jurisdiction over capital crimes such as murder, but Burroughs maintained its own courthouse and system of punishment. For instance, misdemeanor offenders performed roadwork, one of the public services cut off by the county.[83]

The second generation, like the first, placed a high priority on acquiring land. In Burroughs the number of landowners increased slightly between 1910 and 1920. Moreover, the proportion of male landowners increased dramatically. Whereas in 1910 men made up 54.1 percent of the landowners; by 1920 they were 74.5 percent.[84] The "internal land trade" contributed to this increase. David Roulabit, for instance, sold small plots of his twenty-five acres to Flander Grant, John Shellman, and Barney Preston between 1916 and 1919. The amount they paid totaled $180.[85]

For the residents of Burroughs, gaining even a small foothold in the earth held both real and symbolic importance. For rural African Americans landownership was a form of resistance, an attempt to take charge of their own destinies. They continued to rely on landed kin and co-residents to secure small plots of land. On Fort Argyle road, for instance, Richard Lachison, who had received fifteen acres under Sherman's Order, purchased one half acre from Clara and Sam Lowman, who owned fourteen acres.[86] The real and symbolic importance of owning land is underscored by Gertrude Green, who stated that "one lady worked all day for 5 cents, but somehow she managed to buy five acres."[87]

By the early twentieth century, however, unanticipated strains began tugging at rural communities such as Burroughs. Small landholdings, especially those of an acre or less, could support a dwelling and a kitchen garden but left little room to raise an agricultural surplus for sale or even to pasture a cow. Most important, small landholdings did not conveniently subdivide. Moreover, with land becoming scarcer and the price of available land rising, the option of purchasing additional land grew less likely. In the face of this challenge, landholding families devised different strategies. Chief among these was the tacit agreement whereby only one or two grown children (and their spouse and children) continued to live on the family plot while others moved away—to other rural districts in Chatham County, or to Savannah or other urban areas in the North as well as the South.

As a result of this movement, the rural population in Chatham County had begun to decline. Between 1900 and 1910 the rural population declined from 16,995 to 14,626, a decrease of 13.9 percent.[88] As early as 1914 African Americans in Georgia were departing from Savannah on trains destined for northern cities. The exodus was greatest in Southwestern areas of Georgia, where African Americans owned a comparatively small amount of land and where the boll weevil had damaged cotton crops. In Georgia, more African Americans owned land in the wiregrass and coastal regions than in the black belt. In McIntosh County, for instance, 87 percent of African American farm operators owned their land in 1910 compared with only 2 percent in Dougherty County.[89] Migration from the rural areas of Chatham County was not as pronounced as in other areas of Georgia. In these areas, men and women developed their own institutions and struggled to improve their economic condition through landownership. Moreover, although children who could not gain access to land migrated out of Burroughs, the autonomy offered through self-governance and the complementary roles of land, religion, and family played a fundamental part of holding the community together.[90]

During the first decade of the twentieth century, W. E. B. Du Bois traveled extensively throughout Georgia to assess the historical and contemporary problems facing African Americans. His survey of Dougherty County, Georgia, published in the *Souls of Black Folk*, and his study of black landownership in coastal Georgia for the U.S. Labor Department in 1906 illuminate the experiences of African Americans in the post-Civil War South and Reconstruction's legacy for both regions. With a population of one million, Georgia had the highest concentration of African

Americans in the country at the turn of the twentieth century.[91] For Du Bois, one needed to only travel to Dougherty County to understand the race question in America. It was here that 80 percent of the black population worked the same land they had once worked as slaves, where 66 percent of the black population remained illiterate, and where slavery continued under a new form of capitalism.[92] Conversely, in the lowcountry, according to Du Bois, freedmen and freedwomen at Woodville, Ogeechee, and Belmont united and purchased land; they held 56,000 acres by 1909.[93] Half a decade earlier, Booker T. Washington, in his "Atlanta Compromise" speech, articulated a philosophy of separation and accommodation as the best strategy for black advancement, and this influenced the Black town movement in the South. In Georgia, all-Black towns included Archery (Sumter County), Cannonville (Troup County), Greenough (Mitchell County), and Leroy (Burke County).[94]

The formation of Burroughs represented the apogee of African American resistance to political, economic, and social injustice. The town's charter of incorporation advanced the principles of self-help, moral uplift, and racial solidarity through its governing body.[95] The residents of Burroughs accumulated the resources to purchase land and other forms of property in numerous ways. In some cases, pre-Civil War opportunities to accumulate cash and property had existed that placed freedmen and freedwomen in a better position to acquire land. Both the struggle for and the acquisition of land knit families and communities together. Families pooled resources and passed acquired land from one individual to another and from one generation to the next. Mutual and protective associations promoted landownership both rhetorically and by encouraging their members to purchase land with their savings. When church congregations succeeded in purchasing land, the buildings and grounds served as visible reminders of the fruits of frugality and as centers for the perpetuation of a sense of community and other attendant values.

Although it was a mixed blessing, the incorporation of Burroughs further exemplified this independence. Most important, incorporation allowed the community's residents jurisdiction over a wide range of civil affairs. Perhaps none of these prerogatives meant more than adjudication of the law. Communities such as Burroughs represented safe havens from the racial discrimination endemic to local and state government throughout the South at the turn of the century. The struggle of the residents of Burroughs to own land made these and other achievements possible. Few other rural communities in Georgia or elsewhere in the South enjoyed such amenities. In most plantation areas, sharecroppers had comparatively little control over their labor, their dwellings, or the future.[96]

The abysmal status and condition of African Americans throughout the rural South created the impetus for sustained protest movements during what historian Rayford Logan termed the "nadir."[97] Throughout the late nineteenth and early twentieth centuries, African Americans devised strategies and organized institutions to enable them to protest against economic subordination and de jure segregation. These movements were led by both African American elites and grassroots community intellectuals. In twenty-five cities throughout the South, these two groups organized boycotts against segregated public transit systems and engaged in legal assaults against legal disfranchisement.[98]

The deteriorating status of African Americans led to migration to northern cities during the first two decades of the twentieth century.[99] When the strains of growing families and a declining land base began to threaten the strategy of land acquisition, families adapted. Selected family members would continue to occupy and use family land, while other family members moved away. Through the device known as heirs' property, they maintained common interest in the land of their forebears. Over time, heirs' property would prove vulnerable to encroachment by outsiders desiring access to land. But in the early twentieth century, it epitomized a strategy for achieving a measure of independence on the land—one of the highest priorities of African American southerners from the dawn of freedom and even before.

TABLE 6. Landowners and Renters, Burroughs, Georgia 1910–1920

1910	N=100	%	1920	N=89	%
Owned Free Home/Farm	48	48	Owned Free Home/Farm	55	61.7
Rented Home/Farm	52	52	Rented Home/Farm	34	38.2

SOURCE: U.S. Bureau of the Census, Manuscript Population, Chatham County, 6th Militia District, 1910–1920.

TABLE 7. Age of Landowners, Burroughs, Georgia 1910–1920

AGE CATEGORY 1910	N=48	%	AGE CATEGORY 1920	N=55	%
19–29	10	20.8	19–29	5	9.0
30–39	11	22.9	30–39	10	18.1
40–59	10	20.8	40–59	26	47.2
60–90	17	35.4	60–90	14	25.4

SOURCE: U.S. Bureau of the Census, Manuscript Population, Chatham County, 6th Militia District, 1910–1920.

TABLE 8. Gender Analysis of Landowners, Burroughs, Georgia 1910–1920

1910	N=48	%	1920	N=55	%
Female	22	45.8	Female	14	25.4
Male	26	54.1	Male	41	74.5

SOURCE: U.S. Bureau of the Census, Manuscript Population, Chatham County, 6th Militia District, 1910–1920.

CONCLUSION

The importation of over 12,000 Africans from West Africa and the Caribbean over the course of 48 years constituted an important cultural thread shaping the culture of lowcountry Georgia. It led to the creation of a new language structure that had a common semantic and stylistic form. This shared language made possible the reclamation of a territory—of the landscape, the manscape, and the womanscape to establish a sense of place. The cultural identity of these forced transatlantic communities emanated from shared traditions and perspectives and from intersecting relations and languages.[1] Building on both their African background and their American experience, Africans in lowcountry Georgia retained their African culture and established cultural resistance to their enslavement. Cultural resistance represented a salient form of opposition to federally sanctioned enslavement.

The establishment of rice plantations along the coastal and inland areas of Georgia in the eighteenth century created a unique environment for enslaved Africans to re-create social and cultural institutions. Functioning within the constraints of an inhumane system, Africans and African Americans established familial bonds, preserved agricultural techniques, re-created artistic expressions, maintained Islamic practices, and syncretized African religious beliefs with Christianity. In this context, narratives were integral to the cultural politics of slavery and freedom. Narratives of resistance and freedom during the pre-Civil War era occupied the consciousness of enslaved African Americans in lowcountry Georgia. Ideas were fundamental to the reality of bondmen and bondwomen. Ideological resistance combined with the internal economic strategies of African Americans to secure property served as incubators of nationalist unity and springboards for the development of oppositional communities during the era of emancipation when African Americans used cultural politics to shape and define their space in America.

Landownership symbolized African American discursive and conceptual autonomy. The symbolism of land ownership redefined the individual's existence. As Eric Foner argues, freedom rested on the ownership of productive property. In this context, the task labor system shaped the lived experiences of enslaved Africans and created an internal slave economy that informed African American postwar strategies to secure economic independence and establish land based communities.

Gardens were used to supplement diets and in the process became the de facto land and property of the enslaved.[2]

In the lowcountry, African Americans based kinship on fictive and nonfictive blood relationship, which served to make community. The oppression of slavery created and reinforced social ties and community. Thus, kinship and race were inextricably interlinked. Moreover, the very nature of living life in a system of perpetual bondage meant that conflict within the slave community was diminished. Above all else, the majority of enslaved African Americans endeavored to survive slavery. This common experience and identity, as Wilson Moses has argued, was "the basis of a racial unity, unknown among the various African groups before the transatlantic slave trade."[3]

In many parts of coastal Georgia, rice remained a symbol of the postwar lowcountry landscape. Rice production and rice culture structured both the natural environment and the socioeconomic environment of freedmen and freedwomen and thus became an integral part of their emancipatory ideology and cultural ethos. Obtaining proprietary interest in land suitable for cultivating rice for the market, as well as for home consumption, was a significant expression of their freedom during the first decade following emancipation.

African Americans developed several strategies to sustain access to and control of land. Through individual, community, and organizational collective action, they secured modest acreage large enough to build homes and maintain family gardens. In several communities their land supported the growth of rice, which they valued as both a market crop and a dietary staple. The initiatives undertaken by African Americans to secure land through disciplined economic choices is central to understanding how African Americans claimed freedom. The extent to which African Americans were successful depended upon regional demographic factors, the degree of economic elasticity, and the relative fluidity of race relations. The formulation of overt collective acts designed to secure land and establish autonomous communities in opposition to federal land restoration represented a salient effort to translate emancipation into substantive freedom.

The postemancipation conduct of former slaves serves as an important frame of reference for delineating how they created meaningful structures of resistance out of what Clifford Geertz termed "webs of significance." In lowcountry Georgia, these webs of significance consisted of elements of culture that African Americans created and re-created both during their enslavement and after slavery ended.[4] The formation of Burroughs represented the apogee of African American resistance to political, economic, and social injustice and served as an exemplar of these webs of significance. The town's charter of incorporation advanced the principles of self-help, moral uplift, and racial solidarity through its governing body.[5]

African American leaders, many of whom were former slaves, played a pivotal role in postwar politics and grassroots resistance and activism. Race leaders such as Henry McNeal Turner and Martin Delany provided the theoretical underpinnings for discourse on the doctrines of racial uplift, emigrationism, and separatism during the post-Reconstruction period. The doctrine of racial uplift operated as the cohesive force within post-Reconstruction lowcountry communities. Lowcountry leaders such as Aaron A. Bradley, Solomon Farley, William Golding, and J. C. Legree claimed freedom through cultural, community, and kinship networks that formed the basis of oppositional communities. As African Americans claimed freedom for themselves, their culture became political through the active production of cultural meaning to their lived experiences.

Appendix

TABLE A.1. *Savannah Planter Merchants Who Received and Sold West Africans from Rice Growing Regions, 1765–1798*

NAME OF FIRM	ORIGIN OF AFRICANS	QUANTITY SOLD
Ingliss and Hall	Gambia and Sierra Leone	667
Clay and Habersham	Gambia	320
John Graham/Ingliss and Hall	Rice Coast	340
John Graham	Sierra Leone	200
Craig, MacLeod, and Company	Isle of Banana (Sierra Leone)	237
Joseph Clay	Gambia	170
Robert Watts	Bance Island, Africa	95
Cowper and Telfair	Windward Coast	90
Robert Watts	Isle of Goree (Senegal)	84
Broughton and Smith	Senegal	78

SOURCE: *Georgia Gazette,* 1765–1771; Savannah Inward Manifests, Bureau of Customs, Record Group 36, National Archives and Records Administration, Washington, D.C.

TABLE A.2. *Slaves Imported into Savannah by Origin and Time Period, Early Period, 1755–1767*

ORIGIN	NUMBER OF AFRICANS	PERCENT
Senegal and Gambia	328	14
Gambia and Sierra Leone[a]	244	10
Africa	148	6
Jamaica	353	15
St. Christopher's	430	18
Montserrat	137	6
St. Kitts	156	7
St. Croix	76	3
Curacao	92	4

TABLE A.2 *continued*

ORIGIN	NUMBER OF AFRICANS	PERCENT
Grenada	75	3
Other Islands[b]	166	7
Arrivals from US[c]	120	5
Total	2,325	

a. Gambia and Sierra Leone are listed together on the original manifest.

b. Includes Antigua, 45; Barbados, 42; Tortola, 31; St. Vincent, 15; St. Eustatius, 14; St. Martin, 8; Guadeloupe, 7; Isles of Pines, Cuba, 3; St. Thomas, 1.

c. Includes South Carolina, 98; New York, 2; Rhode Island, 2

SOURCE: RG 36, Inward Slave Manifests, NARA, Washington, D.C.; Elizabeth Donnan, *Documents Illustrative of the History of the Slave Trade*, vol. 4 (New York: Octagon, 1935), 612–63.

TABLE A.3. *Slaves Imported into Savannah by Origin and Time Period, Middle Period, 1768–1771*

ORIGIN	NUMBER	PERCENT
Gambia	814	42
Rice and Grain Coast	470	24
Sierra Leone	297	15
Angola	250	13
Caribbean*	105	5
Total	1,936	

*Includes Antigua, 90, and Barbados, 15. The 90 slaves from Antigua are listed as Windward Coast slaves.

SOURCE: RG 36, Inward Slave Manifests, NARA, Washington, D.C.; Elizabeth Donnan, *Documents Illustrative of the History of the Slave Trade*, vol. 4 (New York: Octagon, 1935) 612–63.

TABLE A.4. *Slaves Imported into Savannah by Origin and Time Period, Final Period, 1784–1798*

ORIGIN	NUMBER	PERCENT
Isle of Goree (Senegal)	217	12
Bananas (Sierra Leone)	394	21
Anamaboe (Gold Coast)	149	8
Africa[a]	698	37
Caribbean[b]	402	21
Total	1,860	

a. Specific regions in Africa not listed.

b. Includes Delos Isle, 217; Jamaica, 36; Martinique, 152; St. Croix, 7.

SOURCE: RG 36, Inward Slave Manifests, NARA, Washington, D.C.; Elizabeth Donnan, *Documents Illustrative of the History of the Slave Trade,* vol. 4 (New York: Octagon, 1935), 612–63.

TABLE A.5. *Institutional Property Owned by Selected Mutual Associations, Savannah*

ASSOCIATION	ACRES	COST
Louisville Ten Acre Society (Sons and Daughters of Louisville)	1 lot (#33)	$90
Mary Magdalene Society	1 lot (#41)	75
Sons and Daughters of Jerusalem	1 lot	75
Sons and Daughters of Mount Sinai	1 lot	200
Sons and Daughters of Southville	3 lots	150
Sons and Daughters of Zion	"small lot"	40

SOURCE: Records of the Chatham County Superior Court, Deed Books, 5A, 320; 5N, 332; 6L, 166; 7M, 167; 7'O, 23.

TABLE A.6. *Leadership of African American Women in Selected Benevolent Associations, Savannah, 1867–1868*

BENEVOLENT ASSOCIATION	PRESIDENT
Benevolent Sisters	Sarah Box
Daughters of Nehemiah	Dolly Jackson
Daughters of Light	Dolly Jackson
John the Baptist	Maria Johnson
Ladies Christian Association	Margaret Millidie
Ladies Galatian Society	Sarah Box
Ladies Union Society	Jane Adams
Mary Magdalene Society	Elizabeth Lawrence
Nickel Club	Eugenia Hooker
Poor and Needy Institute	Georgiana Kelly
Rising Daughters of Africa	Sarah Box
Union Republican Association	Susan Carrier

SOURCE: Register of Signatures of Depositors, Freedmen's Savings and Trust, Savannah Branch, M816, Roll 8, RG 101; James Simms, *The First Colored Church of North America* (Philadelphia: J. B. Lippincott, 1888), 211–13.

TABLE A.7. Summary of Cultivation, Landowners

COMMODITY	ACREAGE	YIELDS
Rice	42	35,048 lbs
Corn	3	50 bushels
Cotton	2	300 pounds
Sweet Potatoes	1 1/2	80 bushels

SOURCE: U.S. Bureau of the Census, Manuscript Agricultural Schedules, Chatham County, 6th Militia District, 1880.

TABLE A.8. African American Farms Classified by Size, Chatham County, 1910

FARM SIZE, IN ACRES	NUMBER OF FARMS
3 and under	2
3–9	111
10–19	64
20–49	33
50–99	5
100–174	3
175–259	2
500–999	2
1,000 and over	1

SOURCE: U.S. Bureau of the Census, Negro Population of the United States, 1790–1915 (Washington, D.C., 1918), 710.

TABLE A.9. Occupation of Landowners, Burroughs, Georgia, 1910

OCCUPATION	NUMBER	%
Farmer	21	43.7
Farm Laborer	5	10.4
Laborer*	10	20.8
Carpenter	2	4.1
Real Estate Agent	1	2.0
Washerwoman	1	2.0
Woodcutter, Lumber Mill	1	2.0

*Includes porters, 1; railroad workers, 8; and a sawmill workers, 1.

SOURCE: U.S. Bureau of the Census, 6th Militia District, Chatham County, 1910.

TABLE A.10. Occupation of Landowners, Burroughs, Georgia, 1920

OCCUPATION	NUMBER	%
Farmer	45	81
Farm Laborer	5	9
Laborer (City)	1	1.8
Laborer (Railroad)	1	1.8
Launderer	2	3.6

SOURCE: U.S. Bureau of the Census, 6th Militia District, Chatham County, 1920.

TABLE A.11. Occupation and Real Estate Value, Ogeechee District, 1870

OCCUPATION	N	REAL ESTATE VALUE	PERSONAL PROPERTY
Blacksmith	1	$400	$100
Butcher	1	2,000	300
Carpenter	5	200–4,000	100–200
Carriage Driver	1	500	100
Cotton Sampler	2	300–1,000	100
Farmer	10	200–4,400	100–600
Hackman	1	1500	2000
Laborer*	8	200–1500	50–150
Laborer (Farm)	5	200–500	100
Pilot (steamboat)	2	200–500	100
Preacher	1	400	100
Retail Grocer	1	3,000	550
Sewer/ Launderer	1	400–2,000	100

*Three of the laborers were women.

SOURCE: U.S. Bureau of the Census, Population Manuscript, Chatham County, Seventh Militia District, 1870.

TABLE A.12. Average Daily Wages in Selected Occupations in Savannah, 1874

OCCUPATION	WAGES
Carpenters	$3.25–3.50
Draymen	1.40–2.00
Laborers	1.75–2.00
Longshoreman	5.00
Machinists	3.00–4.00
Moulders	3.00–5.00
Painters	4.20

SOURCE: *Savannah Morning News,* October 9, 1874, p. 3, col. 3.

TABLE A.13. African American Women Landowners, Chatham County, 1876

NAME	VALUE OF LAND	ACREAGE
Mary Aves	$150	
Sarah Banks	100	5
Belle Barclay	500	
Lucy Ann Barnard	100	50
Matilda Beasley	300	
Catherine Beattie	700	
Molly Benge	100	
Nancy Berrien	200	
Stella Blue	200	
Adrianna Boyd	400	
Sarah Brand	100	
Rachel Broomfield	500	20
Catherine Broughton	250	
Anne Parker Brown	550	
Georgia Burke	100	5
Nelly Buggs	250	
Sarah Burke	1400	
Phoebe Butler	200	
Miranda Campbell	800	
Sophia Chipp	300	
Jane Clay	2100	
Susan F. Cox	700	
Eliza Crawford	400	
Euphemia Curry	450	
Amy Cusbert	100	24
Susan David	250	
Susan Deas	400	
Mary C. Degnore	1000	
Dolly DeLoyd	500	
Catherine Deveaux	2000	
Justine Dolly	500	
Anne Dudley	1600	
Eve Early	200	15
Lucy Edwards	200	
Elizabeth Edy	30	
Fanny Fell	35	5
Patience Fenwick	300	

NAME	VALUE OF LAND	ACREAGE
Henrietta Fields	50	5
Fulonia Fuller	700	
Nancy Garret	900	
Claudia Gibbons	5800	
Emma Gibbons	800	
Nancy Golden	500	
Julia Gordon	60	
Sarah Jane Gordon	600	
Miranda Grant	200	
Margaret Green	160	
Matilda Green	75	5
Eliza Habersham	1300	
Matilda Habersham	300	
Matilda Harrison	75	
Patsey Holmes	250	
Rosa Houston	600	
Jane Hull	200	
Amanda Jackson	100	
Betty Jackson	300	5
Luanda Jackson	350	
Maria Johnson	500	
Mary A. Jackson	1200	
Mary Ann Johnson	450	
Rosa Johnson	150	
Clarinda Jourdan	500	
Rose Julien	200	
Katie Marshall	50	5
Nancy Martin	3000	
Virginia McClean	750	
Minerva McDowell	400	
Ellen McFall	400	
Adeline McNichols	240	6
Mary Ann Middleton	300	
Margaret O. Miller	50	
Sarah Miller	475	
Bina Milligan	900	
Anne Mills	350	
Elizabeth Mirault	3500	

TABLE A.13 *continued*

NAME	VALUE OF LAND	ACREAGE
Josephine Mirault	1200	
Tenah H. Moore	50	
Venus Odingsell	900	
Sarah Patrick	400	10
Flora Poley	800	
Charlotte Reid	600	
Harriet Reynolds	800	
Ellen Richardson	1200	
Hetty Ross	250	21
Jane Rutledge	150	
Julia Ryan	200	
Harriet Sanchez	1000	
Estelle Savage	4800	
Cecelia Scarborough	336	15
Elizabeth Scott	300	
Sylvia Screven	1200	
Margaret Sheftall	1000	
Susan Sheftall	1000	
Swan Simmons	400	
Phoebe Smith	200	
Jane Snead	500	20
Maria Sneed	125	
Dolly Williams	600	
Fanny Williams	900	
Polly Williams	40	3.5
Delia Wilson	300	
Nanny Wilson	150	
Nancy Winkler	300	
Mary Woodhouse	500	
Phyllis Young	150	4

SOURCE: Records of the Chatham County Superior Court, Chatham County Tax Digest, Savannah, 1876.

TABLE A.14. Self-Help Societies in the Lowcountry with Accounts Established in the Freedmen's Bank, 1867–1871

Missionary Zion Baptist Association of First Bryan Baptist Church, Ledger No. 621	established by Reverend Andrew Neyle.
Union League of America, Baker Council No. 9, Ledger No. 649	Jackson Brand, president, occupation: grocer, age 44; Gabriel Adams, treasurer, occupation: carpenter, age 35; Aaron A. Bradley, secretary, occupation: lawyer, age 51; Paul S. Reynolds, occupation: carpenter, age 24
Zion Traveler's Society, "connected with the African Methodist Episcopal Church," Ledger No. 648	J. M. Johnson, president; Abram Logan, treasurer, occupation: porter, age 40; Fortune Campbell, secretary, occupation: porter, age 43
American Missionary Society, Ledger No. 668;	Reverend Ira Pettibone, agent, former superintendent of education
Daughters of Zion, First African Baptist Church, Ledger No. 720–721	Frank Williams, president (Miss Hetty Grant, former president); Mrs. C. Wilson, vice president; Mark Grant, secretary; Mrs. Rhoda Smaller, treasurer; Mrs. Chloe Payne, chair; J. H. McDowell, chief
Union Benevolent Society of Second African Baptist Church, Ledger No. 722	Ann Wilson, president; Lydia Edwards, vice president; K. S. Thomas, secretary; Diana Boles, treasurer
Wrestling Jacob Progressive Association, Ledger No. 731	John Jackson, president ("in place of Amos Benjamin); James Jenkins, vice president; James Ball, treasurer
Sons of Zion, Ledger No. 740	
John the Baptist Society, Ledger No. 745	Mrs. Maria Johnson, president
Benevolent Daughters of Savannah, Ledger No. 594	
Union Republican Association, Liberty County, Ledger No. 757	Mrs. Susan Carrier, school teacher

TABLE A.14 *continued*

Children of Eden Society, Ledger No. 779	Cyrus Gordon, secretary; Samuel Coo[?] president, occupation: shoestore, age 45; Mrs. Jane Allen, treasurer
	Abraham Burke, treasurer
Freedman Newspaper Publishing Association, Ledger No. 810	
Mary Magdalene Society, Ledger No. 842	Elizabeth Laurence, president; Diane Williams, vice president; John A. Laurence, secretary; A. Fleming, treasurer
Sisters Prayer Meeting Benevolent Association, Ledger No. 927	Mrs. Susan Dencile[?], president; Mrs. E. Eady, secretary; Mrs. Melina Beryan, treasurer
Ladies Union Socialize Society, Ledger No. 930	Jane Adams, president; John A. Laurence, secretary; Rose Johnson, treasurer
Macedonia Benevolent Society, Ledger No. 963	Robert Wright, president; Sarah Gardner, treasurer
Poor and Needy Institute, Ledger No. 984	Georgiana Kelly, president; Annie Wilson, vice president; Hammond C. Avers, secretary; Priscilla Shigg, treasurer, occupation: teacher

SOURCE: Records of the Office of the Comptroller of the Currency, Registers of Signatures of Depositors in Branches of the Freedmen's Savings and Trust.

Notes

INTRODUCTION

1. Rosanna Williams of Tatemville and Ophelia Baker of Sandfly, in Georgia Writers Project, *Drums and Shadows,* 71, 91.

2. Michael Gomez, *Exchanging Our Country Marks,* 42.

3. Karen Christensen and David Levinson, eds., *Encyclopedia of Community,* 228.

4. *Georgia Gazette,* April 13, 1768, John Stirk; *Georgia Gazette,* July 13, 1774, James Read; and *Georgia Gazette,* March 29, 1775, James Mossman, in Lathan Windley, *Runaway Slave Advertisements,* 29, 53, 62; see entries for Georgia in *The Trans-Atlantic Slave Trade Voyages Database,* accessible at www.slavevoyages.org; Maria Diedrich, Henry Louis Gates Jr., and Carl Pederson, eds., *Black Imagination and the Middle Passage,* 5–10; see also John Thornton, *Africa and Africans.*

5. *Georgia Gazette,* July 13, 1774, James Read, in Windley, *Runaway Slave Advertisements,* 53; Elizabeth Donnan, *Documents Illustrative of the History of the Slave Trade,* vol. 4, 612–63; Lempster, James, Peter, Fanny, and Silvia, mentioned later in the introduction, successfully ran away from James Read's plantation. See entries for Georgia in *The Trans-Atlantic Slave Trade Voyages Database,* accessible at www.slavevoyages.org.

6. Inward Slave Manifests, Savannah, Bureau of Customs, RG 36, National Archives and Records Administration (NARA); Donnan, *Documents,* vol. 4, 612–63. Donnan provides regional documentation that includes listings of slave vessels, merchant or agent's name, owner of vessel, and where the vessel was built. Shipbuilding emerged as a significant industry in Savannah with West Indian linkages. See also Julia Floyd Smith, *Slavery and Rice,* chap. 1–2.

7. Inward Slave Manifests, Savannah, Bureau of Customs, RG 36, NARA; Donnan, *Documents,* vol. 4, 612–63.

8. Donnan, *Documents,* vol. 4, 612–63.

9. Inward Slave Manifests, Savannah, Bureau of Customs, RG 36, NARA; Donnan, *Documents,* vol. 4, 612–63; see entries for Georgia in *The Trans-Atlantic Slave Trade Voyages Database,* accessible at www.slavevoyages.org.

10. *Savannah Georgia Gazette,* November 19, 1766.

11. *Georgia Gazette,* March 7, 1765, Elizabeth Anderson, in Windley, *Runaway Slave Advertisements,* 10.

12. Anthony Balcomb, "The Power of Narrative: Constituting Reality through Storytelling," in *Memory, Orality, and the Past,* 49–53; Forrest D. Colburn, *Everyday Forms of Resistance,* 27–29; William F. Andrews, *To Tell a Free Story;* Frances Smith Foster, *Witnessing*

Slavery; Dwight N. Hopkins and George C. L. Cummings, *Cut Loose Your Stammering Tongue.*

13. *Georgia Gazette,* December 10, 1789, David Leion [*sic*]. Ben and Nancy were twenty-five years old; Nancy was blind in her right eye. See the case of Betty in the *Georgia Gazette,* December 22, 1788, Benjamin Gobert; the case of Patra, Mary, and Judy in the *Georgia Gazette,* January 29, 1789, J. M. Delarocque; and the case of Patty and Daniel in the *Georgia Gazette,* May 21, 1789, Peter Henry Morel, in Windley, *Runaway Slave Advertisements,* 161–62, 172.

14. *Georgia Gazette,* May 21, 1789, Peter Henry Morel, in Windley, *Runaway Slave Advertisements,* 166.

15. Michael Mullin, *Africa in America,* 290.

16. Inward Slave Manifests, Savannah, Bureau of Customs, RG 36, NAB, Washington D.C.; Donnan, *Documents,* 612–63; Lorenzo Dow Turner, *Africanisms in the Gullah Dialect;* Ambrose Gonzalez, *Black Border;* Albert H. Stoddard, "Origin, Dialect, Beliefs."

17. Mary Frances Berry, *Black Resistance, White Law,* xi; Colburn, *Everyday Forms of Resistance,* 27–29.

18. Ira Berlin, "Time, Space, and the Evolution of Afro-American Society; Barbara Jeanne Fields, *Slavery and Freedom.*

19. Peter J. Parish, *Slavery,* 1–3.

20. David Williams, *I Freed Myself,* 9.

21. Eric Foner, *The Story of American Freedom;* Eric Foner, *Reconstruction.*

22. John David Smith, *When Did Southern Segregation Begin?,* 4.

23. Steven Hahn, *A Nation under Our Feet*; Donald Grant, *The Way It Was in the South.*

24. Government Records and Documents: Record Group 105, Records of the Bureau of Refugees, Freedmen, and Abandoned Lands.

25. See Dylan Penningroth, *The Claims of Kinfolk.*

CHAPTER 1: THE SLAVE'S DREAM

1. Chris J. Magoc, *So Glorious a Landscape,* 54.

2. Toni Morrison, *Beloved.*

3. Gervase Phillips, "Slave Resistance in the Antebellum South."

4. William Dusinberre, *Them Dark Days* 460–61; Daniel Heyward, *Seed From Madagascar,* 19–36; Douglas C. Wilms, "The Development of Rice Culture in 18th Century Georgia," 53. The scholarship on slavery has had multiple revisions and reinterpretations since the publication of Ulrich B. Phillips, *American Negro Slavery* (1936). Phillips believed that race determined behavior and that slaves were childlike, lazy, and happy with their enslavement. According to Phillips, resistance was insignificant. Herbert Aptheker, *American Negro Slave Revolts* (1943); Kenneth Stampp, *The Peculiar Institution* (1956); and John Blassingame, *The Slave Community* (1972) established definitive opposing paradigms to Phillips's interpretation of slavery. See also Herbert Gutman, *The Black Family in Slavery and Freedom;* Thomas L. Webber, *Deep Like the Rivers*; George P. Rawick, *From Sundown to Sunup;* and Charles Joyner, *Down by the Riverside.* A recent study that has placed the economic interests of enslaved African Americans above community and cultural interests has diminished the impact of slavery and American institutional oppression on postwar economic advancement. See Dylan Penningroth, *The Claims of Kinfolk,* which argues that African American economic

interests under girded social relationships and social claims to property. See also Richard V. Burks, "A Conception of Ideology for Historians," and Sterling Stuckey, *Slave Culture*, chapter one.

5. Heyward, *Seed From Madagascar*, 19–36; Wilms, "Development of Rice Culture," 53.

6. Gwen McKee, ed., *A Guide to the Georgia Coast;* Kenneth K. Krakow, *Georgia Place Names*, 120, 199–200.

7. McKee, ed., *A Guide to the Georgia Coast;* Karen Christensen and David Levinson, eds., *Encyclopedia of Community*, vol. 4, 1473.

8. United States Population Census, 1790.

9. Records of the Chatham County Superior Court (RCCSC), Deed Book 4F, Arthur Heyward, 157.

10. Ibid.

11. Account Book of Stephen Habersham, Grove Plantation Near Savannah, June 1858–July 11, 1864, M432, roll 89, Georgia Historical Society, Savannah, Georgia.

12. Francis H. MacLeod Estate, File 398, 1864, Records of the Chatham County Probate Court (RCCPC), Savannah, Georgia.

13. RCCSC, Deed Book 3X, John Cheves, 199–200.

14. Ibid.

15. Ibid.

16. S.G. McLendon, *History of the Public Domain of Georgia*, 40–43; U.S. Bureau of the Census, *Statistics of Population* (Washington, D.C., 1870), Table 1.

17. U.S. Bureau of the Census, *Statistics of Population* (Washington, D.C., 1870), Table 1.

18. Ibid.

19. Malcolm Bell, *Major Butler's Legacy*, 106–25.

20. John Solomon Otto, "Slavery in a Coastal Community," 462; Mart A. Stewart, "*What Nature Suffers to Groe*," 31–33.

21. Records of the Glynn County Courthouse (RGCC), DB 10, 142–51, October 1, 1774; Stephen Berry, "More Alluring at a Distance"; Otto, "Slavery in a Coastal Community," 461–64; George Alexander Heard, "St. Simon's Island during the War between the States"; Bell, *Major Butler's Legacy*, 106–7; W. W. Hazzard, *St. Simon's Island Georgia, Brunswick, and Vicinity*. St. Simons Island lies eighteen miles east of Brunswick, Georgia, and is approximately thirteen miles long and two miles wide. Jekyll Island lies south of St. Simons, is ten miles long, and consists of 11,000 acres.

22. RGCC, DB ABEF, 366ff; Bell, *Major Butler's Legacy*, 107; William Dusinberre, *Them Dark Days*, chapter 7.

23. RGCC, DB 10, 142–51, October 1, 1774; Berry, "More Alluring at a Distance"; Otto, "Slavery in a Coastal Community," 461–64; Heard, "St. Simon's Island during the War between the States"; Bell, *Major Butler's Legacy*, 106–7; Hazzard, *St. Simon's Island Georgia, Brunswick, and Vicinity.*

24. RGCC, DB ABEF, 366ff; Bell, *Major Butler's Legacy*, 107; William Dusinberre, *Them Dark Days*, chapter 7.

25. Albert V. House, ed., *Planter Management*, 57; see also Sam B. Hilliard, "Antebellum Tidewater Rice Culture in South Carolina and Georgia," 97–104.

26. House, *Planter Management*, 57.

27. *Darien Gazette*, June 29, 1824.

28. John P. Legare, "An Account of an Agricultural Excursion into Southern Georgia."

29. Julia Floyd Smith, *Slavery and Rice Culture,* chapter 1.

30. Mary R. Bullard, *Robert Stafford of Cumberland Island;* John E. Ehrenhard and Mary R. Bullard, *Stafford Plantation.*

31. Paul Rabinow, ed., *The Foucault Reader.*

32. Inward Slave Manifests, Savannah, Records of the Customs Bureau, RG 36, National Archives and Records Administration (NARA); Melville Herskovits, *The Myth of the Negro Past,* chapter 2; Lorenzo Dow Turner, *Africanisms in the Gullah Dialect;* see also Roswell King to Pierce Butler, May 13, 1803, Butler Family Papers, Historical Society of Pennsylvania, which references the purchase of Ibo and Angola slaves from the Savannah firm Mein and Mackay.

33. Anthony Balcomb, "The Power of Narrative," 49–53. Narratives have been central to the study of slavery. See, for example, William F. Andrews, *To Tell a Free Story;* Frances Smith Foster, *Witnessing Slavery;* and Dwight N. Hopkins and George C. L. Cummings, *Cut Loose Your Stammering Tongue.* During the early twentieth century, historians did not regard slave narratives as proper historical sources for the study of slavery. The first systematic publication of slave narratives occurred during World War 2. The two principal collections of slave narratives are Benjamin Botkin ed., *Lay My Burden Down,* and the Fisk collection, *Unwritten History of Slavery.* The perspective of the enslaved remained absent from the historiography of slavery until the appearance of Blassingame's *The Slave Community* in 1972.

34. Philip D. Morgan, "Work and Culture"; Thomas F. Armstrong, "From Task Labor to Free Labor."

35. Account Book of Stephen Habersham, Grove Plantation near Savannah, June 1858–July 11, 1864, M432, roll 89, Georgia Historical Society (hereafter cited as GHS), Savannah, Georgia; Frances A. Kemble and Frances A. Butler Leigh, *Principles and Privilege,* 245–61; Dusinberre, *Them Dark Days,* 235, 238, 242, 246; Leslie Owens, *This Specie of Property,* 21. For a discussion of enslaved African American children, see Wilma King, *Stolen Childhood,* and Marie Jenkins Schwarz, *Born in Bondage.*

36. Georgia Writer's Project, *Drums and Shadows,* 32, 169, 175–77, 184. See also Lawrence Levine, *Black Culture and Black Consciousness.*

37. Georgia Writer's Project, *Drums and Shadows,* 32, 169, 175–77, 184.

38. George P. Rawick, *The American Slave,* 179; Georgia Writer's Project, *Drums and Shadows,* 79, 81, 99, 185; William Mein to Pierce Butler, May 24, 1803, Butler Family Papers, Historical Society of Pennsylvania; Bell, *Major Butler's Legacy,* 132; Robert Hayden, "Middle Passage."

39. Kemble and Leigh, *Principles and Privilege,* 238–62. Kemble describes Sophy as "pretty with a refined face"; Sophy was the wife of the driver, Morris, (239–40). Pierce Butler to Roswell King Jr., March 17, 1839. Roswell King Jr. to Pierce Butler, March 23, 1839, Butler Family Papers, Historical Society of Pennsylvania; William Dusinberre, *Them Dark Days,* 248–49. For a discussion of enslaved women's response to sexual exploitation, see Melton A. McLaurin, *Celia, a Slave;* Linda Brent, *Incidents in the Life of a Slave Girl.*

40. Brent, *Incidents;* Catherine Clinton, "'Southern Dishonor,'" 52; Hélène Lecaudey, "Behind the Mask," 262. See also Thelma Jennings, "'Us Colored Women Had to Go Through a Plenty'"; Stephanie M. H. Camp, "The Pleasures of Resistance."

41. Roswell King to Pierce Butler, February 12 and 26, 1815, Butler Family Papers, Historical Society of Pennsylvania; John Hope Franklin and Loren Schweninger, *Runaway Slaves,*

42–43; Mary Frances Berry, *Black Resistance,* chapters 4–5; Cornelia Walker Bailey, *God, Dr. Buzzard, and the Bolito Man,* 135. For a discussion of the migration of black Seminoles to the Bahamas following the first Seminole War, see Rosalyn Howard, *Black Seminoles in the Bahamas.*

42. J. Lorand Matory, "The Illusion of Isolation."

43. Rev. C. C. Jones to Mr. Charles C. Jones Jr., Montevideo, Monday, November 17, 1856, and Mr. Charles C. Jones Jr. to Mrs. Mary Jones, in Robert Manson Myers, *Children of Pride,* 263–64, 266; Account Book of Stephen Habersham, Grove Plantation Near Savannah, June 1858–July 11, 1864, M432, roll 89, GHS.

44. James Postell, Kelvin Grove Plantation Book, 1853, Margaret Davis Cate Collection, Hargrett Rare Book and Manuscript Library, University of Georgia Libraries. Nanny, age forty-five, appeared on the list as a three-quarter hand. Jane and Sarah were in their twenties; Hester was nineteen; Hamit's age was unknown. According to Ralph Flanders, ginning was more challenging than fieldwork or picking cotton. Ginning exposed slaves to dust and lint for several hours. Ralph Flanders, *Plantation Slavery in Georgia,* 85; Daina L. Ramey, "She Do a Heap of Work."

45. Loren Schweninger, *Black Property Owners in the South,* 30; Dylan Penningroth, "Slavery, Freedom, and Social Claims to Property"; Betty Wood, *Women's Work, Men's Work;* Morgan, "Work and Culture," 565–66; Philip D. Morgan, "The Ownership of Property by Slaves in the Mid-Nineteenth-Century Low Country," 399–401; Arnold to Dr. Heber Chase, October 13, 1836, in Richard H. Shryock, ed., *Letters to Richard D. Arnold,* 13.

46. Frank W. Klingberg, *The Southern Claims Commission,* 65–72.

47. Penningroth, *Claims of Kinfolk,* 90–91.

48. Wilson Moses, *The Golden Age of Black Nationalism,* 14; Deborah Gray White, *Ar'n't I a Woman?,* 25.

49. Sandy Austin, Claim No. 20636, Southern Claims Commission (SCC), "Approved Claims," Liberty County, Georgia, M1658, Records of the Accounting Officers of the Department of the Treasury, RG 217, NARA. Austin asserted, "I am 70 years of age. I live on Joseph LeCont's plantation. I am a regular Farmer. I lived from the 1st of April 1861 to the 1st of June 1865 right where I live now. I was born on the plantation that I now live on. At the beginning of the rebellion, I was a slave and made free by the Yankee army, when they came to our relief. I continued right on farming on my old master's land and gave him one-third of all that I raised, I worked when a slave for my master by the task in that way I saved time to work for myself. I commenced raising poultry and hogs first and for many years before I bought the mare. I bought the mare when a colt about 15 years before the raid. I raised other mare which the Yankee took from me from the march. I got my hogs and poultry in the same year and by raising and selling the increase."

50. Sambo Jefferson, Claim No. 17020, SCC, "Approved Claims," Chatham County, Georgia, M1658, RG 217, NARA. According to Jefferson, he had enough rails to fence five acres—split pine, middling size. They had been in use two or three years; the fence was ten rails high. Sherman used these rails for campfires. Jefferson asserted that these fence rails belonged to him; "that was one of the conditions of the lease that I should fence the land." All the other property was of his own raising. See also, Samuel Elliott, Claim No. 21448, "Approved Claims," Liberty County, Georgia, M1658, RG 217, NARA. Elliott's property included 15 stock hogs, 7 cattle, 210 pounds clean rice, 30 ducks, and a wagon and harness. See, Ira

Berlin et al., *Freedom: A Documentary History . . .*, series 1, vol. 1, *The Destruction of Slavery*, 149–50.

51. Betty Wood, *Women's Work, Men's Work*, 51. James Anderson, Claim No. 18546, SCC, "Approved Claims," Liberty County, Georgia, M1658, RG 217, NARA. Anderson claimed $248 in property. Testimony of John Crawford, Testimony of Clarinda Lowe, James Anderson, Claim No. 18546, SCC, "Approved Claims," Liberty County, Georgia, M1658, RG 217, NARA; Richard LeCounte, Claim No. 20672, SCC, "Approved Claims," Liberty County, Georgia, M1658, RG 217, NARA. Richard claimed $137 in property, which included cattle, hogs, corn, rice, and potatoes.

52. Adam LeCounte, Claim No. 18545, Liberty County, SCC, 1877–1883, RG 217, NARA.: "I worked 30 or 40 years by the task. I got this horse about a month before the Yankees came. Hercules LeCounte, Claim No. 20667, Liberty County, SCC, RG 217. Joshua LeCounte, Claim No. 20675: "I bought it selling rice, poultry, and hogs." Hercules LeCounte was a slave of John LeCounte. He worked for himself after the task was done. He was seventy years old at the time of his deposition. He had owned property for many years. Hercules claimed property valued at $310, which included cows, pigs, fowl, rice, corn, potatoes, a mare, and clothing. Joshua LeCounte was a slave in Liberty County. He was fifty years old at the time of deposition on July 26, 1874. He was a farmer who resided on LeCounte's plantation. His property included a mare, fowl, ducks, and rice. His claim totaled $172.

53. White, *Ar'n't I a Woman?*, 24–25.

54. Steven Hahn, *A Nation under Our Feet*, 38–39; Will of William Page, February 6, 1827, Margaret Davis Cate Collection, Georgia Historical Society, Savannah, Georgia.

55. Linda Roberts, Claim No. 21467, Charles C. Jones Jr. to William Paine, August 19, 1876, William Wiseham Paine Papers, GHS; Betty Wood, *Women's Work, Men's Work*, 85–88.

56. Rachel Norman, Claim No. 21416, Liberty County, SCC, Settled Claims, 1877–1883, RG 217, NARA. The property was removed to camp at Midway church and used by the army stationed there on December 20, 1864. Rachel was fifty years old at the time of her deposition.

57. Moses Stikes and Binah Butler, Claim No. 17563, Chatham County, SCC, Settled Claims 1877–1883, RG 217, NARA.

58. Ibid. SCC, Approved Claims 1871–1880, Georgia, M1658, Records of the Accounting Officers of the Department of the Treasury, Record Group 217 (Washington, D.C.: National Archives and Records Administration, 1992), 5–18.

59. Michael Gomez makes a very cogent argument for viewing the history of Africans along the South Carolina-Georgia continuum as more complicated than previously understood. According to Gomez, study can no longer be limited to the Gullah language and handicrafts. See Gomez, *Exchanging Our Country Marks* and Gomez, *Black Crescent*. In clear defiance of the 1808 ban on the slave trade, American ships continued to import slaves with impunity. In 1841 the United States dispatched a naval unit, the U.S. African Squadron, to patrol the west coast of Africa. One of the main tasks of the squadron was to enforce the antislaving laws by apprehending American slave vessels. From 1841 to 1863, fifty American ships were taken into custody for slaving. Only one officer ever served a prison term commensurate with the sentence prescribed by law. The extensive antislaving legislation and the efforts of the African Squadron were circumvented by the lenient sentencing of U.S. courts. In spite of consistent overwhelming evidence of guilt, the majority of ship officers brought to trial were exonerated of criminal charges. The failure of the courts to adequately punish flagrant

lawbreakers allowed the continuation of American participation in the illegal transatlantic slave trade. Robert Vinson, "The Law as Law-Breaker"; W. E. B. DuBois, *The Suppression of the African Slave Trade,* Appendix D.

60. Will Coleman, "'Coming through 'Ligion,'" 66–67.

61. Allen D. Austin, *African Muslims in Antebellum America,* 321; Michael A. Gomez, "Muslims in Early America," 696; Lydia Parrish, *Slave Songs of the Georgia Sea Islands,* 24. For an excellent study of Gullah's linkages with the Caribbean, see Frederic G. Cassidy, "The Place of Gullah"; Ian F. Hancock, "Gullah and Barbadian"; and John P. Thomas Jr., "The Barbadians in Early South Carolina." See also Turner's classic study *Africanisms in the Gullah Dialect;* Ambrose Gonzales, *Black Border;* and Albert H. Stoddard, "Origin, Dialect, Beliefs, and Characteristics of the Negroes of the South Carolina and Georgia Coasts."

62. See Robert Farris Thompson, *Flash of the Spirit;* Mechal Sobel, *Trabelin' On;* Herskovits, *Myth of the Negro Past;* Albert Raboteau, *Slave Religion.*

63. Lucy to Charles C. Jones, December 30, 1850, in John W. Blassingame, ed., *Slave Testimony,* 90–91; Andrew to Rev. Charles C. Jones, September 10, 1852, Maybank, in Robert Starobin, ed., *Blacks in Bondage,* 52. Andrew's daughter, Dinah, joined the Baptist church established for slaves at Sunbury.

64. Moses Roper to Thomas Price, London, June 27, 1836, in Blassingame, ed., *Slave Testimony,* 23.

65. *Liberator,* February 4, 1837; Blassingame, ed., *Slave Testimony,* 124–25.

66. John Mbiti, *Introduction to African Religion.*

67. Gomez, "Muslims in Early America," 696; Gomez, *Black Crescent,* 143–84; Gomez, *Exchanging Our Country Marks,* 59–87.

68. Ivor Wilks, "Salih Bilali of Massina," p. 145 in Philip D. Curtin, ed., *Africa Remembered;* Austin, *African Muslims;* Gomez, "Muslims in Early America," 692; Gomez, *Black Crescent,* 143–84; Gomez, *Exchanging Our Country Marks,* 59–87. By 1800 West Africa had undergone significant changes caused by the transatlantic slave trade. These changes can be analyzed in four phases: 1) the emergence of British West African settlements, 1787–1865; 2) French colonial activity in West Africa; 3) Islamic revolutions in the western and central Sudan, which led to the emergence of the Fulani Empire (1795–1809) and the disintegration of the Alafin of Oyo in 1817; and 4) Ashanti expansion caused by their invasion of the coastal states along the Gold Coast, 1824.

69. Georgia Writer's Project, *Drums and Shadows,* 178–83; Gomez, "Muslims in Early America," 697; Annette I. Kashif, "Africanisms upon the Land," 21. Ben Sullivan's father's name was Belali, a direct indication of Salih Bilali's desire to pass on his Islamic identity; Stuckey, *Slave Culture,* chapter four.

70. Georgia Writer's Project, *Drums and Shadows,* 178–79; Gomez, "Muslims in Early America," 697. Daphne had a light complexion and wore one ring in his ear, Sullivan believed, as a talisman. Salih Bilali, while claiming to possess a Qur'an, could not write Arabic coherently.

71. Georgia Writer's Project, *Drums and Shadows,* 178–79.

72. Ibid. Okra resided on the Couper plantation, the same plantation as Salih Bilali. According to Sullivan, he built a twelve-by-fourteen-foot home with a flat roof made from bush and palmetto. Couper made him pull it down. Leland Ferguson, *Uncommon Ground,* 75; Gomez, *Black Crescent,* 154.

73. Austin, *African Muslims,* 268; Gomez, "Muslims in Early America," 699; Joseph H. Greenberg, "The Decipherment of the 'Ben-Ali Diary' a Preliminary Statement." Thomas Astley, in vol. 2 of his *Collection of Voyages and Travels* (1745), gives extracts from various explorers. Their abstracts of Islamic practices in Senegal and the Gambia region provide insights into the practices of slaves on Sapelo Island. Francis Moore, in his travels, stated that the Fuli "are much like the Arabs, whose language is taught in their schools. . . . They are generally more skilled in the Arabic than the Europeans in Latin; for most of them speak it, though they have a vulgar tongue of their own, called Fuli. . . . Their humanity extends to all, but they are doubly kind to their own race." Another traveler stated, "At Day-break, Noon, and at Sunset" they say their prayers."

74. Gomez, "Muslims in Early America," 699. Bailey, *God, Dr. Buzzard, and the Bolito Man,* chapter thirteen; Parrish, *Slave Songs,* 26–27; Mae Ruth Green, "Sapelo Island Families," Liberty Bell Family No. 102, B29, Department of Natural Resources, Real Estate Division, Georgia Department of Archives and History, Atlanta, Georgia. This genealogy source book is over five hundred pages long and contains detailed biographical sketches and descendant charts for forty-four first-generation families brought to Sapelo during the early nineteenth century. The author received a copy of this book from Carolyn Douse, executive director of the Sapelo Island Cultural and Revitalization Society (SICARS), in 2001. Carolyn Douse is the granddaughter of Katie Brown. Terry Alford writes that Muslim slaves were used as "drivers, overseers, and confidential servants with a frequency their numbers did not justify." Terry Alford, *Prince among Slaves,* 56. Also, despite their religious resistance to enslavement, both Ben Ali and Salih Bilali were placed in positions of high authority and jointly used that authority to quell a slave insurrection during the War of 1812. See Alford, *Prince Among Slaves,* 56; Gomez, "Muslims in Early America," 700; Georgia Bryan Conrad, *Reminiscences of a Southern Woman,* 13. According to Bryan, Ben Ali and his family spoke English with the Spaldings, but spoke a different tongue among themselves. See Ruth Mae Green, "Sapelo Island Families," Genealogical Source Book, Carolina Underwood, Family No. 136, Georgia Department of Archives and History, Atlanta, Georgia, copy provided by Dr. Carolyn Douse, SICARS, Sapelo Island, Georgia. The grandchildren of Carolina and Hannah Underwood, interviewed in 1938 by the Works Progress Administration (WPA), recalled how both continued to speak their "funny talk," or native tongue, which their descendants could not understand.

75. Gomez, "Muslims in Early America," 699–700; Gomez, *Black Crescent,* 155; Parrish, *Slave Songs,* 22, 25–28, 28n21; Georgia Writers' Project, *Drums and Shadows,* 159–61. In addition to religious observances, Bilali apparently adhered to Islamic prescriptions on marriage. Brown remarked, "Magret she say Phoebe he wife, but maybe he hab more one wife. I spects des bery possible"; Austin, *African Muslims,* 265–68. Ethnic and religious differences were recounted by both Ben Sullivan and Cornelia Bailey. See Georgia Writers' Project, *Drums and Shadows,* 180–81; Bailey, *God, Dr. Buzzard, and the Bolito Man,* chapter thirteen. According to Bailey, Ben Ali kept his distance from others because he "did not like mixing"; Muslims and non-Muslims tended to keep to themselves; however, they "got along" and could work with others for specific purposes or special occasions. Conrad, *Reminiscences of a Southern Woman,* 13. Ben Ali wore a cap that resembled a Turkish fez and kept himself aloof.

76. Georgia Writers' Project, *Drums and Shadows,* 180–81.

77. Ibid.

78. Georgia Writers' Project, *Drums and Shadows,* 91, 127, 165–66. Naming practices also indicated pride in an Islamic heritage. Shad Hall's grandmother Hestuh bore a son called

Belali Smith, who in turn was the grandfather of Phoebe Gilbert, also a Sapelo resident. Drum beatings served as an important communication device. According to the intergenerational narratives of Josephine Stevens, Madam Truth, and several other coastal Georgians, drums could be heard for miles, and the beats were encoded to symbolize events.

79. Ibid.; Parrish, *Slave Songs*, 26n17.

80. *Columbian Museum and Savannah Advertiser*, May 11, 1802; Gomez, "Muslims in Early America," 696. See also Gomez, *Black Crescent*, 152–63.

81. *Columbian Museum and Savannah Advertiser*, March 27, 1807; Gomez, "Muslims in Early America," 696. Native American communities in the lowcountry provided havens for runaways. According to the *Georgia Gazette*, a "Mahomet" belonging to John Graham of Augustin's Creek "had been seen at a settlement line near the Indian Line on the Ogeechee" three years after his initial flight. *Georgia Gazette*, August 31, 1774.

82. Georgia Department of Archives and History, GRG2–09 and GRG2–29, Atlanta, GA, quoted in Gomez, "Muslims in Early America," 696; Gomez, *Black Crescent*.

83. William Dallam Ames, ed., *Autobiography of Joseph LeCounte*, 29–30; Gomez, "Muslims in Early America," 695. See also Gomez, *Black Crescent*, 143–73.

84. Georgia Writers' Project, *Drums and Shadows*, 76, 120–21, 144–45, 154–56; Gomez, "Muslims in Early America," 699. See also Gomez, *Black Crescent*, 157.

85. Georgia Writers' Project, *Drums and Shadows*, 76, 120–21, 144–45, 154–56.

86. Ibid.

87. Sylvia R. Frey and Betty Wood, *Come Shouting to Zion*; Raboteau, *Slave Religion*, chapter three; Margaret Washington Creel, *"A Peculiar People,"* 259–328; Georgia Writers' Project, *Drums and Shadows*, 62, 67, 71, 159, 168; Parrish, *Slave Songs*; Art Rosenbaum, *Shout Because You're Free*.

88. Georgia Writers' Project, *Drums and Shadows*, 91; Bailey, *God, Dr. Buzzard, and the Bolito Man*, 134; Gomez, "Muslims in Early America," 698; William McFeely, *Sapelo's People*.

89. Gomez, "Muslims in Early America," 699n111; see also Gomez, *Black Crescent*, 143–84.

90. Hahn, *A Nation under Our Feet*, 19.

91. Gomez, "Muslims in Early America," 705; see also Gomez, *Black Crescent*, 143–84.

92. Ibid.

93. Georgia Writers' Project, *Drums and Shadows*, 71, 91. Sophie described the mark as a circle the size of a fifty-cent piece with lines that run toward the center. The narrative of Ophelia Baker reveals a relationship between markings and African secret societies.

94. Ibid, 65–67. The desire to return to Africa is evidenced by the actions of Golla Jones Davis, who left the Tatemville community for Africa around 1932.

95. Ibid. See also Turner, *Africanisms in the Gullah Dialect*.

96. Gomez, "Muslims in Early America," 706; Bailey, *God, Dr. Buzzard, and the Bolito Man*, chapter sixteen; Austin, *African Muslims*, 448; Gomez, *Black Crescent*, 161.

97. Lauren DuBois and Julius Scott, *Origins of the Black Atlantic*, 1–5.

CHAPTER 2: WAR AND FREEDOM

1. Ira Berlin, Marc Favreau, and Steven Miller, eds., *Remembering Slavery*, 8–11, 90–91.
2. Toni Morrison, *Playing in the Dark*, 42.
3. Robert E. Birt, ed., *The Quest for Community and Identity*, 2, 4.
4. Karen B. Bell, "'The Ogeechee Troubles,'" 381.

5. Roderick A. McDonald, *The Economy and Material Culture of Slaves,* 70; James Scott, *Domination and the Arts of Resistance.* For an early study of slavery in Louisiana, see Joe Gray Taylor, *Negro Slavery.*

6. John Hope Franklin and Loren Schweninger, *Runaway Slaves,* 42–43.

7. Mr. Charles C. Jones Jr. to Rev. C. C. Jones, Savannah, Wednesday, October 1, 1856; Rev. C. C. Jones to Mr. Charles C Jones Jr., Maybank, Thursday, October 2, 1856; Mr. Charles C. Jones Jr., to Rev. C. C. Jones, Savannah, Saturday, October 4, 1856; Rev. C. C. Jones to Mr. Charles C. Jones Jr., Maybank, Saturday evening, November 1, 1856; Rev. C. C. Jones to Mrs. Mary Jones, Savannah, Wednesday, December 10, 1856, in Robert Manson Myers, *Children of Pride,* 240–46, 257–58, 270; Franklin and Schweninger, *Runaway Slaves,* 42–43.

8. *U.S. Statutes at Large, Treaties, and Proclamations,* vol. 12 (Boston, 1863), 319.

9. James McPherson, *Ordeal by Fire,* 195–99; Clarence Mohr, *On the Threshold of Freedom;* Thomas Wentworth Higginson, *Army Life in a Black Regiment,* 27–29.

10. *U.S. Population Census, 1860* (Washington, D.C.).

11. *Official Records of the Union and Confederate Navy,* series 1, vol. 13, pp. 21, 159.

12. *Official Records of the War of the Rebellion,* series 1, vol. 44 (Washington, D.C., 1893) 159, 787.

13. Stephanie M. H. Camp, *Closer to Freedom,*119; Rev. C. C. Jones to Lt. Charles C. Jones Jr., July 10, 1862, and July 21, 1862, in Myers, *Children of Pride,* 929, 935.

14. Higginson, *Army Life,* 79, 106–14, 162–63; Ella Forbes, *African American Women,* 46.

15. *U.S. Statutes at Large,* vol. 12, 589–600.

16. Ira Berlin et. al., *Freedom,* series 1, vol. 1, 123.

17. "Louis Manigault Civil War Diary," December 3, 1863, Manigault Family Papers, Reel 2; "List of Negroes at Gowrie," "Hermitage," "East Hermitage," Manigault Family Papers, #484), Southern Historical Collection, Wilson Library, University of North Carolina, Chapel Hill (hereafter cited as SHC).

18. "List of Negroes at Gowrie," Manigault Family Papers, #484, SHC.

19. "Commander of the Department of the South to the Secretary of War," June 23, 1862, in Ira Berlin et al., *Freedom,* series 2; *The Black Military Experience,* 50–53.

20. Ibid.

21. "Superintendent of Contraband in the Department of the South to the Secretary of War," January 25, 1863, in Berlin et al., *Freedom,* series 2: *The Black Military Experience,* 54–55.

22. Ibid. George L. Hendricks, "Union Army Occupation of the Southern Seaboard, 1861–1865," Ph.D. diss., Columbia University, 1954, 80–89; Dudley T. Cornish, *The Sable Arm,* 138.

23. Hendricks, "Union Army Occupation of the Southern Seaboard, 1861–1865."

24. Army Engineer to the Headquarters of the Department of the South, April 3, 1863, and Affadavit of an Impressed Black Recruit, April 28, 1863, in Berlin et al., *Freedom,* series 2: *The Black Military Experience,* 55–58.

25. Commander of the Department of the South to the Superintendent of Contrabands in the Department of the South, August 29, 1864, in Berlin et al., *Freedom,* series 2: *The Black Military Experience,* 61.

26. Ibid. See also Cousins, "A History of the 33rd United States Colored Troops,"" 35–51, 61–64. The activities of Colonel James Montgomery's Second South Carolina Volunteers

(Thirty-fourth U.S.C.T.) are discussed in Rose, *Rehearsal for Reconstruction,* 244–53; Cornish, *Sable Arm,* 138–42, 148–50, 244.

27. Berlin et. al., *Freedom,* series 2: *The Black Military Experience,* 142.

28. Ibid.

29. Mary Hawkesworth, *Political Worlds of Women,* 9.

30. Elinor Barnes and James A. Barnes, eds., *Naval Surgeon,* 247, 254–55.

31. Clarence Mohr, "Before Sherman," 331–52; Commander of the U.S.S. *Mohican* to the Commander of the South Atlantic Squadron," March 30, 1862, in Berlin et al., *Freedom,* series 1, vol. 1: *The Destruction of Slavery,* 118–19.

32. Mohr, "Before Sherman," 331–52.

33. Commander of the U.S.S. *Mohican* to the Commander of the South Atlantic Squadron," March 30, 1862, in Berlin et al., *Freedom,* series 1, vol. 1: *The Destruction of Slavery,* 118–19; Susie King Taylor, *A Black Woman's Civil War Memoirs.*

34. Commander of the U.S.S. Dale to the Commander of the South Atlantic Squadron, June 13, 1862, in Berlin et al., *Freedom,* series 1, vol. 1: *The Destruction of Slavery,* 125–26.

35. Commander of a Confederate Cavalry Battalion to the Headquarters of the 3rd Military District of the Confederate Department of South Carolina, Georgia, and Florida," June 14, 1862, in Berlin et al., *Freedom,* series 1, vol. 1: *The Destruction of Slavery,* 128.

36. Hermitage, April 22, 1860, and East Hermitage, April 21, 1861, Manigault Family Papers, #484, SHC.

37. Louis Manigualt Civil War Diary, September 3, 1863, Manigault Family Papers, Reel 2, SHC; List of Negroes at Gowrie, Hermitage, April 22, 1860, Manigault Family Papers, #484, SHC.

38. Louis Manigualt Civil War Diary, September 3, 1863, Manigault Family Papers, Reel 2, SHC; Higginson, *Army Life,* 74.

39. James Schmidt, *Free to Work,* 95; Bentley, *A History of the Freedmen's Bureau,* 14; *United States Statutes at Large,* vol. 12, 590–92, 599. See also Theda Skocpol, *Protecting Soldiers and Mothers;* Thavolia Glymph, *Out of the House of Bondage.*

40. U.S. Statutes at Large, vol. 12, 599; Ira Berlin, Joseph P. Reidy, Leslie Rowland, *Freedom's Soldiers,* 21n39.

41. U.S. Statutes at Large, vol. 13, 571; Berlin, Reidy, and Rowland, *Freedom's Soldiers,* 21n39. See also Evelyn N. Glenn, *Unequal Freedom.*

42. Captain George G. Davis to Brig. Gen. James Bowen, August 21, 1863, Letter Received, ser. 1845, Provost Marshal, Department of the Gulf, Record Group 393, Pt. 1 [C-768]; Provost Marshal of St. Bernard Parish to the Provost General of the Dept. of the Gulf, St. Bernard [Parish, La.], August 21, 1863, in Ira Berlin, et al., *Freedom,* series 2: *The Black Military Experience,* 157.

43. Affidavit of Mary Wilson, June 17, 1865, filed with H-8 1865, Registered Letters Received, ser. 3379, TN Asst. Comr., Record Group 105 Bureau of Refugees, Freedmen and Abandoned Lands [A-6148], cited in Ira Berlin et al., *Freedom,* series 2: *The Black Military Experience,* 623–24. See also Hannah Rosen, *Terror in the Heart of Freedom;* Kidada E. Williams, *They Left Great Marks on Me.*

44. U.S. Census Bureau, 1860. The slave population in the state of Louisiana in 1860 consisted of 331,726 men and women, compared with a total white population of 351,556. This figure is for 23 parishes in Louisiana and for women between the ages of 15 and 60. There

were a total of 48 parishes with slaves in Louisiana. The total female slave population of all parishes was 159,749. The free colored population was 18,547.

45. Record of Complaints, November 19, 1864, Records of the Field Offices of the State of Louisiana, M1905, vol. 1, roll 7, BRFAL, RG 105, National Archives Building, Washington, D.C. (hereafter cited as NAB).

46. Record of Complaints, November 19, 1864, Records of the Field Offices of the State of Louisiana, M1905, vol. 1, roll 7, BRFAL, RG 105, NAB.

47. Registers and Payrolls of Freedmen Employed on Plantations, Terre-Bonne-West Feliciana, Louisiana, 1864–68, M1905, roll 39, BRFAL, RG 105, NAB.

48. Noralee Frankel, *Freedom's Women,* 2; see also Mary J. Farmer, "'Because They are Women.'" Farmer argues that government officials waged a "war on dependency."

49. Jacqueline Jones, *Labor of Love, Labor of Sorrow,* chapter two.

50. Farmer, "'Because They Are Women,'" 163.

51. Record of Complaints, August 1, 1865, Elizabeth White, Amelie Candole, Caroline Starks, Charlotte Ann Hall, and Henrietta Henderson, Records of the Field Offices of the State of Louisiana, M1905, vol. 1, roll 7, BRFAL, RG 105, NAB; Register of Proceedings in the Freedmen's Court, June 20, 1865, Sarah Moore, Mary DeLisle, Lorina Jones, Cecilia Jones, Records of the Field Offices of the State of Louisiana, M1905, vol. 1, roll 7, BRFAL, RG 105, NAB. See Farmer, "'Because They Are Women.'" For a discussion of the experiences of women in Civil War Mississippi see Frankel, *Freedom's Women.*

52. Taylor, *Black Woman's Civil War Memoirs,* 7–8; Mohr, "Before Sherman," 346.

53. William Tecumseh Sherman, *Memoirs,* vol. 2, 1104–105.

54. *The War of the Rebellion: A Compilation of the Official Records of the Union and Confederate Armies* (Washington, 1880–1902), series 1, vol. 44, pp. 75, 159, 410.

55. *New York Daily Tribune,* December 23, 1864; Malcolm Bell, *Major Butler's Legacy,* 380.

56. Sherman, *Memoirs,* vol. 2, 652–53.

57. Sherman, *Memoirs,* vol. 2, 651; Benjamin Quarles, *The Negro in the Civil War,* 317; Report of Major General Slocum, January 9, 1865, *Official Records of the Union and Confederate Armies* (hereafter cited as *ORUCA*), series 1, vol. 44, 159, 836. Statistics regarding slaves set free in northern and central Georgia by the Army of Tennessee also reference the figure 3,000 from October 4 to December 31, 1864. See *ORUCA,* series 1, vol. 44, 75.

58. Jacob D. Cox, *March to the Sea,* 37–38.

59. Sherman, *Memoirs,* vol. 2, 1106.

60. Report to General Joseph Wheeler, CSA, *ORUCA,* series 1, vol. 44, 410; W. C. Dodson, ed., *Campaigns of Wheeler and His Cavalry,* 301.

61. "The March to the Sea," *Western Reserve Chronicle,* December 28, 1864; "From Rebel Papers," *The Cleveland Morning Leader,* December 5, 1864; "From Sherman," *The Raftsman Journal,* January 21, 1865; "Review of Sherman's Grand Campaign," *The Caledonian,* December 30, 1864.

62. Works Progress Administration (WPA), *Annals of Savannah 1850–1937,* 5; Lisa M. Brady, *War upon the Land,* 93.

63. *The Soldiers Journal,* February 1, 1865; *Cleveland Morning Leader,* December 5, 1864; Sherman, *Memoirs,* 1105–106; List of Possessory Titles Issued to Freed people, Register of Land Titles Issued to Freed people, Records of A. P. Ketchum, Savannah, Georgia, RG 105, BRFAL, NAB.

64. *Savannah Daily Herald,* December 6, 1865; Bell, "'Ogeechee Troubles,'" 376–97.

65. Mohr, "Before Sherman," 349–50; *ORUCA,* series 1, vol. 44, 787, 819. See also Jacqueline Jones, *Saving Savannah.*

66. Mohr, "Before Sherman," 349–50.

67. Eric Foner, *Reconstruction,* 183; Edward Magdol, *A Right to the Land,* 137; Charles L. Hoskins, *The Trouble They Seen,* 28.

68. Magdol, *A Right to the Land,* 137; Register of Land Titles Issued to Freedmen, RG 105, BRFAL, Georgia, Reel 36, (M798), NAB.

69. Foner, *Reconstruction,* 183.

70. Ibid.

71. Allan Kulikoff, *Tobacco and Slaves;* Wm. Tiffany, Supt. of the Ogeechee District to Capt. A. P. Ketchum, July 5, 1865, Records of Ketchum, Applications for the Restoration of Property, List of Possessory Titles Issued to Freedmen, Savannah, RG 105, BRFAL, NAB; Records of the Chatham County Superior Court, Chatham County Courthouse, Savannah, Georgia, Deed Book 3X, 199–200. Hereafter cited as RCCSC.

72. "An Account of the Capture of Fort McAllister," by Lt. Col. William E. Armstrong, December 30, 1864, Miscellaneous, Reel 51, William T. Sherman Papers, Library of Congress; Lillian C. Bragg and Margaret Godley, *Stories of Old Savannah,* 13. The Bureau also controlled the rice mill on George Screven's Mifflin plantation.

73. Articles of Incorporation, Burroughs, Georgia, 1898, Charter Book 4, pp. 123–24, RCCSC.

74. List of Possessory Titles Issued to Freedmen, Savannah, RG 105, BRFAL, NAB.

75. Ibid. Robert Habersham to Capt. A. P. Ketchum, February 6, 1866, Letters Received; Capt. A. P. Ketchum to Wm. H. Tiffany, Ogeechee District, October 30, 1865, Letters Sent, RG 105, BRFAL, NAB. RCCSC Deed Book 4F, 157. Francis MacLeod, the owner of Wild Horn, died in 1864. The plantation did not meet the definition of "abandoned" set forth in Section 2 of the July 2, 1864, Act of Congress. Similar circumstances probably occurred at Vallambrosia, whose owner was Arthur Heyward. The children of MacLeod and Heyward inherited the property. Francis H. MacLeod Estate, File 398, 1864, Records of the Chatham County Probate Court, Savannah, Georgia, Chatham County Courthouse. Hereafter cited as RCCPC.

76. Paul Cimbala, *Under the Guardianship of the Nation,*167.

77. Ibid.

78. Register of Land Titles Issued to Freedmen, Savannah, RG 105, BRFAL, Georgia, Reel 36, (M798), NAB; *Savannah Daily Republican,* June 19, 1865; Hoskins, *Trouble They Seen,* 28; Magdol, *Right to the Land,* 105;

79. Register of Land Titles Issued to Freedmen, Savannah, RG 105, BRFAL, Georgia, Reel 36, (M798), NAB; Bell, *Major Butler's Legacy,* 395.

80. Wilson Moses, *The Golden Age of Black Nationalism,* 17; see also Paul Connerton, *How Societies Remember.*

81. Slave Inventory, File 398, RCCPC; Mae Ruth Green, "Sapelo Island Families," Department of Natural Resources, Real Estate Division, Georgia Department of Archives and History, Atlanta, Georgia. See also Register of Land Titles Issued to Freedmen, Savannah, Georgia, Records of A. P. Ketchum, Record Group 105, BRFAL, NAB, for references to African Americans' ancestral ties to lowcountry plantations.

82. *Compendium of the Ninth U.S. Census,* 1870, 139.

83. Bell, "'Ogeechee Troubles.'"

84. A. P. Ketchum to Moses Bentley, July 6, 1865, Savannah, Records of A. P. Ketchum, Letters Sent, RG 105, BRFAL, Georgia, Reel 36, (M798), NAB; Magdol, *Right to the Land,* 104.

85. Judith Carney, *Black Rice;* U.S. Bureau of the Census, Manuscript Agricultural Returns, Chatham County, Ogeechee District, 1880. The largest quantity produced by an African American rice planter in 1880 was 10,208 pounds from sixteen acres. See Plenty Ancrum, Frank Gladding, Mingo Broughton, Jacob Grant, Fortune Watson, and Richard Crawford, who each produced over 10,000 pounds of rice. In 1872 one thousand African Americans who cultivated rice assembled on Bay Street, the center of market activity in Savannah, to protest a possible repeal of the duty on foreign rice. African American leader Aaron A. Bradley stated that the repeal would touch the pocket of every rice planter, white and black. *Savannah Morning News,* January 23, 1872 (hereafter cited as *SMN*); Joseph P. Reidy, "Aaron A. Bradley."

86. Mohr, *On the Threshold of Freedom,* chapter four; Eric Foner, *Nothing But Freedom,* 75–79; U.S. Bureau of the Census, Manuscript Agricultural Returns, Chatham County, Bryan County, Liberty County, McIntosh County, Glynn County, Camden County, 1860; George Alexander Heard, "St. Simons Island during the War between the States."

87. Mart A. Stewart, "Rice, Water, and Power," 47–48; see also Mart A. Stewart, *What Nature Suffers to Groe.*

88. "Sketches on a Rice Plantation," *Harpers Weekly,* January 5, 1867, 6; Douglas C. Wilms, "The Development of Rice Culture in 18th Century Georgia." See also Albert V. House, ed., *Planter Management and Capitalism,* 24–28; Daniel Heyward, *Seed From Madagascar,* 19–36; and Julia Floyd Smith, *Slavery and Rice Culture,* 35–36. For the African origins of planting rice according to the task labor system see John Blassingame, *The Slave Community,* 101, and Carney, *Black Rice.* See also Lydia Parrish, *Slave Songs,* 225–36 for African cultural expressions that accompanied rice cultivation.

89. "Sketches on a Rice Plantation, *Harper's Weekly,* January 5, 1867, 6.

90. For a discussion of the "Port Royal Experiment," see Rose, *Rehearsal for Reconstruction.* In her early assessment of the land issue, Rose argued that land distribution would have had a negligible effect in alleviating African American poverty. See also Cimbala, *Under the Guardianship of the Nation,* 167.

91. Cimbala, *Under the Guardianship,* 167.

92. A. P. Ketchum to Wm. Tiffany, October 30, 1865, re George P. Screven's Mifflin plantation, Permission Given to Freedmen of Ogeechee to Sell Rice, December 4, 1865, H.F. Sickles, Letters Sent, Records of Ketchum, Savannah, RG 105, NAB.

93. Cimbala, *Under the Guardianship of the Nation,* 173. For the Bureau's position on cases involving freedmen, see Complaint of Mungo Davis against Mr. Miller, June 30, 1865; A.P. Ketchum to Harris Phillips, June 24, 1865; and Notice to Mrs. Julia Spiers of Effingham County, June 28, 1865, in Letters Sent, Records of Ketchum, Savannah, RG 105, BRFAL, NAB. Ketchum acknowledged the "right of the freed people" in each of these cases. Judge Benedict and General Grover of the Bureau were identified by Reverend James Simms of Savannah as hostile to freed people. Ketchum replaced Judge Benedict. Capt. A. P. Ketchum to Bvt. Major Stuart M. Taylor, July 1, 1865, Letters Sent, Records of Ketchum, RG 105, BRFAL, NAB. See also Paul A. Cimbala, "The Freedmen's Bureau, the Freedmen, and Sherman's Grant," 598; Paul A. Cimbala, "On the Front Line of Freedom," 577–89.

94. *SMN,* December 31, 1868; RCCSC, Deed Book 3T, 301–2; RCCPC Slave Inventory, File 398. Langdon Cheves had previously owned Southfield plantation. A deed dated February 17, 1860, lists 116 slaves whose names correspond with those on the riot list related to the Ogeechee troubles. The names of slaves in the inventory of the estate of Francis MacLeod, owner of Wild Horn, also correspond with those listed on the riot list.

95. Daily accounts of the revolt and court records of the preliminary trial that followed appeared in the *SMN,* December 31, 1868, to February 1, 1869. Sworn affidavits of witnesses were also published in the *SMN.*

96. A. P. Ketchum to Moses Bentley, July 6, 1865, Savannah, Records of A. P. Ketchum, RG 105 NAB; Civil Minutes, *State v. Moses H. Bentley,* Docket 26, 440, RCCSC; Magdol, *Right to the Land,* 104. The criminal minutes of the Chatham County Superior Court for 1868–1869 are combined with civil minutes.

97. *SMN,* January 26, 1869.

98. *SMN,* December 31, 1868; January 1–2, 1869.

99. *SMN,* December 31, 1868.

100. *SMN,* January 2, 1869.

101. *SMN,* January 4, 1869.

102. *Compendium of the Ninth U.S. Census,* 1870, 139.

103. Russell Duncan, *Freedom's Shore,* 21–27.

104. *SMN,* December 31, 1868, and January 2–6, 1869; *Savannah, Florida, and Western Railway Company Guide to Southern Georgia and Florida* (Savannah, Georgia, 1879), 7–9.

105. *SMN,* January 7, 1869, and January 23, 1872. The occupation "rice planter" appears in the ledgers of the Freedmen's Bank. See Captain Shigg, Ledger #138, Index to Deposit Ledgers, Savannah, Records of the Freedmen's Savings and Trust, RG 101, National Archives and Records Administration (NARA). Black labor activist Aaron A. Bradley, in speeches to rice workers, referred to them as rice planters.

106. Joseph P. Reidy, "Aaron A. Bradley: Voice of Black Labor in the Georgia lowcountry," in Howard N. Rabinowitz, ed., *Southern Black Leaders,* 281–86.

107. *SMN,* January 4–6, 1869; Georgia Federal Writers' Project, *Drums and Shadows,* 212; Art Rosenbaum, *Shout Because You're Free,* 4–8, 137–39.

108. *SMN,* January 4–6, 1869.

109. Ibid.

110. Ibid. The robbery charges stemmed from the pilfering of rice.

111. Ibid; *SMN,* January 7–15, 1869.

112. Kenneth Coleman, ed., *A History of Georgia,* 213–14.

113. RCCSC, Civil Minutes, *State v. Captain Green,* Docket 27, 52–53, 108–9, 117, 228–29; *SMN,* January 25, 1869; February 1, 1869.

114. *SMN,* January 15–February 1, 1869.

115. Ibid.

116. Ibid.

117. Russell Duncan, *Entrepreneur for Equality,* 118–20; *SMN,* January 23, 1869.

118. RCCSC, *State v. Captain Green [et al.], State v. Ned Edwards, State v. Dandy McNeil,* Civil Minutes, Docket 27, 52, 67, 108–9, 117; RCCSC, *State v. Captain Green [et al.],* Civil Minutes, Docket 26, 498; *SMN,* July 12, 1869; Georgia General Assembly, *Committee to Investigate the Official Conduct of Rufus Bullock Late Governor of Georgia* (Atlanta, 1872), 76–77, 162–67.

119. Foner, *Reconstruction,* 41.

120. Mohr, "Before Sherman," 351.

121. U.S. Bureau of the Census, Montgomery, Alabama, roll 43, District 6, 1930. In 1930 Delia Garlic was a widow who resided with her daughter's family in Montgomery, Alabama.

CHAPTER 3: "FULL AND FAIR COMPENSATION"

1. Records of the Chatham County Superior Court (RCCSC), Deed Book 3S, pp. 247–55; Malcolm Bell, *Major Butler's Legacy,* 311–40; William Dusinberre, in *Them Dark Days,* argues that slavery in the rice kingdom was much harsher and more horrific than has been acknowledged. See also Frances Butler Leigh, *Ten Years on a Georgia Plantation.* The *New York Daily Tribune* provided multipage coverage of the March 11, 1859, auction and sale. See also Kwesi DeGraft-Hanson, "Unearthing the Weeping Time."

2. U.S. Manuscript Population Census, Glynn County, 1870; Bell, *Major Butler's Legacy,* 407.

3. Ira Berlin, *Freedom,* series 1 vol. 3: *The Wartime Genesis of Free Labor,* 111–12; *U.S. Statutes at Large, 1863–1864,* chapter 225, second section, 375–78; Letters Sent by the Commissioner of Customs Relating to Captured and Abandoned Property, M498, roll 1, Records of the U.S. General Accounting Office, RG 217, National Archives Building, Washington, D.C. (hereafter cited as NAB). See also Steven F. Miller et al., *Land and Labor.*

4. Peter A. Coclanis and Stuart Bruchey, eds., *Ideas, Ideologies, and Social Movements,* 49; General Carl C. Schurz, "Observations on the Labor of Freedmen," Bureau of Free Labor, Montgomery, Alabama, August 19, 1865, Carl Schurz Papers, Library of Congress, Washington, D.C.

5. U.S. Bureau of the Census, Population Manuscript, Chatham County, Seventh Militia District, 1870; *Savannah Morning News,* October 9, 1874, p. 3 col. 3. The occupation "rice planter" appears in the ledgers of the Freedmen's Bank; Index to Deposit Ledgers, Savannah, Records of the Freedmen's Savings and Trust, RG 101, NAB. For a discussion of the significance of spatial dialectics on plantations, see Theresa A. Singleton, "Slavery and Spatial Dialectics."

6. "A Disaster to the Rice Crop," Manigault Family Papers, #484, Southern Historical Collection, Manuscript Department, Wilson Library, the University of North Carolina at Chapel Hill. Daniel Heyward, *Seed from Madagascar,* 19–36; Douglas C. Wilms, "The Development of Rice Culture," 53. See also Julia Floyd Smith, *Slavery and Rice Culture;* Stewart, "*What Nature Suffers to Groe.*"

7. "Some Previous Floods," Manigault Family Papers, #484, Southern Historical Collection, Manuscript Department, Wilson Library, University of North Carolina at Chapel Hill.

8. Leigh, *Ten Years,* 1, 14.

9. Ibid., 15. The *Savannah Daily Herald,* October 31, 1865, reported that 7,000 sick and helpless former slaves in Georgia were under the care of the newspaper. The *Savannah Daily Herald* had replaced the *Daily Morning News* in December 1864 after General Sherman's arrival in Savannah.

10. Works Progress Administration, *Annals of Savannah 1850–1937,* vol. 16, 5. See also Jacqueline Jones, *Saving Savannah.*

11. Works Progress Administration, *Annals of Savannah 1850–1937,* vol. 16, 5.

12. Robert Birt, ed., *The Quest for Community and Identity,* 2, 4; William T. Sherman, *Memoirs,* vol. 2, 250–52.

13. In the Bible, see Exodus 6:1–8, Exodus 7–14, and Matthew 5:5; "Sketch of a Sermon by Rev. H. M. Turner LL.D., Delivered in St. James Tabernacle," *Savannah Tribune,* November 28, 1875; Lydia Parrish, *Slave Songs of the Georgia Sea Islands;* John Langston Gwaltney, *Drylongso,* xxvi; Will Coleman, "'Coming through 'Ligion'"; Wayne E. Croft, "'You Jes' Wait a Little.'" For an excellent discussion of reparations during the period immediately following the Civil War, see Mary Frances Berry, *My Face Is Black.*

14. Capt. A. P. Ketchum to Wm. H. Tiffany, Ogeechee District, October 30, 1865, Letters Sent, RG 105; List of Possessory Titles Issued to Freed People, Savannah, Georgia; Records of A. P. Ketchum, February 6, 1866, Letters Received, RG 105, NAB. See also Leslie A. Schwalm, *A Hard Fight for We.*

15. *Savannah Daily Herald,* February 3, 1865; *Savannah Tribune,* August 12, 1876.

16. The term "full and fair compensation" appears in speeches given by lowcountry African American leaders, many of whom served as agents of the Freedmen's Bureau; the term also appears in Bureau correspondence. See, for instance, Eric Foner, *Freedom's Lawmakers,* 88; Claim of W. A. Golding, Claim No. 18129, Liberty County, Georgia, Records of the Southern Claims Commission, RG 217, NAB; Letter to Capt. S. Soper, July 5, 1865, Contracts, Savannah, Georgia, Records of A. P. Ketchum, Bureau of Refugees, Freedmen, and Abandoned Lands (hereafter cited as BRFAL), RG 105, NAB. For a full discussion of labor laws, see James Schmidt, *Free to Work,* 2.

17. John R. Cheves to Col. H. L. Sickles, Letters Received, November 17, 1865, Savannah, Records of A. P. Ketchum, RG 105, NAB; Eric Foner, *Politics and Ideology in the Age of the Civil War,* 97–99; Karen Cook Bell and Peter J. Breaux, "Robert Smalls and the Politics of Race and Freedom."

18. *The National Freedmen,* June 1, 1865; Senate Report 693, 46th Congress, 2nd Session; *The New Era,* March 3, 1870; *New Orleans Tribune,* October 31, 1867; Heather Cox Richardson, *The Death of Reconstruction,* chapter one. See also Steven F. Miller et. al, "Between Emancipation and Enfranchisement," 1069–71.

19. Richardson, *Death of Reconstruction,* chapter one. For a discussion of the relationship between the Thirteenth Amendment and slave marriage, see Amy Dru Stanley, "Instead of Waiting for the Thirteenth Amendment"; Noralee Frankel, *Freedom's Women.*

20. William Cohen, *At Freedom's Edge,* 4; Eric Foner, *The Story of American Freedom,* 177. See also Patricia G. Davis, "Ripping the Veil."

21. For a discussion of the polarity created by skin color and the construction of blackness in the white imagination, see Toni Morrison, "Romancing the Shadow," in *Playing in the Dark,* 31–59.

22. S. Ryan Johansson, "Status Anxiety and Demographic Contraction of Privileged Populations."

23. State of Georgia Constitution (1865), art. 2, sec. 5; Georgia Acts 1865–1866; The Condition of Affairs in the State of Georgia, Report of the Joint Select Committee, February 19, 1872; Proceedings of the Freedmen's Convention of Georgia, Assembled at Augusta, January 10, 1866. For a discussion of central Georgia, see Joseph P. Reidy, *From Slavery to Agrarian Capitalism,* chapter six.

24. Mississippi Constitution (1832, as amended in 1865), art. 1, sec. 12; State of South Carolina Constitution (1865), art. 3, sec. 1; Laws of the State of Mississippi (1866), 82–86; W. E. B. DuBois, *Black Reconstruction;* Eric Foner, *Reconstruction,* 199–200.

25. A. P. Ketchum to Harris Phillips, June 24, 1865, Contracts, Savannah, Georgia, Records of Ketchum, Letters Sent, May-Oct. 1865, BRFAL, RG 105, NAB; George R. Bentley, *A History of the Freedmen's Bureau,* chapter ten.

26. Senate Documents, 39th Cong., 1st Sess., No. 27, p. 60; Senate Documents, 39th Cong. 2ne Sess., No. 6, p. 127; House Executive Documents, 39th Cong. 1st Sess., No. 70, pp. 45, 57, 77, 231; House Executive Documents, 39th Cong. 2nd Sess. No. 1, pp. 718–19; Douglass Risley to J. Rowe, May 20, 1867, Letters Sent, Brunswick (Subassistant Commissioner), vol. 1, March 1867–June 1868; National Archives Microfilm Publication M1903, roll 52; Records of the Field Offices for the State of Georgia, BRFAL, RG 105, NAB.

27. A. P. Ketchum to Harris Phillips, June 24, 1865; Contracts, Savannah, Georgia; Records of Ketchum, Letters Sent, May-October 1865; BRFAL, RG 105, NAB; Bentley, *History of the Freedmen's Bureau,* chapter ten.

28. Reidy, *From Slavery to Agrarian Capitalism,* 143. See also Susan E. O'Donovan, *Becoming Free.*

29. Reidy, *From Slavery to Agrarian Capitalism,* chapter six.

30. Letter to Capt. S. Soper, July 5, 1865, Contracts, Savannah, Georgia, Records of A. P. Ketchum, BRFAL, RG 105, NAB.

31. Land Report and Report of Planters Who Had Sent Their Freedmen Away Unpaid, August-September 1865, St. Simons (Agent), National Archives Microfilm Publication M1903, roll 77, Records of the Field Offices for the State of Georgia; BRFAL, RG 105, NAB.

32. Notices to Mrs. Julia Spiers of Effingham County, June 18, 1865; Letters Sent by A. P. Ketchum, May-October 1865, Records of A. P. Ketchum, Savannah, Georgia, BRFAL, RG 105, NAB.

33. Wm. Royal to Jesse Butler, June 24, 1868; Wm. Royal to Jesse Butler, July 30, 1868; Letters Sent, St. Mary's (Agent), vol. 1, September 1867–July 1868; National Archives Microfilm Publication M1903, roll 77, Records of the Field Offices for the State of Georgia, BRFAL, RG 105; NAB.

34. Complaint of Mungo Davis against Mr. Miller, Contracts, Savannah, Georgia, 1865–1872, Records of A. P. Ketchum, BRFAL, RG 105, NAB; Order of restoration to W. R. Nelson of "Modena" plantation Skidaway Island, January 29, 1866, Contracts, Savannah, Georgia, Records of A.P. Ketchum, 1865–1872, BRFAL, RG 105, NAB.

35. Complaint of Mungo Davis against Mr. Miller, Contracts, Savannah, Georgia, 1865–1872, Records of A. P. Ketchum, BRFAL, RG 105, NAB. See also Wm. Royal to Major J. Booth, December 26, 1867, Letters Sent, St. Mary's (Agent), vol. 1, September 1867–July 1868, National Archives Microfilm Publication M1903, roll 77; Records of the Field Offices for the State of Georgia, BRFAL, RG 105, NAB.

36. Letter to Bvt. Major Stuart M. Taylor, July 1, 1865, Contracts, Savannah, Georgia, 1865–1872, Records of A. P. Ketchum, BRFAL, RG 105, NAB.

37. Notification to Mr. Andrew T. Eyck, Contracts, Savannah, Georgia, June 30, 1865, Records of A. P. Ketchum, BRFAL, RG 105, NAB. See also, Wm. Royal to J. Booth, June 26, 1868, Letters Sent, St. Mary's (Agent), vol. 1, September 1867–July 1868, National Archives

Microfilm Publication M1903, roll 77; Records of the Field Offices for the State of Georgia, BRFAL, RG 105, NAB.

38. Gerald D. Jaynes, *Branches without Roots,* 121–27.

39. *Raymond R. Kay v. Charles Walthour, Peter Way, and Billy Gillman,* November 1865, Contracts, Savannah, Georgia, Records of A. P. Ketchum, BRFAL, RG 105, NAB.

40. Eliza F. Andrews, *The War-Time Journal of a Georgia Girl* (New York, 1908), 319; A. P. Ketchum to Mr. W. H. Tiffany, Agt. Ogeechee, October 28, 1865, Contracts, Savannah, Georgia, Records of A. P. Ketchum, BRFAL, RG 105, NAB; Communication from W.C.G. to Langdon Cheves in Regard to Land Owned by Him and Other Parties, May 11, 1865, Savannah, Georgia, Contracts, Records of A. P. Ketchum, BRFAL, RG 105, NAB.

41. Senate Documents, 39th Cong., 2nd Sess., No. 6, pp. 44, 54, 90; House Executive Documents, 40th Cong., 3rd Sess., vol. 3, No. 1, pp. 1040, 1044.

42. Schmidt, *Free to Work,* 94–95. Schmidt argues that emancipation was a "legal event that destroyed a legal apparatus that had been instituted and perpetuated in the South." My study argues that racial biases regarding contracts, apprenticeships, and exploitative wages remained firmly fixed as legal restraints on free labor.

43. See Winthrop D. Jordan, *The White Man's Burden;* Gerald Horne, *The Deepest South,* chapters three and eight; Paul A. Cimbala, *Under the Guardianship of the Nation,* 7.

44. House Executive Documents, 40th Cong., 3rd Sess., vol. 3, No. 1, p. 1052; Report on Reconstruction, Part 2, pp. 28, 290; Oliver Otis Howard, Circular Letter, October 14, 1865, Senate, Orders Issued by the Freedmen's Bureau, 1865–1866, 39th Cong., 1st Sess. Senate Executive Doc. 6, 197–98; Schmidt, *Free to Work,* 1.

45. House Executive Documents, 40th Cong., 2nd Sess., No. 1, pp. 669, 664, 684; House Executive Documents 40th Cong., 3rd Sess., No. 1, pp. 1038, 1044; Senate Documents, 39th Cong., 2nd Sess., No. 6, pp. 48, 101, 123, 127; House Executive Documents, 39th Cong., 1st Sess., No. 70, pp. 173, 264, 313; see also Christopher R. Bean, "The Freedmen's Bureau and Logistical Problems"; Cimbala, *Under the Guardianship of the Nation,* 14.

46. Bentley, *History of the Freedmen's Bureau,* 136.

47. John and LaWanda Cox, "General O. O. Howard and the Misrepresented Bureau," 430; Bentley, *History of the Freedmen's Bureau,* 136.

48. James McPherson, *Ordeal by Fire,* 253–54.

49. Ibid., 253–55; Works Progress Administration, *Louisiana: Past and Present,* 47.

50. Ibid.

51. Schmidt, *Free to Work,* 95; Bentley, *History of the Freedmen's Bureau,* 14; *United States Statutes at Large, Volume XII,* 590–92, 599. See also Skocpol, *Protecting Soldiers and Mothers.*

52. Schmidt, *Free to Work,* 95. At Coco Bend Plantation in West Feliciana Parish, amid the disorder and chaos of war numerous slaves across the age spectrum left the plantation, and the Red River uprising led to the deaths of several enslaved men. Letter to Mrs. Henrietta Matthews, Bayou Sara, December 5, 1864, and "List of Slaves Killed in Red River Uprising," Charles L. Matthews and Family Papers, Mss. 910, Louisiana and Lower Mississippi Valley Collections, Special Collections, Louisiana State University, LSU Libraries, Baton Rouge. The Matthews family owned Greenwood, Georgia, Coco Bend, and Chaseland plantations, located on the Red River in Rapides Parish. See also Auguste Le Blanc Family Papers, Mss. 214; Special Collections, LSU Libraries. In his study of Louisiana, C. Peter Ripley argues that

the rivers, bayous, and swamps precluded the likelihood and success of running away. See C. Peter Ripley, *Slaves and Freedmen,* 7.

53. Registers and Payrolls of Freedmen Employed on Plantations, Terre Bonne, Louisiana, M1905, roll 39, BRFAL, RG 105, NAB.

54. Ibid.; Schmidt, *Free to Work,* 2.

55. Julie Saville, *The Work of Reconstruction,* 68.

56. Amy Dru Stanley, *From Bondage to Contract Labor,* 29.

57. Schmidt, *Free to Work,* 5. See also William E. Nelson, *The Roots of American Bureaucracy,* 1–8. Nelson argues that the origins of the modern state lie in the "tension between the idea of majority self-rule and the concern for protecting minority and individual rights." The contract system developed by the Freedmen's Bureau sought to strike a balance between these two ideas, but ultimately protecting the interests of the majority prevailed.

58. W. N. Ginn, "New History of the Rice Industry in America," vol. 3, pp. 1–2 in Louisiana Sugar and Rice Trade Collection, Mss. 784, Louisiana and Lower Mississippi Valley Collections, Special Collections, Louisiana State University, LSU Libraries, Baton Rouge.

59. Ibid., 2.

60. Ibid., 5.

61. An Agreement Between William H. Gibbons and 119 Colored People, Contracts, Savannah, Georgia, Records of A. P. Ketchum, BRFAL, RG 105, NAB.

62. Ibid. See also George P. Screven, October 30, 1865, Contracts, Savannah, Georgia, Letters Received, Records of A. P. Ketchum, 1865–1872, BRFAL, RG 105, NAB; Contract between George P. Screven and Certain Freedmen, February 20, 1866, Contracts, 1865–1872, Savannah, Georgia, BRFAL, RG 105, NAB; George P. Screven, March 22, 1866, Savannah, Georgia, Contracts, Records of A. P. Ketchum, 1865–1872, BRFAL, RG 105, NAB; Article of Agreement between Richard McLeod and Certain Freedmen, Contracts, Savannah, Georgia, 1865–1872, BRFAL, RG 105, NAB.

63. An Agreement between William H. Gibbons and 119 Colored People, Contracts, Savannah, Georgia, Records of A. P. Ketchum, BRFAL, RG 105, NAB.

64. For a discussion of the economic effects of uncompensated emancipation within a legal framework, see Paul Finkleman, *Law of Freedom and Bondage.*

65. Thomas V. Scriven and Certain Freedmen, Contracts, Savannah, Georgia, Records of A. P. Ketchum, BRFAL, RG 105, NAB.

66. Ibid.

67. Peter Wallenstein, *From Slave South to New South,* 131–32.

68. William H. Burroughs and Certain Freedman, Contracts, Savannah, Georgia, February 26, 1866, Records of A. P. Ketchum, BRFAL, RG 105, NAB.

69. J. Rowe, Esq., May 20, 1867, Brunswick, Georgia, Registered Letters Received, St. Mary's, May 1867–November 1868, National Archives Microfilm Publication M1903, roll 77; Records of the Field Offices for the State of Georgia, BRFAL, RG 105, NAB.

70. Jaqueline Jones, *Labor of Love,* 53. Henry L. Swint, ed., *Dear Ones at Home,* 203–4; Douglass Risley to Captain Eugene Pickett, June 4, 1867; Letters Sent, Brunswick (Subassistant Commissioner), vol. 1, March 1867–June 1868; National Archives Microfilm Publication M1903, roll 52, Records of the Field Offices for the State of Georgia, BRFAL, RG 105, NAB; Darlene Clark Hine, *Hine Sight,* 3–4. Risley discusses the conditions of women and their needs in lowcountry Georgia.

71. Jones, *Labor of Love,* 53. Douglass Risley to James F. Blain, Mayor of Brunswick, June

21, 1867, Letters Sent, Brunswick (Subassistant Commissioner), National Archives Microfilm Publication M1903, roll 52, Records of the Field Offices for the State of Georgia, RG 105. For a similar discussion of how Freedmen's Aid societies treated freed women see, Carol Faulkner, *Women's Radical Reconstruction,* chapter seven.

72. Jones, *Labor of Love,* 53. "Testimony by a Georgia Freedwoman before the Southern Claims Commission," Savannah, March 22, 1873, in Ira Berlin et al., *Freedom,* vol. 3, 150–54.

73. Jones, *Labor of Love,* 53. Ira Berlin et al., *Freedom,* vol. 3, 92–97.

74. Jones, *Labor of Love,* 53. John R. Dennett, *The South As It Is,* 105.

75. Jones, *Labor of Love,* 53. Douglass Risley to O. A. Dodge, Wayne County, Georgia, June 6, 1867, Letters Sent, Brunswick (Subassistant Commissioner), vol. 1, September 1867–July 1868, National Archives Microfilm Publication M1903, roll 52, Records of the Field Offices for the State of Georgia, BRFAL, RG 105, NAB.

76. Wm. Royal to Wm. Dickson, November 15, 1867, Letters Sent, St. Mary's (Agent), vol. 1, September 1867–July 1868, National Archives Microfilm Publication M1903, roll 77, Records of the Field Offices for the State of Georgia, BRFAL, RG 105, NAB. See also Wm. Royal to Francis Adams, December 30, 1867, Letters Sent, St. Mary's (Agent), vol. 1, September 1867–July 1868, Records of the Field Offices for the State of Georgia, BRFAL, RG 105, NAB. Wm. Royal to James Dampier, July 29, 1868, Letters Sent, St. Mary's (Agent), vol. 1, September 1867–July 1868, Records of the Field Offices for the State of Georgia, BRFAL, RG 105, NAB.

77. Wm. Royal to Wm. Dickson, November 15, 1867, Letters Sent, St. Mary's, vol. 1, September 1867–July 1868, National Archives Microfilm Publication M1903, roll 77, Records of the Field Offices for the State of Georgia, BRFAL, RG 105, NAB.

78. Wm. Royal to Dr. W.B. Folks, April 14, 1868, Letters Sent, St. Mary's, vol. 1, September 1867–July 1868, National Archives Microfilm Publication M1903, roll 77; Records of the Field Offices for the State of Georgia, BRFAL, RG 105, NAB. Wm. Royal to William Murray, February 24, 1867, Letters Sent, St. Mary's, vol. 1, September 1867–July 1868, National Archives Microfilm Publication M1903, roll 77; Records of the Field Offices for the State of Georgia, BRFAL, RG 105, NAB.

79. Wm. Royal to Dr. W.B. Folks, April 14, 1868, Letters Sent, St. Mary's, vol. 1, September 1867–July 1868, National Archives Microfilm Publication M1903, roll 77, Records of the Field Offices for the State of Georgia, BRFAL, RG 105, NAB. Wm. Royal to James Dampier, July 29, 1868, Letters Sent, St. Mary's (Agent), vol. 1, September 1867–July 1868, Records of the Field Offices for the State of Georgia, NAB.

80. Douglass Risley to Mitchell August, June 4, 1867, Letters Sent, St. Mary's (Agent), National Archives Microfilm Publication M1903, roll 52, Records of the Field Offices for the State of Georgia, BRFAL, RG 105, NAB.

81. Wm. Royal to D. J. Dillion, June 4, 1868; Letters Sent, St. Mary's, vol. 1, September 1867–July 1868; National Archives Microfilm Publication M1903, roll 77, Records of the Field Offices for the State of Georgia, BRFAL, RG 105, NAB.

82. Douglass Risley to E. P. Smith, August 15, 1867, Reel 32, Georgia, American Missionary Association Archives, 1839–1882, Amistad Research Center, Tulane University, New Orleans.

83. Jones, *Labor of Love,* 53–54. Letters Sent, St. Mary's (Agent), vol. 1, September 1867–July 1868, National Archives Microfilm Publication M1903, roll 77, Records of the Field Offices for the State of Georgia, BRFAL, RG 105, NAB.

84. Jones, *Labor of Love,* 53–54. Case 104, September 9, 1867, Register of Complaints, Cuthbert, Georgia, Agent No. 238, BRFAL, RG 105, NAB; Mary Farmer-Kaiser, *Freedwomen and the Freedmen's Bureau,* chapter one; Jacqueline Jones, *Labor of Love, Labor of Sorrow,* 55.

85. Jones, *Labor of Love,* 55. Case 104, September 9, 1867, Register of Complaints, Cuthbert, Georgia, Agent No. 238, BRFAL, RG 105, NAB.

86. Douglass Risely to Col. C. A. Reynolds, June 28, 1867, Letters Sent, Brunswick (Subassistant Commissioner), vol. 1, March 1867–June 1868, National Archives Microfilm Publication M1903, roll 52; Records of the Field Offices for the State of Georgia, BRFAL, RG 105, NAB.

87. William Royal to Miller B. Grant, December 16, 1867, Letters Sent, St. Mary's, vol. 1, September 1867–July 1868; National Archives Microfilm Publication M1903, roll 77, Records of the Field Offices for the State of Georgia, BRFAL, RG 105, NAB.

88. William Royal to Miller B. Grant, December 16, 1867, Letters Sent, St. Mary's, vol. 1, September 1867–July 1868; National Archives Microfilm Publication M1903, roll 77, Records of the Field Offices for the State of Georgia, BRFAL, RG 105, NAB.

89. Works Progress Administration, *Annals of Savannah 1850–1937,* vol. 17, 5. For a discussion of the significance of 1866, see Patrick W. Riddleberger, *1866.*

90. Reidy, *From Slavery to Agrarian Capitalism,* 144.

91. "Petition of the Colored Washerwomen," *Jackson* (Mississippi) *Daily Clarion,* June 24, 1866, in Philip S. Foner and Randolph Lewis, *Black Workers;* Tera Hunter, *To Joy My Freedom,* chapter four.

92. Interview with Benjamin Lewis, February 3, 2001, Savannah, Georgia. Lewis is the grandson of Sapelo Island resident Katie Brown, who is featured in Georgia Writers' Project, *Drums and Shadows,* and Lydia Parrish, *Slave Songs.* Born during slavery, Brown cultivated rice on Sapelo Island, as did previous generations of women. Lewis described rice as his grandmother's "money crop." Recording in possession of the author.

93. Judith Carney, *Black Rice,* 107–8, 135; Leigh, *Ten Years on a Georgia Plantation,* 51. See also, Judith Carney and R. N. Rosomoff, *In the Shadow of Slavery;* Daina Ramey Berry, *"Swing the Sickle for the Harvest Is Ripe."*

94. Leigh, *Ten Years,* 58–59.

95. Jones, *Labor of Love,* 57. Leigh, *Ten Years,* 58–59.

96. Carol Faulkner, *Women's Radical Reconstruction,* chapter seven; Edmund Drago, "Militancy and Black Women in Reconstruction Georgia."

97. Register of Signature of Depositors, Freedmen's Savings and Trust, Savannah Branch, M816, roll 8: Acct. 722, Union Benevolent Society of Second African Baptist Church; Acct. 745, John the Baptist Society; Acct. 757, Union Republican Association; Acct. 842, Mary Magdalene Society; Acct. 927, Sisters Prayer Meeting Benevolent Association; Acct. 930, Ladies Union Society; Acct. 984, Poor and Needy Institute; Records of the Office of the Comptroller of the Currency, Record Group 101, NAB. James Simms, *First Colored Church of North America,* 211–13, lists additional benevolent societies organized and headed by women.

98. Leigh, *Ten Years,* 25–26, 51, 55–56, 57, 59, 65–67; Lawrence Powell, *New Masters,* 109; Jones, *Labor of Love,* 57, 70; Eric Foner, *Nothing but Freedom,* 87. See also Elizabeth Hayes Turner, *Women and Gender in the New South.*

99. Mae Ruth Green, Sapelo Island Families, Pheobe Robinson Family #130, Genealogical Source Book (unpublished); copy provided by Carolyn Douse, Sapelo Isalnd Cultural and

Revitalization Society (SICARS), Sapelo Island, Georgia; Barbara Omolade, *The Rising Song,* 39; Leigh, *Ten Years,* 54.

100. Records of the Chatham County Superior Court, Chatham County Tax Digest, 1876; Register of Signature of Depositors, Freedmen's Savings and Trust, RG 101, M816, roll 8, #777; U.S. Bureau of the Census, Manuscript Population, Savannah, #1039, 1870; Simms, *First Colored Church,* 206–7, lists contributors to the building fund.

101. Records of the Chatham County Superior Court, Chatham County Tax Digest, 1876; U.S. Bureau of the Census, Manuscript Population, Savannah, #1692.

102. I.W. Avery, "The City of Savannah, Georgia," *Harper's New Monthly Magazine,* January 1888, 261; Register of Signature of Depositors, Freedmen's Savings and Trust, Savannah Branch, M816, roll 8, #590, RG 101; Records of the Chatham County Superior Court, Chatham County Tax Digest, 1876, Savannah, Georgia.

103. Leigh, *Ten Years,* 54. For a comparative response in the Georgia cotton belt, see Susan E. O'Donovan, *Becoming Free.*

104. Leigh, *Ten Years,* 54.

105. Mae Ruth Green, Sapelo Island Families, Sampson Hillery, William Hillery, Family No. 116, unpublished Genealogical Source Book; copy provided by Carolyn Douse, SICARS, Sapelo Island, Georgia.

106. Mae Ruth Green, Sapelo Island Families, Family No. 116.

107. Mae Ruth Green, Sapelo Island Families, Sampson Hillery, William Hillery, Family No. 116. See also McFeely, *Sapelo's People.*

108. RCCSC, Deed Books 4K, 530–33, Salsbury Barnard and Apollo Blunt; 4N, 222–23, Richard Crawford; 4O, 138–39, 153, 401–2, Frank Gladden, Pierce Neil, John Shellman, Caroline Ealy; 4P, 194, 212–13, 267, Charles Banks, Wally Large, Jeremiah Jones; 4Q, 352, James Grant; 4R, 361, 372–73, John Shellman and Plenty Ancrum; 4S, 277, January Stoney; 4V, 206, Fortune Watson; 4Z, 454–56, Mingo Bro[ug]hton, trustee for Hannah Green, Norris Weston; 5M, 68–69, 104–5, 367, Kate Brown and Children, Sarah Davis, Sara Miller; 5O, 324, Sarah Banks; 5P, 175, Tyra Williams; 6Z, 350, David Rolabit.

109. Foner, *Reconstruction,* 374, 379–81.

110. *Savannah Tribune,* January 1, 1876, p. 2, col. 3.

111. "Ku Klux Klan Report, Georgia Testimony: Report of the Joint Committee to Inquire into the Affairs of the Late Insurrectionary States," *Senate Reports of Committees,* 42nd Cong., 2nd Sess., vol. 2, Pt. 7, pp. 1099–1103. *Cong. Globe,* 42nd Cong., 1st Sess., 283; *Cong. Globe,* 42nd Cong., 2nd Sess., 573; U.S. Congress, Senate, *Georgia before the Senate Judiciary Committee, 1970;* John Hope Franklin, *Reconstruction,* 153; Ralph Wardlaw, "Negro Suffrage in Georgia," 38–39; DuBois, *Black Reconstruction,* 580. See also Herman Belz, *A New Birth of Freedom.*

112. Ralph Wardlaw, "Negro Suffrage in Georgia," 38–39, 49.

113. *Savannah Tribune,* January 1, 1876; January 28, 1876; January 5, 1876; August 3, 1876; September 24, 1892.

114. *Savannah Tribune,* August 3, 1876.

115. *Savannah Tribune,* August 12, 1876; Rollin Chambliss, "What Negro Newspapers of Georgia Say," 11–12.

116. Eric Foner, *Freedom's Lawmakers,* 88; Claim of W. A. Golding, Claim No. 18129, Liberty County, Georgia, Records of the Southern Claims Commission, RG 217, NAB; James

Stacy, *History of the Midway Congregational Church,* 209–20, 218–19; Robert Manson Myers, *Children of Pride,* 1613; Peggy Harris, "For the Love of Place," 843n53. An ordained minister in the Congregational church, Golding became a leader in the local slave community. He joined Midway Congregational Church in 1839. His grandfather, Larson Sharper Jones, was reputed to be the "first colored Congregationalist preacher under white Congregationalists." During slavery Golding had been the body servant for John B. Mallard, a planter and educator who owned a plantation near Charles C. Jones's Arcadia plantation in Liberty County.

117. Eric Foner, *Freedom's Lawmakers,* 88; Claim of W. A. Golding, Claim No. 18129, Liberty County, Georgia, Records of the Southern Claims Commission, RG 217, NAB. Politicians who engaged issues concerning labor were also landowners. They included Hamilton Jackson, constable of Darien (McIntosh County) in 1870, who owned $250 in real estate and $250 in personal property; Lewis Jackson, who represented McIntosh County in 1868, owned $800 in real estate and $250 in personal property; Caroline Johnson, member of the Darien City Council in 1870, owned $1,500 in real estate and $200 in personal property; Austin Jones, constable in Isle of Hope, Chatham County, in 1871, also owned land and property. Foner, *Freedom's Lawmakers,* 20, 204, 181, 115, 117, 121. Also, Dandy Stewart of Butler's Island, elected to the Darien County Board of Commissioners in 1878, owned real estate valued at $500 in 1870.

118. Tunis G. Campbell to Hon. E. D. Morgan, Atlanta, July 8, 1872, William E. Chandler Papers, Library of Congress, Washington, D.C. See Joseph P. Reidy, "Aaron A. Bradley," 281–86; Duncan, *Freedom's Shore.*

119. In Chatham County, Superior Court Judge William Schley in March 1869, in the case *State of Georgia ex rel William J. Clements v. Richard W. White,* ruled that the "right to hold office in Georgia does not belong to any person of color." RCCSC, Civil Minutes, Docket 27, 1–13. In a series of court decisions such as *Appling v. Odum (1872),* which defined sharecroppers as wage laborers, the courts separated freedmen and freedwomen from the means of production and accomplished what planters by themselves could not achieve. See Foner, *Nothing but Freedom.*

120. Charles R. Hale, "The Cultural Politics of Identity in Latin America," 568.

121. *Savannah Daily Herald,* July 25, 1865.

122. U.S. Bureau of the Census, Manuscript Population, Ninth Census of the United States, 1870, Darien, McIntosh County, 271st Militia District; Tenth Census of the United States, 1880, Darien, McIntosh County, 27st Militia District; Tad Evans, ed. *Darien, Georgia, Newspaper Clippings,* vol. 1: *1818–1878,* 266, 276, 284–87, and vol. 2: *1879–1890,* 221, 304, 314, 323, 351, 370–74.

123. *Savannah Tribune,* December 7, 1889; Grant, *The Way It Was in the South,* 174.

124. Interview with LeRoy Palmer, Sapelo Island Cultural and Revitalization Society, March 17, 2001, Sapelo Island, Georgia.

125. *Savannah Tribune,* September 17, 1892, 2–3; Grant, *The Way It Was in the South,* 174; Steven Hahn, *A Nation under Our Feet,* 414–15. See also Foner, *The Story of American Freedom; The New York Times,* November 6, 1890, p. 1, col. 1. Democrats were the majority in the 52nd Congress; however Alliance candidates made significant gains, with six elected from Georgia in 1890. Elected representatives included Alliance members Thomas Watson, Charles L. Moses, Thomas E. Winn, L. F. Livingstone, R. W. Everett, and Thomas E. Lawson.

126. Evans, ed., *Darien, Georgia, Newspaper Clippings, 1891–1903,* vol. 3, 16.

127. *Georgia Property Tax Digest,* 1890, Dandy Stewart, 271st Militia District.

CHAPTER 4: THE STATE OF FREEDOM IS THE STATE OF SELF RELIANCE

1. *Registers of Signatures of Depositors in Branches of the Freedmen's Savings and Trust Company, 1865–1874,* National Archives and Records Administration, Washington D.C., microfilm publication M816, Ancestry.com. *Freedmen's Bank Records, 1865–1871* [database online], Provo, Utah, Ancestry.com. *Georgia, Returns of Qualified Voters and Reconstruction Oath Books, 1867–1869,* Ancestry.com. *Georgia, Property Tax Digests, 1793–1892,* Ancestry.com.

2. Clifford Geertz, *Interpretation of Culture.*

3. Charles P. Loomis and J. Allan Beegle, *Rural Social Systems,* 293; Richard R. Myers and J. Beagle, "Delineation and Analysis of the Rural-Urban Fringe," 14–17; Sherwin H. Cooper, "The Rural Settlement of the Lower Savannah River Basin in Georgia," 116; see James Simms, *The First Colored Church,* for the religious origin of the rural-urban link in Chatham County.

4. Myers and Beagle, "Delineation and Analysis of the Rural-Urban Fringe," 14–17.

5. Wilson Moses, *Golden Age of Black Nationalism,* chapters 2–3; Martin Robinson Delany, *Condition, Elevation, Emigration and Destiny,* chapters 8–15; "Emigration to Liberia," *Savannah Morning News* (hereafter cited as *SMN*), January 8, 1878, p. 2, col. 3; Kermit Small, *Yearbook of Colored Savannah,* 15; Edwin S. Redkey, *Black Exodus,* 219, 225–26; James L. Conyers, "Black Nationalism and Pan-Africanism," 37–38. In 1854 at the Emigration Convention, the delegates issued a proclamation demanding that the U.S. government pay reparations for their suffering. Following the Civil War, Henry McNeal Turner asserted that the U.S. government owed Black America 40 billion dollars for their enslavement. See also James Theodore Holly, "A Vindication of the Capacity of the Negro Race."

6. The Jacksonian concept of the essential whiteness of the democratic man defined the way in which postbellum southern society constructed and reconstructed blackness and the heritage of slavery. See Grace Elizabeth Hale, *Making Whiteness,* 4; Winthrop Jordan, *The White Man's Burden;* George Frederickson, *The Black Image in the White Mind,* 71–96; Sean Wilentz, *The Rise of American Democracy;* Mia Bay, *The White Image,* 150–69. Michael D. Harris, *Colored Pictures,* examines how the visual arts have been marshaled in the creation and perpetuation of a racially divided America. According to Harris, early paintings and popular newspaper illustrations outline how physical and behavioral stereotypes were harnessed for the purpose of writing inferiority onto the black body. Patrick Rael, *Black Identity;* Jacqueline Bacon, *The Humblest May Stand Forth;* Moses, *Golden Age of Black Nationalism,* 17–29.

7. Donald L. Grant, *The Way It Was in the South,* 134; Edmund L. Drago, *Black Politicians,* Appendix B. See also Eric Foner, *Freedom's Lawmakers,* for detailed biographies of African Americans in politics at the local, state, and national levels.

8. Georgia Office of the Governor, Return of Qualified Voters under the Reconstruction Act, 1867, Georgia State Archives, Morrow, Georgia; 1880 Census, St. Mary's, Camden County, Georgia, roll 137; Georgia Property Tax Digests, 1871–1877, District 22, McIntosh County; Georgia Property Tax Digests, 1872–1876, Militia District 18, Camden County.

9. Grant, *The Way It Was in the South,* 134.

10. W. E. B. DuBois, *The Souls of White Folk;* Reiland Rabaka, "The Souls of White Folk: W. E. B. Du Bois's Critique."

11. Mark Weiner, *The Black Trials,* 152.

12. Kidada E. Williams, *They Left Great Marks,* 101–44.

13. See Melbourne S. Cummings, "The Rhetoric of Bishop Henry McNeal Turner"; Delany, *Condition, Elevation, Emigration, and Destiny.*

14. Liberian Exodus Association, *The Liberian Exodus,* 8–11 accessible at http://docsouth.unc.edu/church/liberian/menu.html; Carter G. Woodson, *The Mind of the Negro;* Redkey, *Black Exodus,* 226–27; James H. Cone, *A Black Theology of Liberation;* John Ernest, *Liberation Historiography,* 13.

15. Carter G. Woodson, *The Mind of the Negro,* 4–7; Cummings, "Rhetoric of Bishop Henry McNeal Turner," 462–63; Edwin S. Redkey, ed., *Respect Black.* See also Edwin S. Redkey, "Bishop Turner's African Dream"; E. Merton Coulter, "Henry M. Turner"; Andre E. Johnson, "Is the Negro Like Other People?" Redkey argues that middle-class African Americans generally opposed nationalism and emigration. See, Redkey, *Black Exodus,* 289.

16. Redkey, *Black Exodus,* 219, 225–26; "Emigration to Liberia," *SMN,* January 8, 1878, p. 2, col. 3; Small, *Yearbook of Colored Savannah,* 15.

17. Allen Batteau, "The Contradictions of Kinship," 28; Monroe Work, "The Negroes of Warsaw, Georgia"; Norman Crockett, *The Black Towns.*

18. Loomis and Beegle, *Rural Social Systems,* 293; Records of the U.S. Bureau of the Census, Manuscript Population Returns, Chatham County, 6th Militia District, 1880, Record Group 29, National Archives and Records Administration, Washington, D.C. See also Dianne Swann-Wright, *A Way Out of No Way.*

19. W. E. B. Du Bois, "The Negro Landholder of Georgia," 699; Enoch Banks, *The Economics of Land Tenure,* 62–75.

20. Du Bois, "The Negro Landholder," 699. The total value of real and personal property in 1870 was 425,013. John Blassingame, "Before the Ghetto," 469. The Ogeechee road was the main artery connecting these communities, with the exception of Dittmersville.

21. Chatham County Tax Digest, 1873–74, RCCSC: DB 4F, 89–90, William Morgin; DB 4H, 428, Robert Watts; DB 4B, 472, Diamond Williams.

22. *SMN,* February 24, 1874, p. 3, col. 4; *SMN,* September 27, 1881, p. 4, col. 2; RCCSC, Deed Book 6I 166, Sons and Daughters of Southville.

23. U.S. Bureau of the Census, Population Manuscript, Chatham County, Seventh Militia District, 1870.

24. William Morgin, Records of the Office of the Comptroller of Currency, Index to Deposit Ledgers, Savannah, Record Group 101, National Archives Building (NAB), Washington, D.C. In the bank ledger, Morgin lists his occupation as a carpenter. RCCSC, DB 4F, 89–90, William Morgin; U.S. Census Bureau, 1870, Seventh Militia District, #913, Record Group 29, NAB. Morgin's real estate was valued at five hundred dollars in 1870.

25. RCCSC, DB 4B, 472, Diamond Williams; U.S. Bureau of the Census, 1870, Seventh Militia District, #1005; RCCSC, DB 4H, 428, Robert Watts; U.S. Census Bureau, 1870, Seventh Militia District, #905, Record Group 29, NAB.

26. U.S. Bureau of the Census, Manuscript Population Returns, Chatham County, 6th Militia District, 1880, RG 29, NARA, Washington D.C. Gutman, *The Black Family in Slavery and Freedom,* 448; Arnold H. Taylor, *Travail and Triumph,* 161–67. Only fifteen of

the twenty-four landowners could be located in the census. The 13 percent of landowners who did not have nuclear households maintained augmented nuclear families, with either a grandchild or niece living within the household. For an examination of kinship solidarity among rural African Americans, see Crandall A. Shiflett, "The Household Composition of Rural Black Families: Louisa County, Virginia, 1880.".

27. Work, "Negroes of Warsaw, Georgia," 36.

28. U.S. Bureau of the Census, Population Manuscript Returns, Chatham County, 6th Militia District, #729, 1880; Manuscript Agricultural Returns, Chatham County, 6th Militia District, 20–21, 1880; "Burroughs Seeks Historic Status," *Georgia Gazette,* February 11, 1981, p. 1, col. 3.

29. Loomis and Beagle, *Rural Social Systems,* 293; Records of the Chatham County Probate Court, Index to General Wills, File No. 849, Samuel Black. Samuel Black received fifteen acres of land at Grove Point plantation in 1865 under Sherman's Field Order. Toby Roberts received ten acres at Grove Hill plantation. Black remained landless until 1890, when his real property was listed in the Chatham County Tax Digest as worth seventy-five dollars. Chatham County Tax Digest, 1880, 1890, Sam Black, Toby Roberts; U.S. Census Bureau, Population Manuscript Returns, 1870, Chatham County, Seventh Militia District, #1420, #1225.

30. Loomis and Beagle, *Rural Social Systems,* 293.

31. RCCSC, Deed Books, 4S, 318, January Stoney to Matilda Ferguson et al., 5E, 366.

32. James Grant to Adam Young, 5H, 474–75, Hobby and Dell to James Grant 5H 473–74. According to the latter deed, the land was located in the Ogeechee Ward, "four and one-half miles from Savannah."

33. James Grant to Adam Young, 5H, 474–75.

34. Deed Book 6L, 350, David Roulabit; Deed Book 6M, 18, David Roulabit to Elze Green.

35. Edgar A. Schuler, "Some Regional Variations in Levels and Standards of Living," 139. Schuler distinguishes between level of living and standard of living. Level of living refers to the "the content of goods and services utilized by a particular population . . . with regard to space, time, and income."

36. Eric Foner, *Nothing But Freedom,* 108–10; Thomas F. Armstrong, "From Task Labor to Free Labor," 443; Cooper, "Rural Settlement," 132; Jacqueline Jones, *The Dispossessed.*

37. RCCSC, Deed Books 4'O, 401–2, Caroline Ealy.

38. RCCSC, Deed Book 4Z, 454–55, Hannah Green; 5M, 104–5, Sarah Davis; Farris W. Cadle, *Georgia Land Surveying History and Law* (Athens: University of Georgia Press, 1991), 356; RCCSC, Deed Book 5M, 68–89, Kate Brown and children. Brown's property was "bounded on the west by Chevis Road . . . and on the south by lot number twenty one, sold to Robin Davis and Prince Wright, trustees for Sarah Davis."

39. Register of Signatures of Depositors, Freedmen's Savings and Trust, Savannah Branch, 1866–1874, M816, roll 8, #499, Records of the Office of the Comptroller of the Currency, Record Group 101, National Archives Building, Washington, D.C. (hereafter cited as RG 101). The signature books contain information on the account holders that includes age, color, occupation, birthplace, master's name, current residence, marital status, and family history (names and ages of children, parents' name, and siblings' name). For a cogent discussion of the role of Black women in community development, see Tera W. Hunter, *To Joy My Freedom;* Sharon Harley and Rosalyn Terborg Penn, eds., *The Afro-American Woman;*

Rosalyn Terborg Penn, *African American Women;* Evelyn Brooks Higginbotham, *Righteous Discontent;* Jacqueline Jones, *Labor of Love, Labor of Sorrow.*

40. *Savannah Tribune,* February 5, 1876, p. 2, col. 1–2; RCCSC, Deed Book 5D, 320, Mt. Zion CME; U.S. Bureau of the Census, Manuscript Population, Chatham County, Seventh Militia District, 1870, Record Group 29, National Archives, Washington, D.C. James Stewart's real estate was valued at one thousand dollars in 1870.

41. *Savannah Tribune,* February 5, 1876, p. 2, col. 1–2; RCCSC Deed Books 5H, 550, Colored Methodist Episcopal Church; 7N, 477, Mount Olive Baptist Church; 7Z, 58, New Ogeechee Baptist Church. The Great Ogeechee was one of several sister churches of the First Colored Baptist Church, established in 1788; RCCSC, DB 5A, 320, Mary Magdalene Society; *SMN,* October 7, 1873, p. 3, col. 1; *SMN,* July 22, 1881, p.4, col. 3; *Savannah Tribune,* May 27, 1876, p. 3, col. 2; Mechal Sobel, *Trabelin' On,* 319–23; Simms, *First Colored Church,* 59. African Americans in the Ogeechee district also attended St. Bartholomew's Episcopal Church, which was formed in 1832 to provide religious services for rice planters and slaves. *Georgia Gazette,* "Burroughs Seeks Historic Status," February 21, 1981.

42. Elsa Barkley Brown, "'Not Alone to Build This Pile of Bricks,' cited in Robin D. G. Kelley, "'We Are Not What We Seem,'" 80.

43. Register of Signatures of Depositors, Freedmen's Savings and Trust, Savannah Branch, M816, roll 8; Simms, *The First Colored Church,* 211–13.

44. Register of Signature of Depositors, Freedmen's Savings and Trust, Savannah Branch, M816, roll 8, Acct. 722, Union Benevolent Society of Second African Baptist Church; Acct. 745, John the Baptist Society; Acct. 757, Union Republican Association; Acct. 842, Mary Magdalene Society; Acct. 927, Sisters Prayer Meeting Benevolent Association; Acct. 930, Ladies Union Society; Acct. 984, Poor and Needy Institute; Simms, *First Colored Church,* 211–13, which lists additional benevolent societies organized and headed by women. Robert Perdue, *The Negro in Savannah,* 89; Brown, "'Not Alone to Build This Pile of Bricks,'" 80.

45. RCCSC, DB 7M, Sons and Daughters of Mount Sinai; DB 5N, 332, Sons and Daughters of Jerusalem; 6L, 333, Sons and Daughters of Zion.

46. Chatham County Tax Digest, 1876, Chatham County Courthouse, Savannah, Georgia; Loren Schweninger, *Black Property Owners in the South,* 149. Schweninger contends that the vast majority of the Lower South's landowners were ex-slaves. See also John Simpson, "A Reflection of Black Enterprise in the Old South," 35–38, which examines "virtually free slaves" in Savannah who participated in the free-market system.

47. John Blassingame, "Before the Ghetto," 469; W. E. B. DuBois, "The Negro Landholder of Georgia," 699.

48. U.S. Bureau of the Census, Manuscript Population, Savannah 1870; Register of Signatures of Depositors, Freedmen's Savings and Trust, Savannah, RG 101; John Blassingame, "A Social and Economic Profile of the Negro in Savannah," 94. A corollary body of records that sheds insight into the economic dimensions of the Reconstruction period is the Records of the Comptroller of the Currency. This record group contains the records of the Freedmen's Bank, which operated thirty-seven branches in seventeen states and the District of Columbia. Over its nine-year history the bank had more than seventy thousand depositors, and deposits totaling more than $57 million. The Savannah branch of the Freedmen's Bank operated until 1871. Bank branches collected an enormous amount of personal information

about each depositor and his or her family. The Registers of Signatures of Depositors include place of residence, occupation, spouse, siblings, and remarks, which often contain invaluable personal information.

49. RCCSC, Deed Book 4A, 475–78, William Sheftall, Susan Sheftall, and Eve Johnson. William Sheftall worked as porter. His real property was valued at three hundred dollars in 1880. U.S. Bureau of the Census, Population Manuscript, Chatham County, Seventh District, #612, 1880. *Savannah City Directory*, 1874–1875. William Sheftall also purchased land from Margaret Sheftall's estate. The surname Sheftall is associated with a prominent planter in Chatham County, Abraham Sheftall, who once owned Beverly-Berwick plantation. According to the deed, they were "heirs of Adam Sheftall, freedman." See also Robert Perdue, *Negro in Savannah*, 117.

50. RCCSC, DB 5M, 68–69, Kate Brown and children.

51. RCCSC, DB 6U, 329, Nancy Singleton's children. See Ira Berlin and Leslie Rowland, eds., *Families and Freedom*.

52. RCCSC, DB 5M, 356, Plenty Ancrum to Tenah Murray. All deeds must contain words of conveyance. Whether or not Tenah actually paid five dollars did not affect the validity of the deed.

53. *Compendium of the Tenth U.S. Census*, Washington, D.C., 1880, 385; W. E. B. DuBois, "The Negro Landholder of Georgia," 699; Banks, *The Economics of Land*, 62–75; John Blassingame, "Before the Ghetto," 468–69; *Compendium of the Tenth U.S. Census*, Washington, D.C., 1880, 385. In the state of Georgia, African Americans owned 1,251,714 acres of the 31,103,973 acres of improved land, or four percent of the farming area by 1900. Lowcountry African Americans owned the largest percentage of this land.

54. "Resolution Adopted at the Liberty County Meeting," *Savannah Tribune*, May 6, 1876, p. 3, col. 3. This resolution offering cheap land to the illiterate appeared for several weeks in the *Tribune*. Du Bois, "Negro Landholder of Georgia."

55. "Burroughs Seeks Historic Status," *Georgia Gazette*, February 11, 1981, p. 1, col. 3; Personal Scrapbook of Mrs. Gertrude Green, Chatham County, Georgia, in possesion of the author; Crockett, *Black Towns*, 15; Harold M. Rose, "The All Negro Town," 362–64; Booker T. Washington, "Town Owned by Negroes," *World's Work*, 14 (July 1907): 9125–134. Other, more prominent, incorporated black towns included Mound Bayou, Mississippi; Nicodemus, Kansas; Boley, Oklahoma; and Clearview, Oklahoma.

56. Elizabeth R. Bethel, *Promiseland;* U.S. Bureau of the Census, Manuscript Population, Chatham County, 6th Militia District, 1880, #941 and #688; RCCSC, Deed Books 6T, 11, Apollo Blount to Elizabeth Agnew; 7Q, 149, Frank Gladden to C. K. Nelson, Bishop.

57. The habendum clause, which describes the boundaries of the property, indicates that at least three African Americans whose names do not appear in the grantor index for the Burroughs family purchased land in the settlement. Among them were Sukey Boles, wife of Thomas Boles, whose name is listed in the grantor index; however, the deed is between Nina Burroughs and Rebecca Tillman. Tillman lived in very close proximity to Boles. Also not listed in the index but with lands that are mentioned as boundaries are James Washington and Jake Grant. All were cross-referenced with the 1880 population census.

58. RCCSC, DB 6U, 329, Nancy Singleton's children; 6U, 372–73, Hester Shepperd; DB, 6U 373, Abraham Williams; DB 6Z, 57–58, J.C. Legree et al.; DB 7R, 329, Jane Solomon;

DB 7R, 32–33, Rebecca Tillman; DB 9A, 204, Hercules Barnard; DB 8R, 400, Jacob Shellman; DB 8N, 125, Priscilla Robinson; DB 9I, 245, Betsey Field; DB 9G, 370, Mollie Baker; DB 9'O, 277, Comfort Blake; DB 9I, 246, Sambo Crawford; DB 9'O, 157, Celia Prior.

59. DB 9'O, 277, Comfort Blake.

60. Ibid.

61. DB 6Z, 57–58, J. C. Legree et al. The latter deed specifies "heirs of Sallie Legree," which indicates that Sallie Legree or her husband, Amos, who may have predeceased her, had worked as agricultural laborers and were both sixty-five years of age in 1880. U.S. Bureau of the Census, Manuscript Population Returns, Chatham County, 6th Militia District, 1880, #723, #735, #897, #920, #923, #930.

62. Interview with Gertrude Green, March 17, 1993, Chatham County, Georgia.

63. Personal scrapbook of Gertrude Green, "Burroughs School," in possession of the author; Sydney Nathans, "Fortress Without Walls," 58–60; John Dittmer, *Black Georgia,* 51.

64. "Resolution of Condolence," *Savannah Tribune,* May 14, 1892, p. 3, col. 2. At Howard's funeral, members of the Mt. Olive church "turned out in full regalia." "Tenth Session," *Savannah Tribune,* August 27, 1892, p. 3, col. 2. The *Tribune* also reported the anniversary celebration of the New Ogeechee Baptist Church at Burroughs station. Deacons of churches in Savannah and Chatham County were invited to bring two guests.

65. Interview with Peter Warner, March 17, 1993, Chatham County, Georgia. (All interviews were conducted by the author unless otherwise stated, with tapes of same in possession of the author.) Peter Warner has been a resident of Grove Point Road for over a century. His grandfather, Winter Warner, signed labor contracts at Vallambrosia in 1866. His knowledge about the previous mayor of Burroughs and about Masonic secret societies is corroborated by London Lowman, a third-generation resident of the Ogeechee Neck whose grandfather received ten acres under Sherman's Field Order No. 15. Interview directed with the assistance of W. W. Law, local historian and former director of the Beach African American Cultural Center. "L.U.P.A.," *Savannah Tribune,* June 23, 1892, p. 3, col. 3; Perdue, *Negro in Savannah,* 113; "Ogeechee Notes," *Savannah Tribune,* March 19, 1892, p. 3, col. 2; Work, "Negroes of Warsaw, Georgia," 33. During the oyster season, 65.8 percent of African American women in the county migrated to the oyster factories of Thunderbolt for employment. See also, "Honored: Peter Warner, Jr.," *Georgia Gazette,* June 24, 1981, p. 6, col. 2.

66. RCCSC, DB 5D, 70, Mt. Zion CME; RCCPC, Estate of Mars Ward, File 673. James Stewart's real estate was valued at one thousand dollars in 1870. U.S. Bureau of the Census, Manuscript Population, Chatham County, Seventh Militia District, 1870, RG 29, NAB.

67. RCCSC DB 5A, 320; 5N, 332; 6L, 166, 333; 7M, 167; 7'O, 23; 10F, 97; Chatham County Tax Digest, 1910; W. E. B. Du Bois, *The Negro American Family,* chapter 3.

68. *Savannah Tribune,* May 27, 1876, p. 3, col. 2.

69. See William H. Grimshaw, *Official History of Freemansonry,* and H. R. Butler, *The History of Freemasonry* for the socioeconomic makeup of the Masons.

70. *SMN,* October 7, 1873, p. 3, col. 1; *SMN,* July 22, 1881, p. 4, col. 3; *Savannah Tribune,* May 27, 1876, p. 3, col. 2. The Poor and Needy Institute, which maintained an account with the Freedmen's Bureau, contributed two and twenty dollars, respectively, to yellow fever relief in Shreveport, Louisiana, and Memphis, Tennessee. Poor and Needy Institute, Priscilla Shigg, Treasurer, Ledger #984, Savannah, Records of the Freedmen's Savings Bank, RG 101, NAB. The press identifies churches and mutual associations as "colored." Way's Station across the

Ogeechee River was the area most frequented for summer picnics by both rural and urban African Americans. See *SMN,* July 19, 1881, p. 4, col.1.

71. Georgia Society of Colonial Dames of America, *Georgia,* 213.

72. Walter Richard Hamlin, "Rural Black Kinship"; Kay Young Day, "Kinship in a Changing Economy," 15.

73. Bethel, *Promiseland,* 107.

74. RCCSC Deed Book 8R, 125–26, 186, Emanuel Heidt to Crispy Arkwright, Martha Crawford, and Pinkey Sheppard. Martha Crawford was the wife of Sambo Crawford whose name is listed in the grantor index but is not a party to the transaction. Pinkey Sheppard's deed states, "deed made in accordance with the will of Heidt."

75. DB 8R, 400, Jacob Shellman.

76. RCCSC, DB 9Q, 137, Richard Crawford to Fountain, H. A. According to the deed, John Burroughs served as witness. In 1910 there were only three white residents in Burroughs. U.S. Bureau of the Census, Manuscript Population, Chatham County, 6th Militia District, 1910. John Dittmer, *Black Georgia in the Progressive Era,* 26.

77. Cooper, "Rural Settlement," 119.

78. Ibid.

79. U.S. Bureau of the Census, Manuscript Population, 6th Militia District, Chatham County, 1910, 1920.

80. Eric Foner, *Reconstruction,* 109.

81. Monroe Work, *The Negro Yearbook,* 165

82. Crockett, *Black Towns,* 15; interview with W. W. Law, March 17, 1993; Carter G. Woodson, *The Rural Negro,* 120.

83. Interview with Peter Warner, March 17, 1993.

84. Manuscript Population Returns, 6th Militia District, Chatham County, Georgia, 1910, 1920.

85. RCCSC, DB 13A, 124–25, Flander Grant; 13N, 180, John Shellman; DB 13Z, 298, Barney Preston.

86. RCCSC, DB 14K, 222, Clara and Sam Lowman to Richard Lachison; Adelbert H. Jenkins, *The Psychology of Afro-Americans,* 2–20.

87. Interview with Gertrude Green, March 17, 1993.

88. Dittmer, *Black Georgia,* 25, 186–87.

89. Ibid; W. E. B. Du Bois, *The Souls of Black Folk,* chapter four.

90. Gertrude Green described the Burroughs community as an "African village" because it remained cohesive and tight-knit. Interview with Gertrude Green, March 17, 1993.

91. U.S. Population Census, 1900.

92. W. E. B. Du Bois, *Souls of Black Folk;* Manning Marable, *How Capitalism Underdeveloped Black America.*

93. W. E. B. Du Bois, "Georgia Negroes and Their Fifty Millions of Savings," 11552; Du Bois, "Negro Landholder of Georgia," 735.

94. Monroe Work, "Principal Negro Towns and Settlements," 165; Schweninger, *Black Property Owners in the South,* 165, lists Burroughs with several other farming communities. See also Woodson, *Rural Negro,* 119, which lists Burroughs and four other black towns in Georgia.

95. "Burroughs Charter of Incorporation," 1898. The town council met for meetings at

the mayor's place. The government of Burroughs consisted of Mayor J. C. Legree, described as heavy and tall; Judge C. B. Sheppard, a full and heavy man; and Sheriff Eddie Gardner, "grandson of Steven Gardner." All of the men were dark in complexion. Interview with Peter Warner, March 3, 1993, Chatham County, Georgia. The adjudication of the law reinforced the political, artistic, and spiritual values of Burroughs by reinforcing manhood, freedom, and self-reliance. According to the town charter, persons found guilty of misdemeanors were required to perform road work. Conversely, capital crimes required a trip to the courthouse in Savannah.

96. Interview with Peter Warner, March 3, 1993. Early surveys of African Americans in Georgia provide a useful comparison with the achievements of the town of Burroughs. See T. J. Woofter, "The Negroes of Athens Georgia"; W.B. Hill, "Rural Survey of Clarke County, Georgia"; Ruth Reed, "The Negro Women of Gainsville, Georgia."

97. Rayford Logan, *The Negro in American Life and Thought.*

98. Jones, *Labor of Love, Labor of Sorrow,* 149.

99. For a comparison between northern cities the Georgia lowcountry see, Clyde Vernon Kiser, *Sea Island to City.*

CONCLUSION

1. Françoise Charras, "Robert Hayden's and Kamau Brathwaite's Poetic Renderings," 68.
2. Dylan Penningroth, "Slavery, Freedom, and Social Claims."
3. Moses, *The Golden Age of Black Nationalism,* 14.
4. Clifford Geertz, *Interpretation of Culture.*
5. "Burroughs Charter of Incorporation," 1898.

Bibliography

MANUSCRIPTS

Butler Family Papers, Historical Society of Pennsylvania, Philadelphia, Pennsylvania.

Margaret Davis Cate Collection, Hargrett Rare Book and Manuscript Library. University of Georgia Libraries. Athens, Georgia.

Account Book of Stephen Habersham, Grove Plantation Near Savannah, 1858. Georgia Historical Society. Savannah, Georgia.

Manigault Family Papers, Southern Historical Collection, Wilson Library, University of North Carolina Chapel Hill

Charles L. Matthews Family Papers, Louisiana and Lower Mississippi Valley Collections; Special Collections Louisiana State University Libraries, Baton Rouge, Louisiana.

Carl Schurz Papers, Library of Congress, Washington, D.C.

Louisiana Sugar and Rice Trade Collection, Louisiana and Lower Mississippi Valley Collections; Special Collections, Louisiana State University Libraries, Baton Rouge, Louisiana

William T. Sherman Papers, Library of Congress, Washington, D.C.

William Wiseham Paine Papers, Georgia Historical Society, Savannah, Georgia.

GOVERNMENT RECORDS AND DOCUMENTS

Chatham Country Tax Digest, 1870–1920, Chatham County, Georgia.

Cong. Globe, 42nd Congress, 1st Sess.

Georgia Department of Archives and History, Atlanta, Georgia.

Georgia Property Tax Digest, Atlanta, Georgia.

House Executive Documents, 40th Cong., 3rd Sess.

Record Group 101, Records of the Comptroller of Currency, Registers of Signatures of Depositors in Branches of the Freedmen's Savings and Trust, National Archives and Records Administration, Washington, D.C.

Record Group 105, Records of the Bureau of Refugees, Freedmen, and Abandoned Lands, National Archives and Records Administration, Washington, D.C.

Record Group 21, Records of the District Courts of the United States, National Archives and Records Administration, Washington, D.C.

Record Group 217, Records of the Accounting Officers of the Department of the Treasury, Southern Claims Commission Approved Claims, 1871–1880: Georgia, National Archives and Records Administration, Washington, D.C.

Record Group 29, Records of the United States Bureau of the Census, Manuscript Population, National Archives and Records Administration, Washington, D.C.

Record Group 36, Records of the Bureau of Customs, National Archives and Records Administration, Washington, D.C.

Records of the Chatham County Probate Court, Chatham County Courthouse, Savannah, Georgia.

Records of the Chatham County Superior Court, Chatham County, Georgia.

Records of the Glynn County Courthouse, Glenn County, Georgia

Report of the Joint Select Committee on the Condition of Affairs in the Late Insurrectionary States, Georgia, February 19, 1872.

Savannah City Directory, 1870–1871.

Senate Documents, 39th Cong. 2nd Sess.

Senate Executive Documents, 35th Congress, 2nd Session, 1858–59, vol., 7, Document No. 8, "Message of the President of the U.S. in answer to a resolution of the Senate relative to the landing of the barque Wanderer on the coast of Georgia with a cargo of Africans

United States Bureau of the Census, Agricultural Schedules, National Archives and Records Administration, Washington, D.C.

Works Progress Administration, *Annals of Savannah 1850–1937: A Digest and Index of the Newspaper Record of Events and Opinions in Eighty-Seven Volumes* (Savannah, 1937).

PUBLISHED MATERIALS

Adekunle, Julius O., and Hettie V. Williams, eds. *Converging Identities: Blackness in the Modern African Diaspora.* Durham, N.C.: Carolina Academic Press, 2013.

Alford, Terry. *Prince Among Slaves.* New York: Harcourt, Brace, Jovanovich, 1977.

Ames, William Dallam, ed. *The Autobiography of Joseph LeCounte.* New York: D. Appleton, 1903.

Andrews, Eliza F. *The War-Time Journal of a Georgia Girl.* New York: D. Appleton and Company, 1908.

Andrews, William F. *To Tell a Free Story: The First Century of Afro-American Autobiography, 1760–1865.* Urbana: University of Illinois Press, 1986.

Aptheker, Herbert. *American Negro Slave Revolts.* New York: International Publishers, 1943.

Armstrong, Thomas F. "From Task Labor to Free Labor: The Transition along Georgia's Rice Coast, 1820–1880." *Georgia Historical Quarterly* 64, no. 4 (1980): 432–47.

Astley, Thomas. *Collection of Voyages and Travels.* London: T. Astley, 1745.

Austin, Allen D. *African Muslims in Antebellum America.* New York: Routledge, 1997.

Bacon, Jacqueline. *The Humblest May Stand Forth: Rhetoric, Empowerment, and Abolition.* Columbia: University of South Carolina Press, 2002.

Bailey, Cornelia Walker. *God, Dr. Buzzard, and the Bolito Man: A Saltwater Geechee Talks about Life on Sapelo Island.* New York: Doubleday, 2000.

Balcomb, Anthony. "The Power of Narrative: Constituting Reality Through Storytelling." *Memory, Orality, and the Past,* Philippe Denis, ed. 49–53. Pietermaritzburg, South Africa: Cluster Publications, 2000.

Banks, Enoch M. *The Economics of Land Tenure in Georgia.* New York: Columbia University Press, 1905.

Barnes, Elinor, and James A. Barnes, eds. *Naval Surgeon: Blockading the South, 1862–1866: The Diary of Samuel Pellman Boyer.* Bloomington: Indiana University Press, 1963.

Batteau, Allen. "The Contradictions of Kinship." In *Holding on to the Land and the Lord: Kinship, Ritual, Tenure, and Social Policy in the Rural South,* ed. Robert Hall and Carol Stack. Athens: University of Georgia Press, 1982.

Bay, Mia. *The White Image in the Black Mind: African-American Ideas about White People, 1830–1925.* New York: Oxford University Press, 2000.

Bean, Christopher R. "The Freedmen's Bureau and Logistical Problems in Texas, 1865–1868." *Military History of the West* 39 (2009), 1–20.

Bell, Howard H., ed. *Black Separation and the Caribbean.* Ann Arbor: University of Michigan Press, 1970.

Bell, Karen B. "'The Ogeechee Troubles': Federal Land Restoration and the 'Lived Realities' of Temporary Proprietors, 1865–1868." *Georgia Historical Quarterly* 85, no. 3 (2001): 375–97.

Bell, Karen Cook, and Peter J. Breaux. "Robert Smalls and the Politics of Race and Freedom in Low Country South Carolina, 1865–1890." In *Before Obama: A Reappraisal of Black Reconstruction Era Politicians,* ed. Matthew Lynch. New York: Praeger, 2012.

Bell, Malcolm. *Major Butler's Legacy: Five Generations of a Slave Holding Family.* Athens: University of Georgia Press, 1987.

Belz, Herman. *A New Birth of Freedom: The Republican Party and Freemen's Rights, 1861–1866.* Westport, Conn.: Greenwood Press, 1976.

Bentley, George. *A History of the Freedmen's Bureau.* Philadelphia: University of Pennsylvania, 1955.

Berlin, Ira. "Time, Space, and the Evolution of the Afro-American Society on British Mainland North America." *American Historical Review* 85 (1980): 47–78.

Berlin, Ira, et al., eds. *Freedom: A Documentary History of Emancipation, 1861–1867,* Series 1, vol. 1: *The Destruction of Slavery.* New York, Cambridge University Press, 1985.

Berlin, Ira, et al., eds. *Freedom: A Documentary History of Emancipation, 1861–1867,* Series 1, vol. 3: *The Wartime Genesis of Free Labor: The Lower South.* New York: Cambridge University Press, 1991.

Berlin, Ira, et al., eds. *Freedom: A Documentary History of Emancipation, 1861–1867,* Series 2: *The Black Military Experience.* New York: Cambridge University Press, 1982.

Berlin, Ira, Marc Favreau, and Steven Miller, eds. *Remembering Slavery: African Americans Talk about Their Personal Experiences of Slavery and Emancipation.* New York: New Press, 1998.

Berlin, Ira, Joseph P. Reidy, and Leslie Rowland. *Freedom's Soldiers: The Black Military Experience in the Civil War.* New York: Cambridge University Press, 1988.

Berlin, Ira, and Leslie Rowland, eds. *Families and Freedom: A Documentary History of African American Kinship in the Civil War Era.* New York: Cambridge University Press, 1997.

Berry, Daina Ramey. *"Swing the Sickle for the Harvest Is Ripe": Gender and Slavery in Antebellum Georgia.* Urbana: University of Illinois Press, 2010.

Berry, Mary Frances. *Black Resistance, White Law: A History of Constitutional Racism.* New York: Penguin, 1995.

———. *My Face Is Black Is True: Callie House and the Struggle for Ex-Slave Reparations.* New York: Vintage, 2005.

Berry, Stephen. "More Alluring at a Distance: Absentee Patriarchy and the Thomas Butler King Family." *Georgia Historical Quarterly* 81, no. 4 (1997): 863–96.

Bethel, Elizabeth R. *Promiseland: A Century of Life in a Negro Community.* Philadelphia: Temple University Press, 1982.

Birt, Robert, ed. *The Quest for Community and Identity: Critical Essays in Africana Social Philosophy.* Lanham, Md: Rowman and Littlefield, 2002.

Blassingame, John. "Before the Ghetto: The Making of the Black Community in Savannah, Georgia, 1865–1880." *Journal of Social History* 64 (1973).

———. *The Slave Community: Plantation Life in the Antebellum South.* New York: Oxford University Press, 1972.

———, ed. *Slave Testimony: Two Centuries of Letters, Speeches, Interviews, and Autobiographies.* Baton Rouge: Louisiana State University Press, 1977.

———. "A Social and Economic Profile of the Negro in Savannah, 1865–1880." Unpublished paper cited in Robert Perdue, *The Negro in Savannah, 1865–1900* (New York: Exposition Press, 1973).

Blesser, Carol, ed. *In Joy and Sorrow: Women, Family, and Marriage in the Victorian South, 1830–1900.* New York: Oxford University Press, 1991.

Botkin, Benjamin, ed. *Lay My Burden Down: A Folk History of Slavery.* Chicago: University of Illinois Press, 1945.

Brady, Lisa M. *War upon the Land: Military Strategy and the Transformation of Southern Landscapes during the American Civil War.* Athens: University of Georgia Press, 2012.

Bragg, Lillian C., and Margaret Godley. *Stories of Old Savannah.* n.p., 1948.

Brent, Linda. *Incidents in the Life of a Slave Girl.* New York: Harcourt, Brace, 1973.

Brown, Elsa Barkley. "'Not Alone to Build This Pile of Bricks': Institution Building and Community in Richmond, Virginia." Paper presented at the conference The Age of Booker T. Washington, at University of Maryland, College Park.

Bullard, Mary R. *Robert Stafford of Cumberland Island: Growth of a Planter.* Athens: University of Georgia Press, 1995.

Burks, Richard V. "A Conception of Ideology for Historians." *Journal of the History of Ideas* 10 (1949): 183–98.

Butler, H. R. *The History of Freemasonry among Colored Men in Georgia.* Atlanta, n.p., 1911.

Cadle, Farris W. *Georgia Land Surveying History and Law.* Athens: University of Georgia Press, 1991.

Camp, Stephanie M. H. *Closer to Freedom: Enslaved Women and Everyday Resistance in the Plantation South.* Chapel Hill: University of North Carolina Press, 2004.

———. "The Pleasures of Resistance: Enslaved Women and Body Politics in the Plantation South, 1830–1861." *Journal of Southern History* 68, no. 3 (2002): 533–72.

Carney, Judith. *Black Rice: The African Origins of Rice Cultivation in the Americas.* Cambridge, Mass.: Harvard University Press, 2001.

Carney, Judith, and R. N. Rosomoff. *In the Shadow of Slavery: Africa's Botanical Legacy in the Atlantic World.* Berkeley: University of California Press, 2009.

Cassidy, Frederic G. "The Place of Gullah." *American Speech* 55, no. 1 (1980): 3–33.

Chambliss, Rollin. "What Negro Newspapers of Georgia Say about Some Social Problems, 1933." *Bulletin of the University of Georgia, Phelps-Stokes Fellowship Studies,* no. 13 (1934).

Charras, Françoise. "Robert Hayden's and Kamau Brathwaite's Poetic Renderings of the Middle Passage in Comparative Perspective." In *Black Imagination and the Middle Passage,* ed. Maria Diedrich, Henry Louis Gates Jr., and Carl Pederson. New York: Oxford University Press, 1999.

Christensen, Karen, and David Levinson, eds. *Encyclopedia of Community*. Thousand Oaks, Calif.: Sage, 2003.

Cimbala, Paul A. "The Freedmen's Bureau, the Freedmen, and Sherman's Grant in Reconstruction Georgia, 1865–1867." *Journal of Social History* 15 (1989): 597–632.

Cimbala, Paul A. "On the Front Line of Freedom: Freedmen's Bureau Officers and Agents in Reconstruction Georgia, 1865–1868." *Georgia Historical Quarterly* 76 (1992): 577–611.

Cimbala, Paul A. *Under the Guardianship of the Nation: The Freedmen's Bureau and the Reconstruction of Georgia, 1865–1870*. Athens: University of Georgia Press, 1997.

Cimbala, Paul A., and Randall Miller. *The Freedmen's Bureau and Reconstruction: Reconsiderations*. New York: Fordham University Press, 1999.

Clinton, Catherine. "'Southern Dishonor': Flesh, Blood, Race, and Bondage." Pp. 52–68 in *In Joy and Sorrow: Women, Family, and Marriage in the Victorian South, 1830–1900*, ed. Carol Blesser. New York: Oxford University Press, 1991.

Coclanis, Peter A., and Stuart Burchey, eds. *Ideas, Ideologies, and Social Movements: The U.S. Experience since 1800*. Columbia: University of South Carolina Press, 1999.

Cohen, William. *At Freedom's Edge: Black Mobility and the Southern White Quest for Racial Control, 1861–1915*. Baton Rouge: Louisiana State University Press, 1991.

Colburn, Forrest D. *Everyday Forms of Resistance*. New York: M.E. Sharpe, 1989.

Coleman, Kenneth. *Colonial Georgia: A History*. New York: Charles Scribner's Son, 1976.

———. *A History of Georgia*. Athens: University of Georgia Press, 1991.

Coleman, Will. "'Coming through 'Ligion': Metaphor in Non-Christian and Christian Experiences with the Spirit(s) in African American Slave Narratives." Pp. 47–71 in *Cut Loose Your Stammering Tongue: Black Theology in the Slave Narratives*, ed. Dwight N. Hopkins and George C. L. Cummings. New York: Orbis, 1991.

Cone, James H. *A Black Theology of Liberation*. Maryknoll, N.Y.: Orbis Books, 2010.

Connerton, Paul. *How Societies Remember*. New York: Cambridge University Press, 1989.

Conrad, Georgia Bryan. *Reminiscences of a Southern Woman*. Hampton, Va.: Hampton Institute Press, 1901.

Conyers, James L. "Black Nationalism and Pan-Africanism." In *African American Sociology*, ed. James L. Conyers and Alua P. Barnett. Chicago: Nelson-Hall, 1999.

Conyers, James L., and Alua P. Barnett, eds. *African American Sociology*. Chicago, Nelson-Hall, 1999.

Cooper, Sherwin H. "The Rural Settlement of the Lower Savannah River Basin in Georgia." Ph.D. diss., University of Michigan, 1959.

Cornish, Dudley T. *The Sable Arm: Negro Troops in the Union Army, 1861–1865*. New York, W.W. Norton, 1966.

Coulter, E. Merton. "Henry M. Turner: Georgia Preacher, Politician during the Reconstruction Era." *Georgia Historical Quarterly* 48, no. 4 (1964): 371–410.

Cousins, Phillis M., "A History of the 33rd United States Colored Troops." M.A. thesis, Howard University, 1961.

Cox, Jacob D. *March to the Sea*. New York: C. Scribner's Sons, 1882.

Cox, John, and Lawanda Cox. "General O. O. Howard and the Misrepresented Bureau." *Journal of Southern History* 19 (1953): 427–56.

Creel, Margaret Washington. *"A Peculiar People": Slave Religion and Community-Culture among the Gullahs*. New York: New York University Press, 1988.

Crockett, Norman L. *The Black Towns*. Lawrence, Kansas: Regents University Press, 1979.

Croft, Wayne E. "'You Jes' Wait a Little': A Comparison of the Motif of Hope in African American Preaching during the Slave and Post-Civil War Periods." Ph.D. diss., Drew University, 2009.

Cummings, Melbourne S. "The Rhetoric of Bishop Henry McNeal Turner." *Journal of Black Studies* 12, no. 4 (1982): 457–67.

Curtin, Philip D. ed., *Africa Remembered: Narratives by West Africans from the Era of the Slave Trade.* Madison: University of Wisconsin Press, 1967.

———. *The Atlantic Slave Trade: A Census.* Madison: University of Wisconsin Press, 1969.

———. *Economic Change in Pre-Colonial Africa: Senegambia in the Era of the Slave Trade.* Madison: University of Wisconsin Press, 1975.

Davis, Patricia G. "Ripping the Veil: Collective Memory and Black Southern Identity." Ph.D. diss., University of California, San Diego, 2009.

Day, Kay Young. "Kinship in a Changing Economy." In *Holding on to the Land and the Lord: Kinship, Ritual, Tenure, and Social Policy in the Rural South,* ed. Robert Hall and Carol Stack. Athens: University of Georgia Press, 1982.

DeGraft-Hanson, Kwesi. "Unearthing the Weeping Time: Savannah's Ten Broeck Race Course and 1859 Slave Sale." *Southern Spaces,* February 18, 2010. http://southernspaces.org/2010/unearthing-weeping-time-savannahs-ten-broeck-race-course-and-1859-slave-sale.

Delany, Martin Robinson. *The Condition, Elevation, Emigration, and Destiny of the Colored People of the United States.* Philadelphia: n.p., 1852.

Dennett, John R. *The South As It Is, 1865–1866.* Tuscaloosa, Alabama: University of Alabama Press, 2010.

Diedrich, Maria, Henry Louis Gates Jr., and Carl Pederson, eds. *Black Imagination and the Middle Passage.* New York: Oxford University Press, 1999.

Dittmer, John. *Black Georgia in the Progressive Era, 1900–1920.* Urbana: University of Illinois Press, 1979.

Dodson, W. C., ed. *Campaigns of Wheeler and His Cavalry.* Atlanta: Hudgins Publising Company, 1899.

Donnan, Elizabeth ed. *Documents Illustrative of the History of the Slave Trade,* vol. 4. New York: Octagon, 1935.

Drago, Edmund L. *Black Politicians and Reconstruction in Georgia: A Splendid Failure.* Athens: University of Georgia Press, 1986.

———. "Militancy and Black Women in Reconstruction Georgia." *Journal of American Culture* 1 (1978): 838–44.

DuBois, Lauren, and Julius Scott. *Origins of the Black Atlantic: Rewriting Histories.* New York: Routledge, 2009.

Du Bois, W. E. B. *Black Reconstruction in America, 1860–1880.* New Brunswick, New Jersey: Transaction Publshers, 2012.

———."Georgia Negroes and Their Fifty Millions of Savings." *The World's Work* 18 (1909): 11550–554.

———. *The Negro American Family.* Atlanta University, no, 13, 1907.

———. "The Negro Landholder of Georgia." *U.S. Department of Labor Bulletin,* no. 35, July 1901.

———. *The Souls of Black Folk.* New York, Bantam, 1989.

———. "The Souls of White Folk" in DuBois, *Darkwater: Voices from Within the Veil*. New York: Schocken Books, 1969.

———. *The Suppression of the African Slave Trade to the United States of America, 1638–1870*. New York: Russell and Russell, 1896; repr. New York: Russell and Russell, 1965.

Duncan, Russell. *Entrepreneur for Equality: Governor Rufus Bullock, Commerce, and Race in Post Civil War Georgia*. Athens: University of Georgia Press, 1991.

———. *Freedom's Shore: Tunis Campbell and the Georgia Freedmen*. Athens: University of Georgia Press, 1986.

Dusinberre, William. *Them Dark Days: Slavery in the American Rice Swamp*. New York: Oxford University Press, 1996.

Ehrenhard, John E., and Mary R. Bullard. *Stafford Plantation: Cumberland Island National Seashore: Archeological Investigations of a Slave Cabin*. Tallahassee, Fla.: Southeast Archeological Center, National Park Service, 1981.

Ernest, John. *Liberation Historiography: African American Writers and the Challenge of History*, 1794–1861. Chapel Hill: University of North Carolina Press, 2004.

Evans, Tad. *Darien, Georgia, Newspaper Clippings*, vol. 1: *1818–1878*, vol. 2: *1879–1890*, and vol. 3: *1891–1903*. Savannah, Georgia, 2001–2002.

Farmer, Mary J. "'Because They Are Women': Gender and the Virginia Freedmen's Bureau's 'War on Dependency.'" In *The Freedmen's Bureau and Reconstruction: Reconsiderations*, ed. Paul A. Cimbala and Randall M. Miller. New York: Fordham University Press, 1999.

Farmer-Kaiser, Mary. *Freedwomen and the Freedmen's Bureau: Race, Gender, and Public Policy in the Age of Emancipation*. New York: Fordham University Press, 2010.

Faulkner, Carol. *Women's Radical Reconstruction: The Freedmen's Aid Movement*. Philadelphia: University of Pennsylvania Press, 2007.

Ferguson, Leland. *Uncommon Ground: Archaeology and Early African America, 1650–1800*. Washington, D.C.: Smithsonian Institution, 1992.

Fields, Barbara Jeanne. *Slavery and Freedom on the Middle Ground: Maryland during the Nineteenth Century*. New Haven, Conn.: Yale University Press, 1986.

Finkleman, Paul. *Law of Freedom and Bondage: A Casebook*. New York: Oceana, 1986.

Fisk University. *Unwritten History of Slavery*. Nashville, Tenn.: Fisk Univeristy, 1945.

Flanders, Ralph. *Plantation Slavery in Georgia*. Chapel Hill: University of North Carolina, 1933.

Foner, Eric. *Freedom's Lawmakers: A Directory of Black Officeholders during Reconstruction*. Baton Rouge: Louisiana State University Press, 1996.

———. *Nothing but Freedom: Emancipation and Its Legacy*. Baton Rouge: Louisiana State University Press, 1983.

———. *Politics and Ideology in the Age of the Civil War*. New York: Oxford University Press, 1980.

———. *Reconstruction: America's Unfinished Revolution, 1863–1877*. New York: Harper and Row, 1988.

———. *The Story of American Freedom*. New York: W.W. Norton, 1998.

Foner, Philip S., and Randolph Lewis. *Black Workers: A Documentary History from Colonial Times to the Present*. Philadelphia: Temple University Press, 1989.

Forbes, Ella. *African American Women during the Civil War*. New York: Garland, 1998.

Foster, Frances Smith. *Witnessing Slavery: The Development of Antebellum Slave Narratives.* Madison: University of Wisconsin Press, 1994.

Frankel, Noralee. *Freedom's Women: Black Women and Families in Civil War Era Mississippi.* Bloomington: University of Illinois Press, 1999.

Franklin, John Hope. *Reconstruction: After the Civil War.* Chicago: University of Chicago Press, 1961.

Franklin, John Hope, and Loren Schweninger. *Runaway Slaves: Rebels on the Plantation.* New York: Oxford University Press, 1999.

Frederickson, George. *The Black Image in the White Mind.* New York: Harper and Row, 1971.

Frey, Sylvia R., and Betty Wood. Come Shouting to Zion. Chapel Hill: University of North Carolina Press, 1998.

Geertz, Clifford. *Interpretation of Cultures.* London: Hutchinson Press, 1975.

Georgia General Assembly. *Committee to Investigate the Official Conduct of Rufus Bullock Late Governor of Georgia.* Atlanta, 1872.

Georgia Society of Colonial Dames of America. *Georgia: A Pageant of Years.* Richmond, Va.: Garret and Massie, 1933.

Georgia Writers' Project. *Drums and Shadows: Survival Stories among the Georgia Coastal Negroes.* 1940; repr., Athens: University of Georgia Press, 1940.

Gibson, James R., ed. *European Settlement and Development in North America: Essays on Geographical Change in Honour and Memory of Andrew Hill Clark.* Toronto: University of Toronto Press, 1978.

Glymph, Thavolia. *Out of the House of Bondage: The Transformation of the Plantation Household.* New York: Cambridge University Press, 2008.

Glynn, Evelyn N. *Unequal Freedom: How Race and Gender Shaped American Citizenship and Labor.* Cambridge, Mass.: Harvard University Press, 2002.

Gomez, Michael. *Black Crescent: The Experience and Legacy of African Muslims in the Americas.* New York: Cambridge University Press, 2005.

———. *Exchanging Our Country Marks: The Transition of African Identities in the Colonial and Antebellum South.* Chapel Hill: University of North Carolina Press, 1998.

———. "Muslims in Early America." *The Journal of Southern History* 40, no. 4 (1994): 671–710.

Green, Mae Ruth. Sapelo Island Families. N.p., n.d. Georgia Department of Archives and History, Atlanta, Georgia.

Greenberg, Joseph H. "The Decipherment of the 'Ben-Ali Diary,' a Preliminary Statement." *Journal of Negro History* 25, no. 3 (1940): 372–75.

Grimshaw, William H. *Official History of the Freemasonry among the Colored People in North America.* New York: Broadway, 1903.

Gutman, Herbert G. *The Black Family in Slavery and Freedom, 1750–1925.* New York: Vintage, 1976.

Gwaltney, John Langston. *Drylongso: A Self-Portrait of Black America.* New York: New Press, 1993.

Hahn, Steven. *A Nation under Our Feet: Black Political Struggles in the Rural South from Slavery to the Great Migration.* Cambridge: Harvard University Press, 2003.

Hale, Charles R. "The Cultural Politics of Identity in Latin America." *Annual Review of Anthropology* 26 (1997): 567–90.

Hale, Grace Elizabeth. *Making Whiteness: The Culture of Segregation in the South, 1890–1940.* New York: Pantheon, 1998.

Hall, Robert, and Carol Stack, ed. *Holding on to the Land and the Lord: Kinship, Ritual, Tenure, and Social Policy in the Rural South.* Athens: University of Georgia Press, 1982.

Hamline, Walter Richard. "Rural Black Kinship: A Study of the Black Community of Calvert County, Maryland." Ph.D. diss., University of Rochester, 1980.

Hancock, Ian F. "Gullah and Barbadian: Origins and Relationships." *American Speech* 55, no. 1 (1980): 17–35.

Harley, Sharon, and Rosalyn Terborg Penn, eds. *The Afro-American Woman: Struggles and Images.* New York, Kennikat, 1978.

Harris, Michael D. *Colored Pictures: Race and Visual Representation.* Chapel Hill: University of North Carolina Press, 2003.

Harris, Peggy. "For the Love of Place: Paternalism and Patronage in the Georgia Lowcountry, 1865–1898." *Journal of Southern History* 70, no. 4 (2004): 825–64.

Hawkesworth, Mary. *Political Worlds of Women: Activism, Advocacy, and Government in the Twenty-First Century.* New Jersey: Rutgers University Press, 2012.

Hayden, Robert. "Middle Passage." In *Black Voices: An Anthology of Afro-American Literature.* Abraham Chapman ed., 164–65. New York: New American Library, 1968.

Hazzard, W. W. *St. Simon's Island Georgia, Brunswick, and Vicinity.* 1825; repr., Belmont, Mass.: Oak Hill, 1974.

Heard, George Alexander. "St. Simons Island during the War between the States." *Georgia Historical Quarterly* 22, no. 3 (1938): 249–72.

Hendricks, George L. "Union Army Occupation of the Southern Seaboard, 1861–1865." Ph.D. diss., Columbia University, 1954.

Herskovits, Melville. *The Myth of the Negro Past.* Boston: Beacon, 1941.

Heyward, Daniel. *Seed From Madagascar.* Chapel Hill: University of North Carolina Press, 1937.

Higginbotham, Evelyn Brooks. *Righteous Discontent: The Women's Movement in the Black Baptist Church, 1880–1920.* Cambridge, Mass.: Harvard University Press, 1993.

Higginson, Thomas Wentworth. *Army Life in a Black Regiment.* New York: Houghton, Mifflin, 1870.

Hill, W. B. "Rural Survey of Clarke County, Georgia, with Special Reference to the Negroes," *Bulletin of the University of Georgia* 15, no. 3 (1915).

Hilliard, Sam B. "Antebellum Tidewater Rice Culture in South Carolina and Georgia." Pp. 91–115 in *European Settlement and Development in North America: Essays on Geographical Change in Honour and Memory of Andrew Hill Clark,* ed. James R. Gibson. Toronto: University of Toronto Press, 1978.

Hine, Darlene Clark. *Hine Sight: Black Women and the Reconstruction of American History.* Indianapolis: University of Indiana Press, 1994.

Holly, James Theodore. "A Vindication of the Capacity of the Negro Race." Pp. 21–66 in *Black Separation and the Caribbean,* ed. Howard H. Bell. Ann Arbor: University of Michigan Press, 1970.

Hopkins, Dwight N., and George C. L. Cummings. *Cut Loose Your Stammering Tongue: Black Theology in the Slave Narratives.* New York: Orbis, 1991.

Horne, Gerald. *The Deepest South: The United States, Brazil, and the African Slave Trade.* New York: New York University Press, 2007.

Hoskins, Charles L. *The Trouble They Seen: Profiles in the Life of Colonel John H. Deveaux 1848–1909.* Savannah, Ga.: St. Matthews Episcopal Church, 1989.

House, Albert V., ed. *Planter Management and Capitalism in Antebellum Georgia: The Journal of Hugh Fraser Grant, Ricegrower.* New York: Columbia University Press, 1937.

Howard, Rosalyn. *Black Seminoles in the Bahamas.* Gainesville: University Press of Florida, 2002.

Hunter, Tera. *To Joy My Freedom: Southern Black Women's Lives and Labor after the Civil War.* Cambridge, Mass.: Harvard University Press, 1997.

Jaynes, Gerald D. *Branches without Roots: Genesis of the Black Working Class in the American South, 1862–1882.* New York: Oxford University Press, 1986.

Jenkins, Adelbert H. *The Psychology of the Afro-Americans: A Humanistic Approach.* New York: Pergamon, 1978.

Jennings, Thelma. "'Us Colored Women Had to Go Through a Plenty': Sexual Exploitation of African American Slave Women." *Journal of Women's History* 1, no. 3 (1990): 45–74.

Johansson, S. Ryan. "Status Anxiety and Demographic Contraction of Privileged Populations." *Population and Development Review* 13, no. 13 (1987): 439–70.

Johnson, Andre E. "Is the Negro Like Other People?" In *Converging Identities: Blackness in the Modern African Diaspora,* ed. Julius O. Adekunle and Hettie V. Williams. Durham, N.C.: Carolina Academic Press, 2013.

Jones, Jacqueline. *The Dispossessed: America's Underclass from the Civil War to the Present.* New York: HarperCollins, 1992.

———. *Labor of Love, Labor of Sorrow: Black Women, Work, and the Family from Slavery to the Present.* New York: Basic Books, 1985.

———. *Saving Savannah: The City and the Civil War.* New York: Alfred A. Knopf, 2008.

Jordan, Winthrop D. *The White Man's Burden: Historical Origins of Racism in the United States.* New York: Oxford University Press, 1974.

Joyner, Charles. *Down by the Riverside: A South Carolina Slave Community.* Urbana: University of Illinois Press, 1984.

Kashif, Annette I. "Africanisms upon the Land: A Study of African Influenced Place Names of the USA." In *Places of Cultural Memory.* Washington, D.C.: U.S. Department of the Interior, National Park Service, 2001.

Kelley, Robin D. G. "'We Are Not What We Seem': Rethinking Black Working Class Opposition in the Jim Crow South." *Journal of American History* 80, no. 1 (1993): 75–112.

Kemble, Francis A., and Frances A. Butler Leigh. *Principles and Privilege: Two Women's Lives on a Georgia Plantation.* Ann Arbor: University of Michigan Press, 1995.

King, Wilma. *Stolen Childhood: Slave Youth in Nineteenth-Century America.* Bloomington: Indiana University Press, 1995.

Kiser, Clyde Vernon. *Sea Island to City: A Study of St. Helena Islanders in Harlem and Other Urban Centers.* New York: Columbia University Press, 1932.

Klingberg, Frank W. *The Southern Claims Commission.* Berkeley: University of California Press, 1955.

Krakow, Kenneth K. *Georgia Place Names.* Macon, Ga.: Winship, 1975.

Kulikoff, Allan. *Tobacco and Slaves: The Development of Southern Cultures in the Chesapeake, 1680–1800.* Chapel Hill: University of North Carolina Press, 1986.

Ledaudey, Hélène. "Behind the Mask: Ex-Slave Women and Interracial Sexual Relations." Pp. 260–77 in *Discovering the Women in Slavery,* ed. Patricia Morton. Athens: University of Georgia Press, 1996

Legare, John P. "An Account of an Agricultural Excursion into Southern Georgia." *Southern Agriculturalist* 6 (1833).

Leigh, Frances Butler. *Ten Years on a Georgia Plantation Since the War.* London: R. Bentley and Son, 1883.

Levine, Lawrence. *Black Culture and Black Consciousness: American Folk Thought from Slavery to Freedom.* New York: Oxford University Press, 1977.

Liberian Exodus Association. *The Liberian Exodus: First Voyage of the Azor, Liberia. Delightful Country, Climate, Soil, and Productions, Character of the People in Liberia and How They Live. Full Information of the Exodus Movement.* Charleston, S.C.: W. J. Oliver's Print, 1878.

Logan, Rayford. *The Negro in American Life and Thought: The Nadir, 1877–1901.* New York, Dial, 1954.

Loomis, Charles P., and J. Allan Beegle. *Rural Social Systems: A Textbook in Rural Sociology and Anthropology.* New York: Prentice-Hall, 1950.

Lynch, Matthew. *Before Obama: A Reappraisal of Black Reconstruction Era Politicians.* New York: Praeger, 2012.

Magdol, Edward. *A Right to the Land: Essays on the Freedmen's Community.* Westport, Conn.: Greenwood, 1977.

Magoc, Chris J. *So Glorious a Landscape: Nature and the Environment in American History and Culture.* Wilmington, Del.: Scholarly Resources, 2002.

Marable, Manning. *How Capitalism Underdeveloped Black America: Problems in Race, Political Economy, and Society.* Cambridge, Mass.: South End Press, 2000.

Matory, J. Lorand. "The Illusion of Isolation: The Gullah/Geechees and the Political Economy of African Culture in the Americas." *Comparative Studies in Society and History* 50, no. 4 (2008): 949–80.

Mbiti, John. *Introduction to African Religion.* London: Heinemann, 1991.

McDonald, Roderick A. *The Economy and Material Culture of Slaves: Goods and Chattels on the Sugar Plantations of Jamaica and Louisiana.* Baton Rouge: Louisiana State University Press, 1993.

McFeely, William. *Sapelo's People: A Long Walk into Freedom.* New York: W.W. Norton, 1994.

McLaurin, Melton A. *Celia, a Slave.* Athens: University of Georgia Press, 1991.

McLendon, S.G. *History of the Public Domain of Georgia.* Atlanta: Foote and Davis, 924.

McKee, Gwen, ed. *A Guide to the Georgia Coast.* Alpharetta, Ga.: Georgia Conservancy, 1993.

McPherson, James. *Ordeal by Fire: The Civil War and Reconstruction.* New York: Knopf, 2001.

Miller, Steven F., et al. "Between Emancipation and Enfranchisement: Law and the Political Mobilization of Black Southerners during Presidential Reconstruction, 1865–1867." *Chicago-Kent Law Review* 70 (1995): 1059–77.

———. *Land and Labor, 1865.* Chapel Hill: University of North Carolina Press, 2007.

Mohr, Clarence. "Before Sherman: Georgia Blacks and the Union War Effort, 1861–1864." *Journal of Southern History* 45 (1979): 331–52.

———. *On the Threshold of Freedom: Masters and Slaves in Civil War Georgia.* Athens: University of Georgia Press, 1986.

Morgan, Philip D. "The Ownership of Property by Slaves in the Mid-Nineteenth-Century Low Country." *Journal of Southern History* 49, no. 3 (1983): 399–420.

———. "Work and Culture: The Task System and the World of Lowcountry Blacks, 1700–1880." *William and Mary Quarterly* 39, no. 4 (1982): 564–99.

Morrison, Toni. *Beloved*. New York: Vintage, 2004.

———. *Playing in the Dark: Whiteness and the Literary Imagination*. New York: Vintage, 1993.

Morton, Patricia, ed. *Discovering the Women in Slavery: Emancipating Perspectives on the American Past*. Athens: University of Georgia Press, 1996.

Moses, Wilson. *The Golden Age of Black Nationalism*. New York: Oxford University Press, 1978.

Mullin, Michael. *Africa in America: Slave Acculturation and Resistance in the American South and British Caribbean, 1736–1831*. Urbana: University of Illinois Press, 1992.

Myers, Richard R., and J. Beegle. "Delineation and Analysis of the Rural-Urban Fringe." *Applied Anthropology* 6, no. 2 (1947): 14–22.

Myers, Robert Manson, ed. *Children of Pride: A True Story of Georgia and the Civil War*. New Haven, Conn.: Yale University Press, 1972.

Nathans, Sydney. "Fortress without Walls." In *Holding on to the Land and the Lord: Kinship, Ritual, Tenure, and Social Policy in the Rural South*, ed. Robert Hall and Carol Stack. Athens: University of Georgia Press, 1982

Nelson, William. *The Roots of American Bureaucracy, 1830–1900*. Cambridge, Mass.: Harvard University Press, 1982.

O'Donovan, Susan W. *Becoming Free in the Cotton South*. Cambridge, Mass.: Harvard University Press, 2007.

Omolade, Barbara. *The Rising Song of Afro-American Women*. New York: Routledge, 1986.

Otto, John Solomon. "Slavery in a Coastal Community—Glynn County (1790–1860)," *Georgia Historical Quarterly* 63, no. 4 (1979): 461–68.

Owens, Leslie. *This Specie of Property: Slave Life and Culture in the Old South*. New York: Oxford University Press, 1976.

Parish, Peter J. *Slavery: History and Historians*. New York: Harper and Row, 1989.

Parrish, Lydia. *Slave Songs of the Georgia Sea Islands*. Athens: University of Georgia Press, 1992.

Penningroth, Dylan. *The Claims of Kinfolk: African American Property and Community in the Nineteenth Century*. Chapel Hill: University of North Carolina Press, 2003.

———. "Slavery, Freedom, and Social Claims to Property among African Americans in Liberty County, Georgia, 1850–1880." *Journal of American History* 84, no. 2 (1997): 405–35.

Perdue, Robert. *The Negro in Savannah, 1865–1900*. New York: Exposition Press, 1973.

Phillips, Gervase. "Slave Resistance in the Antebellum South." *History Review* 59 (2007): 34–35.

Phillips, Ulrich B. *American Negro Slavery: A Survey of the Supply, Employment, and Control of Negro Labor as Determined by the Plantation Regime*. New York: D. Appleton-Century, 1936.

Powell, Lawrence. *New Masters: Northern Planters during the Civil War and Reconstruction*. New Haven, Conn.: Yale University Press, 1980.

Quarles, Benjamin. *The Negro in the Civil War*. Boston: Little Brown, 1969.

Rabaka, Reiland. "The Souls of White Folk: W. E. B. Du Bois's Critique of White Supremacy and Contributions to Critical White Studies." *Journal of African American Studies* 11, no. 1 (2007): 1–15.

Rabinow, Paul, ed. *The Foucault Reader*. New York: Pantheon, 1984.

Rabinowitz, Howard, ed. *Southern Black Leaders of the Reconstruction Era.* Urbana: University of Illinois Press, 1982.

Raboteau, Albert J. *Slave Religion: The "Invisible Institution" in the American South.* New York: Oxford University Press, 1978.

Rael, Patrick. *Black Identity and Black Protest in the Antebellum North.* Chapel Hill: University of North Carolina Press, 2002.

Ramey, Daina L. "'She Do a Heap of Work': Female Slave Labor on Glynn County Rice and Cotton Plantations." *Georgia Historical Quarterly* 82, no. 4 (1998): 707–34.

Rawick, George P. *From Sundown to Sunup: The Making of the Black Community.* Westport, Conn.: Greenwood, 1972.

———, ed. *The American Slave: A Composite Autobiography, Supplement I.* Westport, Conn.: Greenwood, 1977.

Redkey, Edwin S. "Bishop Turner's African Dream." *Journal of American History* 54, no. 2 (1967): 217–90.

———. *Black Exodus: Black Nationalists and Back to Africa Movements, 1890–1910.* New Haven: Yale University Press, 1969.

———, ed. *Respect Black: The Writings and Speeches of Henry McNeal Turner.* New York: Arno Press and The New York Times, 1971.

Reed, Ruth. "The Negro Women of Gainsville, Georgia," M.A. Thesis, *Bulletin of the University of Georgia* 22, no. 1 (1921).

Reidy, Joseph P. "Aaron A. Bradley: Voice of Black Labor in Lowcountry Georgia." In *Southern Black Leaders of the Reconstruction Era,* ed. Howard Rabinowitz. Urbana: University of Illinois Press, 1982.

Richardson, Heather Cox. *The Death of Reconstruction: Race, Labor, and Politics in the Post Civil War North, 1865–1901.* Cambridge, Mass.: Harvard University Press, 2001.

———. *From Slavery to Agrarian Capitalism in the Cotton Plantation South.* Chapel Hill: University of North Carolina Press, 1992.

Riddleberger, Patrick W. *1866: The Critical Year Revisited.* New York: University Press of America, 1984.

Ripley, C. Peter, Slaves and Freedmen in Civil War Louisiana. Baton Rouge: Louisiana State University Press, 1976.

Rose, Harold M. "The All Negro Town: Its Evolution and Function." *Geographic Review* 55 (1955): 362–81.

Rose, Willie Lee. *Rehearsal for Reconstruction: The Port Royal Experiment.* New York: Oxford University Press, 1964.

Rosen, Hannah. *Terror in the Heart of Freedom: Citizenship, Sexual Violence, and the Meaning of Race in the Postemancipation South.* Chapel Hill: University of North Carolina Press, 2009.

Rosenbaum, Art. *Shout because You're Free: The African American Ring Shout Tradition in Coastal Georgia.* Athens: University of Georgia Press, 1998.

Savannah, Florida, and Western Railway Company Guide to Southern Georgia and Florida. Savannah, Georgia, 1879.

Saville, Julie. *The Work of Reconstruction: From Slave Labor to Wage Labor in South Carolina, 1860–1870.* New York: Cambridge University Press, 1996.

Savitt, Todd L., and James Harvey Young, eds. *Disease and Distinctiveness in the American South.* Knoxville: University of Tennessee Press, 1988.

Schmidt, James. *Free to Work: Labor Law, Emancipation, and Reconstruction, 1815–1880.* Athens: University of Georgia, 1999.

Schuler, Edgar A. "Some Regional Variations in Levels and Standards of Living." *Rural Sociology* 9 (1944): 122–41.

Schwalm, Leslie A. *A Hard Fight for We: Women's Transition from Slavery to Freedom in South Carolina.* Urbana: University of Illinois Press, 1997.

Schwarz, Marie Jenkins. *Born in Bondage: Growing Up Enslaved in the Antebellum South.* Cambridge, Mass.: Harvard University Press, 2000.

Schweninger, Loren. *Black Property Owners in the South, 1795–1910.* Urbana: University of Illinois Press, 1991.

Scott, James. *Domination and the Arts of Resistance: Hidden Transcripts.* New Haven, Conn.: Yale University Press, 1990.

Sherman, William T. *Memoirs of General William T. Sherman,* vol. 2. New York: D. Appleton, 1990.

Shiflett, Crandall A. "The Household Composition of Rural Black Families: Louisa County, Virginia, 1880." *Journal of Interdisciplinary History* 6, no. 2 (1975): 235–60.

Shryock, Richard H., ed., *Letters to Richard D. Arnold, M.D., 1808–1876.* Durham, N.C.: Duke University Press, 1929.

Simms, James. *The First Colored Church of North America.* Philadelphia: J. B. Lippincott, 1888.

Simpson, John. "A Reflection of Black Enterprise in the Old South." *Lincoln Review* 10 (1990).

Singleton, Theresa A. "Slavery and Spatial Dialectics on Cuban Coffee Plantations." *The Archaeology of Slavery* 33, no. 1 (2001): 98–114.

Skocpol, Theda. *Protecting Soldiers and Mothers: The Political Origins of Social Policy in the U.S.* Cambridge: Harvard University Press, 1992.

Small, Kermit. *Yearbook of Colored Savannah.* n.p., 1934. Savannah Public Library, Savannah, Georgia.

Smith, John David. *When Did Southern Segregation Begin?.* Boston: Bedford/St. Martin's, 2002.

Smith, Julia Floyd. *Slavery and Rice Culture in Low Country Georgia, 1750–1860.* Knoxville: University of Tennessee Press, 1985.

Sobel, Mechal. *Trabelin' On: The Slave Journey to an Afro-Baptist Faith.* Princeton, N.J.: Princeton University Press, 1988.

Stacy, James. *History of the Midway Congregational Church, Liberty County, Georgia.* 1903; repr., Newnan, Georgia: S.W. Murray, 1951.

Stampp, Kenneth. *The Peculiar Institution: Slavery in the Antebellum South.* New York: Vintage, 1956.

Stanley, Amy Dru. *From Bondage to Contract: Wage Labor, Marriage, and the Market in the Age of Slave Emancipation.* Cambridge, Mass.: Harvard University Press, 1998.

Stanley, Amy Dru. "Instead of Waiting for the Thirteenth Amendment: The War Power, Slave Marriage, and Inviolate Human Rights." *American Historical Review* 115 (2010): 732–65.

Starobin, Robert, ed. *Blacks in Bondage: The Letters of American Slaves.* New York: New Viewpoints, 1974.

Stewart, Mart A. "Rice, Water, and Power: Landscapes of Domination and Resistance in the Low Country, 1790–1880." *Environmental History Review* 15, no. 3 (1991): 47–64.

———. *"What Nature Suffers to Groe": Life, Labor, and Landscape on the Georgia Coast, 1860–1920*. Athens: University of Georgia Press, 1996.

Stoddard, Albert H. "Origin, Dialect, Beliefs, and Characteristics of the Negroes of the South Carolina and Georgia Coasts." *Georgia Historical Quarterly* 28 (1944): 187–95.

Stuckey, Sterling. *Slave Culture: Nationalist Theory and the Foundations of Black America*. New York: Oxford University Press, 1987.

Swann-Wright, Dianne. *A Way Out of No Way: Claiming Family and Freedom in the New South*. Charlottesville: University of Virginia, 2002.

Swint, Henry L., ed. *Dear Ones at Home: Letters from Contraband Camps*. Nashville, Tenn.: Vanderbilt University Press, 1966.

Taylor, Arnold. *Travail and Triumph: Black Life and Culture in the Old South*. Westport, Conn.: Greenwood, 1976.

Taylor, Joe Gray. *Negro Slavery in Louisiana*. Baton Rouge: Louisiana Historical Society, 1963.

Taylor, Susie King. *A Black Woman's Civil War Memoirs: Reminiscences of My Life with the 33rd U.S. Colored Troops, Late 1st South Carolina Volunteers*, ed. Patricia Romero. New York: M. Wiener Publishers, 1988.

Terborg Penn, Rosalyn. *African American Women in the Struggle For the Vote*. Bloomington, Indiana University Press, 1998.

Thomas, John P. "The Barbadians in Early South Carolina." *South Carolina Historical and Genealogical Magazine* 31 (1930): 75–93.

Thompson, Robert Farris. *Flash of the Spirit: African and Afro-American Art and Philosophy*. New York: Vintage, 1983.

Thornton, John. *Africa and Africans in the Making of the Atlantic World, 1400–1800*. New York: Cambridge University Press, 2000.

Turner, Elizabeth Hayes. *Women and Gender in the New South, 1865–1945*. Wheeling, Ill.: Harlan Davidson, 2009.

Turner, Lorenzo Dow. *Africanisms in the Gullah Dialect*. Chicago: University of Chicago Press, 1949.

Vinson, Robert. "The Law as Lawbreaker: The Promotion and Encouragement of the Atlantic Slave Trade by the New York Judiciary System, 1857–1862." Unpublished seminar paper, Howard University, 1994.

Wallenstein, Peter. *From Slave South to New South*. Chapel Hill: University of North Carolina Press, 1987.

The War of the Rebellion: A Compilation of the Official Records of the Union and Confederate Armies. Washington, D.C., 1880–1902.

Wardlaw, Ralph. "Negro Suffrage in Georgia, 1867–1930." *Bulletin of the University of Georgia, Phelps-Stokes Fellowship Studies* 33, no. 11 (1932).

Washington, Booker T. "Town Owned by Negroes." *World's Work* 14 (1907): 9125–34.

Webber, Thomas L. *Deep Like the Rivers: Education in the Slave Quarter Community, 1831–1865*. New York: W.W. Norton, 1978.

Weiner, Mark. *The Black Trials: Citizenship from the Beginnings of Slavery to the End of Caste*. New York: Vintage, 2004.

White, Deborah Gray. *Ar'n't I a Woman?: Female Slaves in the Plantation South.* New York: W. W. Norton, 1985.

Wilentz, Sean. *The Rise of American Democracy: Jefferson to Lincoln.* New York: W. W. Norton, 2005.

Williams, David. *I Freed Myself: African American Self-Emancipation in the Civil War Era.* New York: Cambridge University Press, 2014.

Williams, Kidada E. *They Left Great Marks on Me: African American Testimonies of Racial Violence from Emancipation to World War I.* New York: New York University Press, 2012.

Wilms, Douglas C. "The Development of Rice Culture in 18th Century Georgia." *Southeastern Geographer* 12 (1972): 45–57.

Windley, Lathan. *Runaway Slave Advertisements: A Documentary History from the 1730s to 1790.* Westport, Conn.: Greenwood, 1983.

Wood, Betty. *Women's Work, Men's Work: The Informal Slave Economies of Lowcountry Georgia.* Athens: University of Georgia Press, 1995.

Woodson, Carter G. *The Mind of the Negro as Reflected in His Letters.* New York: Dover, 1926.

———. *The Rural Negro.* Washington, D.C.: Association for the Study of Negro Life and History, 1930.

Woofter, T. J. "The Negroes of Athens Georgia," *Bulletin of the University of Georgia* 14, no. 4 (1913).

Work, Monroe. *The Negro Yearbook.* Tuskegee, Ala.: Tuskegee Institute, 1912.

Work, Monroe. "The Negroes of Warsaw, Georgia." *World's Work* 37 (1908).

Work, Monroe. "Principal Negro Towns and Settlements." *Negro Yearbook.* Tuskegee, Ala.: Tuskegee Institute, 1912.

Works Progress Administration, *Annals of Savannah, 1850–1937: A Digest and Index of the Newspaper Record of Events and Opinions, in Eighty-Seven Volumes,* vol. 16. Savannah: Savannah Public Library, 1937.

———. *Louisiana: Past and Present.* New York: Hastings House, 1971.

Wright, Donald. *African Americans in the Colonial Era.* Illinois: Harlan Davison, 1990.

Index

Page numbers in italics refer to illustrations.

About the Author

KAREN COOK BELL is an associate professor of history at Bowie State University. She received a Ph.D. in history from Howard University. Her scholarship has appeared in the *Journal of African American History, Georgia Historical Quarterly, Passport, The United States and West Africa: Interaction and Relations, Before Obama: A Reappraisal of Black Reconstruction Era Politicians, Converging Identities: Blackness in the Contemporary Diaspora,* and *Slavery and Freedom in Savannah.* Bell is a former American Association of University Women Dissertation Fellow.